D0339118

CHAOS OR COMMUNITY?

PRAISE FOR OTHER SOUTH END PRESS BOOKS BY HOLLY SKLAR

STREETS OF HOPE: THE FALL AND RISE OF AN URBAN NEIGHBORHOOD
(with Peter Medoff)

"Stories a novelist would envy." —*Boston Globe*

"Inspiring...*Streets of Hope* is a must read." —*The Neighborhood Works*

"One of the best books ever on neighborhood organizing and community development."
—Professor Norman Krumholz, former president of the American Planning Association

TRILATERALISM: THE TRILATERAL COMMISSION AND ELITE PLANNING FOR WORLD MANAGEMENT

"Excellent."—*Library Journal*

"A book that is central to what historian Henry Adams called 'learning to see' in order to react 'not at haphazard, but by choice.'"
—William Appleman Williams, former president of the Organization of American Historians

WASHINGTON'S WAR ON NICARAGUA

"Well-written...well-documented and comprehensive."—*Choice*

"Sklar makes an excellent case."—*Library Journal*

CHAOS OR COMMUNITY?

SEEKING SOLUTIONS, NOT SCAPEGOATS FOR BAD ECONOMICS

HOLLY SKLAR

SOUTH END PRESS
BOSTON

©1995 Holly Sklar
Cover design by Matt Wuerker
All cartoons by Matt Wuerker except page 68 by Joseph Farris
Text design and production by South End Press collective
Printed in the U.S.A.

Any properly footnoted quotation of up to 500 sequential words may be used without permission, as long as the total number of words quoted does not exceed 2,000. For longer quotations or for a greater number of total words, please write for permission to South End Press.

Library of Congress Cataloging-in-Publication Data
Sklar, Holly, 1955-
    Chaos or Community? : seeking solutions, not scapegoats for bad economics / Holly Sklar
        p. cm.
    Includes index.
    ISBN 0-89608-512-0 — ISBN 0-89608-511-2 (pbk.)
    1. Income distribution—United States. 2. Discrimination—United States. 3. United States—Economic conditions—1981- 4. United States—Politics and government—1989- 5. Economic history—1980-
I. Title.
HC110.I5S57   1995
339.2'0973—dc20

                                                                    95-8800
                        ® GCIU 745-C   CIP

South End Press, 116 Saint Botolph Street, Boston, MA 02115
01 00 99 98 97 96   4 5 6 7 8 9

CONTENTS

"Winners Take All" • Persistent Impoverishment
• The Undervalued

Downwardly Mobile • The Underpaid • Falling Floor
• Lower Wages and Higher Education • Union-Free
Labor • Disposable Workers

Global Webs • "Race to the Bottom" • Free Trading
on Cheap Labor • Uncle Sam's Helping Hand • Global
Loan Sharks • Child Laborers

Leaner and Meaner • Overtime for Some, No Time
for Others • Behind the Unemployment Rate
• Technological Unemployment

The Regression Curve • The Raw Deal • Blaming
Women for Illegitimate Economics • The Wages of
Discrimination • Welfare Queens and Worker Bees
• Ending Welfare Instead of Poverty

TABLES AND FIGURES

ACKNOWLEDGMENTS

Special thanks to Matt Wuerker for his wonderful art and the enjoyable opportunity to collaborate on some cartoons. Thanks also to Chip Berlet, Sue Dorfman, Ros Everdell, Saralee Hamilton, Jean Hardisty, Ed Herman, Maya Miller, Andrew Sarpard, Jana Schroeder, Beth Sims, my computer, and Loie Hayes and South End Press for speedily publishing two books in two years.

For my mother, Elayne Kardeman,
who encourages the creative best in people as a parent,
innovative art teacher/therapist and fun-loving grandma

INTRODUCTION

The American Dream—always an impossible dream for many—is dying a slow death. As the systemic causes go untreated, a host of local and national leaders are peddling the snake oil of scapegoating. We don't have to swallow it. Together, we can find real remedies for our common problems.

Three decades ago, in *Where Do We Go From Here,* Martin Luther King spoke prophetically about polarizing national and international trends. He urged us to choose community over chaos:

> A true revolution of values will soon look uneasily on the glaring contrast of poverty and wealth. With righteous indignation, it will look at thousands of working people displaced from their jobs with reduced incomes as a result of automation while the profits of the employers remain intact, and say "This is not just."...
>
> America, the richest and most powerful nation in the world, can well lead the way in this revolution of values. There is nothing to prevent us from paying adequate wages to schoolteachers...There is nothing but a lack of social vision to prevent us from paying an adequate wage to every American citizen whether he be a hospital worker, laundry worker, maid or day laborer. There is nothing except shortsightedness to prevent us from guaranteeing an annual minimum—and livable—income for every American family. There is nothing, except a tragic death wish, to prevent us from reordering our priorities, so that the pursuit of peace will take precedence over the pursuit of war. There is nothing to keep us from remolding a recalcitrant status quo with bruised hands until we have fashioned it into a brotherhood...
>
> The oceans of history are made turbulent by the ever-rising tides of hate. History is cluttered with the wreckage of nations and individuals who pursued this self-defeating path of hate...

We are now faced with the fact that tomorrow is today...We still have a choice today: nonviolent coexistence or violent coannihilation. This may well be mankind's last chance to choose between chaos and community.[1]

In the last three decades, humankind has taken giant steps toward community—and chaos. The Cold War threat of coannihilation has faded, but many nations are wracked by internal conflict. The United States grows increasingly disunited. The ruinous social and economic trends that King warned us about have intensified. Wealth is not trickling down. It is flooding upward. Real wages for average workers have plummeted—despite rising productivity. Many corporate executives make more in a week than their workers make in a year. Unemployment is high whether the economy is in recession or "recovery." The "War on Poverty" has given way to the escalating war on the poor. Once-thriving communities are in decline.

Economic inequality is now so extreme that the richest 1 percent of American families have nearly as much wealth as the entire bottom 95 percent. More than a fifth of all children are living in poverty in this, the world's richest nation. That's according to the government, which undercounts both poverty and unemployment. Downward mobility has become the legacy for younger generations. Neither two incomes, nor college degrees assure that younger families will ever match their parents' living standards.

For more and more people, a job is not a ticket out of poverty, but into the ranks of the working poor. Jobs and wages are being downsized in the "leaner, meaner" world of global corporate restructuring. Corporations are aggressively automating and shifting operations among cities, states and nations in a continual search for greater public subsidies and lower-cost labor. Full-time jobs are becoming scarcer as corporations shape a cheaper, more disposable workforce of temporary workers, part-timers and other "contingent workers."

Workers are increasingly expected to migrate from job to job, at low and variable wage rates, without paid vacation, much less a pension. How can they care for themselves and their families, maintain a home, pay for college, save for retirement, plan a future? How do we build strong communities? What about the millions of people without jobs? This brand of economics is a prescription for chaos.

The cycle of unequal opportunity is intensifying. Its beneficiaries often slander those most systematically undervalued, underpaid, underemployed, underfinanced, underinsured, underrated and otherwise underserved and undermined—as undeserving and underclass, impoverished in moral values and lacking the proper "work ethic."

The angry, shrinking middle class is misled into thinking that those lower on the economic ladder are pulling them down, when in reality those on top are rising at the expense of those below. People who should be working together to transform the economic policies that are hurting them are instead turning hatefully on each other.

Instead of full employment, the United States has full prisons. It imprisons Black men at a much higher rate than South Africa did under apartheid. The military budget continues consuming resources at Cold War levels, while programs to prevent violence and invest in people, infrastructure and the environment are sacrificed on the altar of deficit reduction.

Instead of dedicating itself to equal opportunity for children, society is living a self-fulfilling prophecy: labeling more children as illegitimate, expecting more children to fail, and declaring more children the enemy. A society which sees a great number of its children as hopeless, is a society without hope for the future.

To realize community over chaos we must revitalize democracy with plain talk about who really benefits and who loses from government policy. We need vigorous debate over how to reshape policy in the public interest—not the pseudo debate of false campaign promises, negative political ads and talk radio hate-mongering.

Rights and "entitlements" familiar today—among them the eight-hour day, minimum wage, Social Security and the right of workers to organize and bargain collectively—were obtained in the face of strong opposition. Many of these achievements are being eroded. Demagoguery is threatening democracy. To realize community over chaos we must not only protect old gains, but forge new social, political and economic rights for the 21st century.

1

WEALTH AND POVERTY

The 1980s were the triumph of upper America—an ostentatious celebration of wealth, the political ascendancy of the richest third of the population and a glorification of capitalism, free markets and finance...*No parallel upsurge of riches had been seen since the late nineteenth century, the era of the Vanderbilts, Morgans and Rockefellers.* (Italics in original.)

Kevin Phillips, conservative political analyst,[1]
The Politics of Rich and Poor.

One out of four children is born into poverty in the United States—according to the official measure. The United States is the world's wealthiest nation, but much of that wealth is concentrated at the top. The combined wealth of the top 1 percent of American families is nearly the same as that of the entire bottom 95 percent. (See table 1.) Such obscene inequality befits an oligarchy, not a democracy. The income gap in Manhattan, New York is worse than Guatemala's.[2]

Wealth is being redistributed *upward*. Between 1977 and 1989, the top 1 percent of American families more than doubled their after-tax incomes, adjusting for inflation, while the bottom 60 percent of families lost income. (See figure 2.) Over the 1962-89 period, "roughly three-fourths of new wealth was generated by increasing the value of initial wealth (much of it inherited)." The wealthiest 1 percent owned more than half of all bonds, trusts and business equity; nearly half of all stocks; and 40 percent of non-home real estate in 1989. The bottom 90 percent owned about a tenth of all those assets, except non-home real estate, of which they owned 20 percent.

TABLE 1

Percent Distribution of Household Wealth and Income, 1989

Share of Households	Net Worth (assets minus debt)	Household Income	Financial Net Wealth (net worth minus net equity in owner-occupied housing)
Top 1%	38.9	16.4	48.1
Bottom 95%	39.1	70.5	27.7
Top 0.5%	31.4	13.4	39.3
Next 0.5%	7.5	3.0	8.8
Next 4%	21.9	13.3	24.1
Next 5%	11.5	10.5	11.5
Next 10%	12.2	15.5	10.1
Bottom 80%	15.4	44.5	6.1
Top Fifth	84.6	55.5	93.9
Upper Middle Fifth	11.5	20.7	6.8
Middle Fifth	4.6	13.2	1.5
Lower Middle Fifth	0.8	7.6	0.1
Bottom Fifth	−1.4	3.1	−2.3

Source: Edward N. Wolff, "Trends in Household Wealth in the United States, 1962-83 and 1983-89," *Review of Income and Wealth*, June 1994, Table 4. Also see Wolff, "The Rich Get Increasingly Richer," Economic Policy Institute, *Briefing Paper*, 1992, Table 2. Wolff explains differences with Census data, which understates income and wealth at the top.

Not surprisingly, the gap between Whites and people of color looms much wider in wealth than income. While the average income of families of color was 63 percent that of White families in 1989, their average wealth (measured by the net worth of assets minus debt) was only 29 percent.[3]

It took a minimum of $310 million to make the *Forbes* Four Hundred richest Americans in 1993—a big jump from $90 million in 1982. Billionaires led the pack, starting with Microsoft leader Bill Gates, who has an estimated net worth topping $9.3 billion. Paul Allen, Microsoft's cofounder and owner of the Portland Trail Blazers basketball team, is further down the list with $3.9 billion. After Gates comes stock market investor Warren Buffett, $9.2 billion; media tycoon John Werner Kluge, $5.9 billion; Fidelity Investments' chief executive Ned Johnson

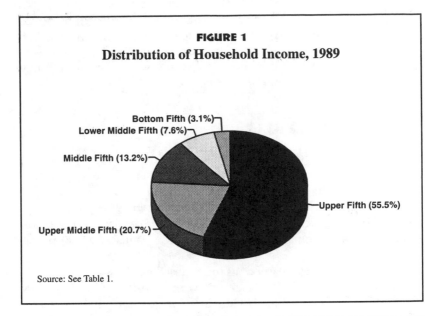

FIGURE 1
Distribution of Household Income, 1989

Bottom Fifth (3.1%)
Lower Middle Fifth (7.6%)
Middle Fifth (13.2%)
Upper Middle Fifth (20.7%)
Upper Fifth (55.5%)

Source: See Table 1.

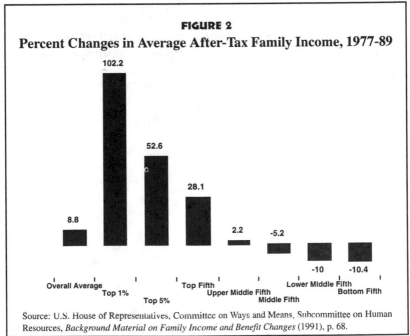

FIGURE 2
Percent Changes in Average After-Tax Family Income, 1977-89

102.2
52.6
28.1
8.8
2.2
-5.2
-10
-10.4

Overall Average
Top 1%
Top 5%
Top Fifth
Upper Middle Fifth
Middle Fifth
Lower Middle Fifth
Bottom Fifth

Source: U.S. House of Representatives, Committee on Ways and Means, Subcommittee on Human Resources, *Background Material on Family Income and Benefit Changes* (1991), p. 68.

and family, $5.1 billion; Amway Corporation founders Richard DeVos (owner of the Orlando Magic basketball team) and Jay Van Andel, $4.5 billion each; and leveraged buyout tycoon Ronald Perelman, also $4.5 billion. The Wal-Mart Walton family holds the world's greatest family fortune, with $21.7 billion.[4]

"WINNERS TAKE ALL"

Paycheck inequality has grown so much that the top 4 percent of Americans make more in wages and salaries than the entire bottom half. Back in the booming fifties, the gap was not as wide: the top 4 percent made as much as the bottom 35 percent in 1959.[5] The average compensation for a chief executive officer (CEO) of a large corporation has skyrocketed to millions of dollars in salary, bonuses, stock options and dividends.

The average CEO "earned" as much as 41 factory workers in 1960, 42 factory workers in 1980, 104 factory workers in 1991 and 157 factory workers in 1992. (See table 3.) The United States leads major industrialized nations with the largest gap in CEO-worker pay. Japan's average CEO, for example, earns less than 32 factory workers. Between 1980 and 1993, American CEO pay increased by 514 percent, workers' wages by 68 percent, consumer prices by 75 percent and corporate profits by

---

TABLE 2

Average Household Net Worth and Income, 1989

in $thousands

	All	Top 0.5%	Next 0.5%	Next 9%	Next 10%	Bottom 80%
Av. Net Worth	199	12,482	2,984	737	243	38
Av. Income	42	1,125	254	111	964	23

	All	Top Fifth	Upper Mid. Fifth	Middle Fifth	Lower Mid. Fifth	Bottom Fifth
Av. Net Worth	199	840	114	45	8	−14
Av. Income	37	116	43	28	16	6

Source: Wolff, "Trends in Household Wealth in the United States, 1962-83 and 1983-89," Table 5, based on Federal Reserve Board, *1989 Survey of Consumer Finances*.

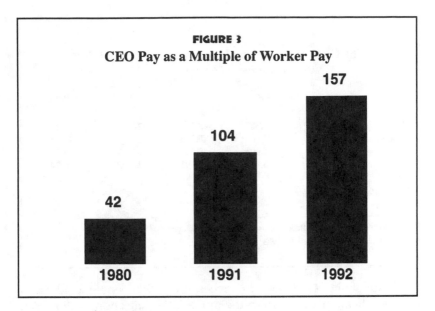

FIGURE 3
CEO Pay as a Multiple of Worker Pay

157

104

42

1980   1991   1992

166 percent.[6] Workers' wages fell way behind inflation. CEO pay zoomed ahead. Yet, CEOs want us to think the problem is overpaid workers.

Lee Iaccoca, one of the best known U.S. business leaders and a key backer of the North American Free Trade Agreement (NAFTA), received about $17 million as Chrysler's CEO in 1992—Chrysler, you may recall, was saved from bankruptcy by the federal government in 1979. Leading the CEO pay pack in 1992 was Thomas Frist Jr. of Hospital Corp. of America, with over $127 million in salary, bonus and long-term compensation. Frist's compensation was so high that *Business Week* excluded it when figuring average CEO pay in its annual survey. Still, 1992 CEO average pay was up 42 percent from 1991.

Business Week editorialized: "At a time when the incomes of 90% of corporate employees are barely growing as work loads get heavier every day and job insecurity is a constant, these multimillion-dollar windfalls are more than unseemly: They are arrogant. They imply that no one else but the CEO is responsible for the good performance of the company...The disparity tears at the social fabric."[7]

In 1993, Disney Chair Michael Eisner broke CEO compensation records with $203 million, "earned" on the joys of children. As *Business Week* noted, his pay that year was "nearly equal to the GNP of Grenada." Eisner "didn't bring about Disney's comeback singlehandedly. It took

TABLE 3

The CEO-Worker Pay Gap, Average Annual Pay

not adjusted for inflation*

	1960	1970	1980	1992
CEO	190,383	548,787	624,996	3,842,247
Factory Worker	4,665	6,933	15,008	24,411
Teacher	4,995	8,626	15,970	34,098
Engineer	9,828	14,695	28,486	58,240
CEO Pay as a Multiple of				
Factory Worker Pay	41	79	42	157

*As seen in other tables, inflation-adjusted worker pay is falling.

Source: *Business Week*, April 26, 1993.

the help of thousands of employees, from the people who keep Disney's theme parks clean to the artists in its animation studios. Yet, Eisner and a few members of his senior management team have reaped most of the rewards."

"That may make Eisner the best example yet," says *Business Week*, "of what economist Robert H. Frank calls a 'winner-take-all' market, in which only a handful of top performers walk away with the lion's share." In 1974, CEOs made 35 times the average salary inside their own company. Today they make about 150 times the average.[8] And thanks to tax changes discussed later, average workers are paying more to the government, while CEOs and their companies are paying less. "We have corporate CEOs who raise their pay 20% or more in years when they lay off thousands of people," remarks Charles Handy, visiting professor of management at the London Business School. "It's obscene."[9]

On top of their pay packages, CEOs commonly enjoy perks such as gourmet dining, chauffeured limousines, corporate jets, luxury hotels, company-paid residences, vacation retreats, country club and health club memberships, and personal financial and legal advice—as well as signing bonuses at the beginning of their tenures and golden parachutes at the end. In the words of longtime compensation consultant Graef Crystal, the modern CEO is pampered and "paid so much more than ordinary workers that he hasn't got the slightest clue as to how the rest of the country lives." The result is more companies "in search of excess," not excellence. Crystal writes:

> CEOs and other senior executives in the United States earn far more than their counterparts in the other major industrialized countries. And they pay the least taxes...By contrast, Japan, the country that gives the United States the greatest competitive fit, pays its CEOs the least, and has the most egalitarian approach to compensation...
> Is there a lesson here?[10]

PERSISTENT IMPOVERISHMENT

For many Americans there is an endless Great Depression. It's covered up with scapegoating terms like "underclass" and Orwellian ones like "jobless recovery," and by officially undercounting the unemployed and impoverished.

The official poverty line understates the real extent of poverty, especially among the working poor. Poverty rates would be much higher if the official measure reflected today's actual cost of living and after-tax income. The official poverty line was established in the 1960s by determining the cost of a minimally adequate diet and multiplying by three, assuming then that the average family spent one-third of its budget on food. The minimal Economy Food Plan underlying the poverty line was designed by the U.S. Department of Agriculture (USDA). The USDA warned that the plan was meant only for "temporary or emergency use when funds are low." It later "stressed that 'the cost of this plan is not a reasonable measure of basic money needs for a good diet,' and suggested that states designing assistance programs for families consider a food plan that cost 'about 25 percent more than the Economy Plan.'" The food plan (now called Thrifty Food Plan) was not only set unreasonably low from the start, but it "still assumes families will bake daily and cook all their food from scratch, never buy fast food or eat out, use dried beans and no canned food, be experts in nutrition, and have a working refrigerator, freezer, and stove," among other things.[11]

The government has not adjusted the poverty formula to reflect the current cost of food, which is now much lower in relation to housing, health care and other necessities, such as child care for working parents. It simply takes the previous year's poverty line (specific poverty thresholds are set for different size households), based on an increasingly inadequate formula, and adjusts it for inflation.

TABLE 4

Percent Below Official and Alternative Poverty Levels, 1993

	Official Poverty Line*	150% of Official Pov. Line	175% of Official Pov. Line	50% of Offical Pov. Line
All Persons	15.1	25.0	30.3	6.9
Men	13.3	22.5	27.7	5.4
Women	16.9	27.4	32.8	6.9
Children under 18	22.7	34.0	39.8	10.1
Related Children under 6	25.6	37.6	43.9	11.8
65 Years & over	12.2	27.4	35.2	2.4
White	12.2	21.3	26.5	4.5
men	10.7	19.2	24.1	3.9
women	13.7	23.4	28.7	5.0
children under 18	17.8	28.3	33.9	6.9
related children under 6	20.1	31.6	37.6	7.9
65 years & over	10.7	25.1	32.9	2.1
Black	33.1	47.2	53.8	16.7
men	29.7	42.9	50.0	15.4
women	36.0	51.0	57.2	17.8
children under 18	46.1	61.2	67.8	26.1
related children under 6	51.7	66.9	74.5	30.6
65 years & over	28.0	51.1	59.4	5.2
Latino**	30.6	48.2	55.5	10.5
men	27.6	45.7	53.3	9.0
women	33.6	50.9	57.9	12.1
children under 18	40.9	60.2	67.3	14.5
related children under 6	43.4	62.8	70.0	15.8
65 years & over	21.4	44.5	52.3	3.7
Asian & Pacific Islander	15.3			
Non-Latino White	9.9			
Am. Indian, Eskimo &				
Aleut, 1990***	30.9			
Persons 15 years & over 1991-92				
with no disability	12.2	20.5		
with a disability	19.3	33.8		
with a severe disability	24.3	41.8		

*Official 1993 poverty thresholds: 1 person under 65, $7,518; 1 person 65 & over, $6,930; 2 persons including 1 child under 18, $9,960; 3 persons including 1 child under 18, $11,631; 4 persons including 2 children under 18, $14,654. Alternative measures vary at about 150 to 170 percent of the official poverty line. Data not available in all categories.

**Latinos may be of any race.

***1990 Census figure from Census Bureau statistician. Latest year available.

Sources: Census Bureau, *Income, Poverty, and Valuation of Noncash Benefits: 1993,* prepublication Table 6, "Age, Sex, Household Relationship, Race, and Hispanic Origin, by Ratio of Income to Poverty Level: 1993"; John M. McNeil, Census Bureau, *Americans With Disabilities: 1991-*92 (December 1993), Table 8. On alternative measures, see Schwarz and Volgy, *The Forgotten Americans*, pp. 35-45.

"Many poor families," observes the Children's Defense Fund, "manage by cutting back on food, jeopardizing their health and the development of their children, or by living in substandard and sometimes dangerous housing. Some do without heat, electricity, telephone service, or plumbing for months or years. Many do without health insurance, health care, safe child care, or reliable transportation to take them to and from work. Confronted with impossible choices and inadequate basics, and lacking any cushion of savings or assets...many are just one illness, job loss, or family crisis away from homelessness or family dissolution."[12] Impoverished two-parent White or Black families are about twice as likely as nonpoor two-parent families to break up, the U.S. Census Bureau reports. "Stresses arising from low income and poverty may have contributed substantially to discontinuation rates for two-parent families."[13]

In their book on the working poor, John Schwarz and Thomas Volgy show that a family of four needed an income of about 155 percent of the official poverty line to buy minimally sufficient food, housing, health care, transportation, clothing and other personal and household items, and pay taxes. They warn that their stringent economy budget does not cover many things, such as paid child care. It does not provide for people who cannot find low-cost housing. Low-income families spend an average one-fourth of their incomes on child care. The gap between low-cost housing units and low-income households is vast; by 1991, there were 4.5 million fewer low-rent units than low-income renters.[14]

Using Schwarz and Volgy's formula, one person in four is living in poverty. By contrast, the official 1993 poverty rate was 15 percent. (See table 4.) That's still about 39 million Americans; one out of seven persons. According to the Children's Defense Fund, "Nearly one in two poor children (46 percent) lives in extreme poverty, in families with incomes below one-half of the poverty line. This proportion has risen steadily—from 31 percent in 1975 (the first year for which data on extreme poverty are available) to its present record-high level."[15]

Some people argue that the official poverty rate overstates poverty because it does not include noncash benefits such as food stamps in measuring income (cash benefits such as Social Security and AFDC are included). However, adjusting the poverty rate for the current cost of necessities has a much greater effect (upward) than the effect (downward) of adding noncash benefits. (See table 5.) It's also important to note that, contrary to common belief, more than one out of four

TABLE 5

Adjusting the Poverty Rate for Food/Housing Costs and Noncash Benefits, 1988

Adjusting for Food Costs	Adjusting for Housing Costs	Official Poverty Rate	Adjusting for Govt. Food and Housing Benefits
25.8%	23.0%	13.0%	11.6%

Note: Noncash medical benefits are omitted. As the U.S. House Committee on Ways and Means *1993 Green Book* explains, "The development of the poverty thresholds did not take into account medical costs. Although poor persons are clearly better off with medical coverage, such benefits cannot be used by recipients to meet other needs of daily living. Also, since health insurance costs are not imputed to the incomes of those above poverty, it seems inappropriate to count health benefits for those below the poverty line." In the words of Mishel and Bernstein, "their inclusion would have the perverse effect of making the ill appear less poor."

Sources: Mishel and Bernstein, *The State of Working America 1994-95*, pp. 255-56, citing Patricia Ruggles; *1993 Green Book*, pp. 1318-20. 1988 is the latest year of available data for comparison.

officially poor people receive *no* government assistance of any kind—cash or noncash. Fewer than one out of five officially poor people live in public or subsidized housing. Half live in households that receive no food stamps. Moreover, according to the Census Bureau, despite the existence of such programs as Medicaid and Medicare, 29 percent of the officially poor had no public or private medical insurance of any kind at any time during 1993.[16] Schwarz and Volgy point out that the issue of whether to include current noncash benefits "largely dissolves if an income significantly above the official poverty line" is recognized as reflecting needed income, because at that level people receive only small amounts, if any, of noncash benefits.[17]

THE UNDERVALUED

The United States is the poorest richest country in the world. Despite its wealth, it lags behind other industrialized democracies in assuring basic human needs—health care being today's best known example. All people and communities need services. In higher-income communities, people needing doctors or psychologists, lawyers or drug treatment, tutors or child care, can afford private practitioners and avoid the stigma that unjustly accompanies public social services. In lower-income communities they cannot. Here, though unemployment is high and wages increasingly low, public social services are commonly stingy, humiliating and punitive. Here, while the income gap is widening and the "safety net" shredded, prisons and other "corrections spending" make up the fastest growing part of state budgets.[18]

When it comes to children, the United States is the poorest of rich nations. A comparison among industrialized democracies showed that U.S. income is the most unevenly distributed and found

> that the child poverty rate in the U.S., after taxes and benefits are considered, was more than twice that in Canada and four times the average child poverty rate in the other nations in the study. It also showed that the poverty rate just among white children in the U.S. was higher than the poverty rate among *all* children in all other countries in the study except Australia. In short, the private economy in the United States generates more relative poverty among children than the private economies of many other western, industrialized nations—and the U.S. then does far less than the other nations to address this problem.[19] (Italics in original.)

If the U.S. government were a parent, it would be guilty of child abuse. As a consequence of unconscionable poverty and governmental neglect, proportionately more children die before their first birthday in the United States than in 20 other countries. The death rate of Black babies in the United States ranks 35th on the global scale, tied with Bulgaria and Chile, and behind such nations as Jamaica, Sri Lanka, Poland, Cuba and Kuwait. In the United States, Black babies are more than twice as likely to die before their first birthday as White babies, and their life expectancy is seven years less.[20]

IN 1960 THE AVERAGE C.E.O. WAS PAID 41 TIMES MORE THAN THE AVERAGE WORKER. BY 1992 THE AVERAGE C.E.O. WAS PAID 157 TIMES MORE.

2

BREAKDOWN OF THE PAYCHECK

By the standards of today, the U.S. offers both cheap energy and cheap labor—and the all-too-rare plus of political stability...In Germany, the Netherlands, Belgium, and Sweden, average wages for manufacturing workers now exceed comparable U.S. wages by as much as 20%.

Business Week, July 9, 1979.

The standard [of living] of the average American has to decline.

Federal Reserve Chair Paul Volcker, October 1979.[1]

It is fashionable to blame the supposed "breakdown of the family" for promoting poverty and ignore the breakdown in wages and employment. The scapegoating stereotype of deadbeat poor people masks the growing reality of dead-end jobs and disposable workers. Living standards are falling for younger generations despite the fact that many households have two wage earners, have fewer children and are better educated than their parents.

DOWNWARDLY MOBILE

The average real (inflation-adjusted) weekly earnings of production and nonsupervisory private sector workers crashed 16 percent

---

TABLE 6

Hourly and Weekly Earnings of Production and Nonsupervisory Workers, 1947-93

in 1993 dollars

Year	Average Hourly Earnings	Average Weekly Earnings
1947	6.75	272.16
1967	10.67	405.40
1973	**12.06**	**445.10**
1979	12.03	429.42
1989	11.26	389.50
1991	10.95	375.55
1993	**10.83**	**373.64**
Percent Change 1973-93	–10.2%	–16.1%

Source: Mishel and Bernstein, *The State of Working America 1994-95*, Table 3.3.

---

between 1973 and 1993—falling below 1967 levels. These workers make up more than 80 percent of wage and salary employment. (See table 6.) The postwar pattern of upward income mobility was broken, beginning with the cohort of Americans born between 1955 and 1964.[2] So-called Yuppies were and are a tiny sliver of the population, whose over-blown image in the 1980s served largely to distract attention from the economic crisis befalling more and more of their peers. Younger generations found themselves blamed for their increasingly obvious downward mobility; they were disparaged as lazy, spendthrift "20-nothings."

The inflation-adjusted median income for young families with children—headed by persons younger than 30—plunged 32 percent between 1973 and 1990. Median income was nearly cut in half for Black families with children headed by persons under 30. (See table 7.)

Forty percent of all children in families headed by someone younger than 30 were *officially* living in poverty in 1990, including one out of four children in White young families and one out of five children in young married-couple families.[3] (See table 8.) If not for the increased work hours and earnings of women since 1973, married-couple families would be significantly poorer.

TABLE 7

Median Income of Families with Children Under 18, Headed by Persons Younger than 30, 1973-90

in 1990 dollars

	1973	1979	1989	1990	Percent Change 1973-89*	Percent Change 1973-90
All young families with children	27,765	25,204	20,665	18,844	–25.6	–32.1
Married-couple	30,947	30,496	28,279	27,000	– 8.6	–12.8
Male-headed	18,547	16,531	17,907	16,000	– 3.5	–13.7
Female-headed	9,962	9,360	7,471	7,256	–25.0	–27.2
White, non-Latino	29,475	28,246	24,858	23,000	–15.7	–22.0
Black, non-Latino	17,958	14,371	11,677	9,286	–35.0	–48.3
Latino	19,704	19,213	16,463	14,200	–16.4	–27.9
Other, non-Latino	25,825	22,336	22,217	15,908	–14.0	–38.4
High School dropout	18,842	16,213	12,543	10,213	–33.4	–45.8
High School grad.	28,410	26,298	21,650	20,000	–23.8	–29.6
Some College	31,710	30,892	26,666	27,000	–15.9	–14.9
College graduate	37,757	36,900	42,181	38,700	+11.7	+ 2.5

Note: Half earn below the median. Half earn above it.

*1973, 1979, 1989 were business-cycle peaks with low official unemployment. Author's calculations for percent change 1973-89.

Source: Children's Defense Fund, *Vanishing Dreams*, Appendix, Table 3.

THE UNDERPAID

Falling wages can't be explained by common rationales such as slow productivity growth, higher-cost fringe benefits or a supposed skills and education deficit. Real wages are dropping because of global corporate restructuring, deunionization, the shift toward lower-paying industries, the lower value of the minimum wage, increased part-time and other contingent work, upsized unemployment and underemployment, automation and other trends.

The Economic Policy Institute shows that taking into account health and pension benefits and payroll taxes, the total inflation-adjusted hourly compensation for private sector employees has declined

TABLE 8

Official Poverty Rates Among Children in Families Headed by Persons Younger than 30, 1973-90

in percent

	1973*	1979	1989	1990	Percent Change 1973-89	Percent Change 1973-90
All children in young families	20.1	23.8	35.0	40.0	74.1	99.0
Married-couple	7.9	10.8	16.5	19.6	108.8	148.1
Male-headed	21.0	22.0	27.8	28.3	32.4	34.8
Female-headed	67.9	61.7	71.2	76.8	4.9	13.1
White, non-Latino	12.1	14.8	23.6	27.2	95.0	124.8
Black, non-Latino	47.4	48.8	59.0	68.4	24.5	44.3
Latino	35.0	36.1	45.2	51.4	29.1	46.9
Other, non-Latino	22.3	33.0	40.6	34.0	82.1	52.5
High School dropout	39.3	44.3	57.9	64.0	47.3	62.8
High School graduate	13.1	19.0	28.4	32.9	116.8	151.1
Some College	8.6	9.6	19.7	21.4	129.0	148.8
College graduate	2.6	4.0	7.3	6.9	180.8	165.4

*1973 was a low point for family poverty rates. Author's calculations for percent change, 1973-89.

Source: Children's Defense Fund, *Vanishing Dreams*, Appendix, Table 7.

by more than 8 percent since 1977. Although "the most commonly mentioned reason for recent wage problems is slow productivity growth," the reality is that wages have fallen behind productivity. According to the Economic Policy Institute, productivity grew a total of 3.6 percent between 1973 and 1979 (0.6 percent annually vs. 2.4 percent annually during 1959-73) and 8.7 percent from 1979 to 1989 (0.8 percent annually), and it grew at 1.5 percent annually between 1989 and 1992.[4] In 1991, annual productivity growth reached 2.3 percent and, in 1992, nearly 3 percent.[5]

Business Week argues that productivity—output per worker—is significantly undermeasured: "The government has no good way of measuring output in a whole range of industries, including banking, software, legal services, wholesale trade, and communication—all of which have invested heavily in information technology...Most economists now believe that productivity growth in these industries is substantially understated by the government figures. As a result, overall productivity growth for the economy is understated by 'something around the order of one-half to one percentage point a year,' says W. Erwin Diewert, an economist at the University of British Columbia."[6]

Rising productivity in the 1990s, says *Fortune*, demonstrates that the "productivity payoff" from information technology and related corporate reengineering has arrived.[7] There has been no wage payoff for most workers. As *Fortune* observed in 1993, before the economy picked up even more speed:

> Many of the productive people driving this slow recovery are going the extra mile for less than they think they deserve...Praise that used to show up in a paycheck is increasingly delivered in the unbankable form of plaques, theater tickets, and thank-you notes from the boss. FedEx sent out over 50,000 such notes last year.
>
> If a pat on the back in lieu of a raise can feel like a slap in the face, who dares complain? These days, having a job is a privilege, and keeping it is the measure of success. With raises few and tiny, FedEx couriers have seen their real wages decline by more than 15% since 1988. Says compensation director Bill Cahill: "What people are saying is, 'Please, keep me employed.' They're not out there clamoring for a raise."[8]

Goodyear CEO Stanley Gault, says *Fortune*, "has watched productivity at his company roll to record levels. Before accounting for retiree benefits, Goodyear earned $352 million [in 1992] on sales of $11.8 billion. The company, Gault says, is producing 30% more tires than in 1988, with 24,000 fewer associates (Gault-speak for employees). Wages have not kept pace with those gains—nor could they, as Gault points out: 'It is essential that companies keep productivity ahead of wage increases. That is the only way to gain on your competitors, bring on new products, and increase the dividend to shareholders.'...Shareholders have seen their dividends triple over the past two years."[9]

Like other CEOs, Goodyear's Stanley Gault has reaped the benefits of rising productivity and shareholder dividends, and downsized worker wages. He pocketed $11.3 million dollars in salary, bonus and long-term compensation in 1993. That put him at number 20 among top-paid chief executives.[10]

"'The only time American workers will get paid on a par with productivity growth,' says [Morgan Stanley economist Stephen] Roach, 'is if the company has an extraordinary global edge on a technology or an idea.' And any such edge, he adds, would probably be short-lived." *Fortune* asserts that higher living standards will come "in the form of

TABLE 9
Low Earners and High Earners, 1979-92
Percent of year-round, full-time civilian workers ages 16 and over
in 1992 dollars

	Percent with Low Earnings* Below $13,091			Percent with High Earnings Above $52,364		
	1979	1992	Percent change	1979	1992	Percent change
Men	7.7	14.1	+6.4	15.0	14.7	–0.3
Women	20.4	23.6	+3.2	1.3	3.4	+2.1
Ages 18-24	22.9	47.1	+24.2	n.a.	n.a.	n.a.
Ages 25-34	8.8	18.4	+9.6	n.a.	n.a.	n.a.
White Men	7.2	11.6	+4.4	15.9	16.4	+0.5
White Women	19.8	21.1	+1.3	1.3	3.8	+2.5
Black Men	14.0	19.4	+5.4	4.2	5.1	+0.9
Black Women	24.3	26.9	+2.6	0.5	1.6	+1.1
Latino Men	13.4	26.4	+13.0	5.2	5.3	+0.1
Latina Women	32.3	36.6	+4.3	1.0	1.8	+0.8
No High School Diploma						
Men	15.3	32.2	+16.9	4.7	2.5	–2.2
Women	40.1	54.7	+14.6	0.3	0.4	+0.1
High School Dipl., no college						
Men	7.8	16.7	+8.9	8.9	5.5	–3.4
Women	21.1	30.0	+8.9	0.5	1.1	+0.6
College Bachelor's or higher						
Men	3.1	6.3	+3.2	34.4	33.5	–0.9
Women	7.2	8.5	+1.3	4.2	9.6	+5.4

n.a. means data not available.

*Earnings is defined by the Census Bureau as "the pre-tax sum of money wages and salary plus any net income from self-employment."

Source: Census Bureau, "The Earnings Ladder: Who's at the Bottom? Who's at the Top?" *Statistical Brief*, March 1994.

cheaper or better goods and services…Workers…will have to make
peace with the fact that their payoff comes not on payday but at the
checkout counter."[11]

Leaving aside the large number of jobless workers, the reality is
that wages are falling further behind price inflation. Discount prices at
places like Wal-Mart, Home Depot, Staples, Circuit City and on-line
shopping services don't compensate for discount wages. Discount
wages aren't enough to cover items like rent, mortgages, cars, insurance, health care and child care, much less college, vacations and
retirement. Not to mention the repair and replacement bills for mer-
chandise that is often cheap in quality as well as cost. Moreover, there's
no guarantee that today's discount prices won't rise once smaller
competitors are driven out of business.

FALLING FLOOR

Good jobs at good wages are becoming harder to find and keep.
Between 1979 and 1992, the proportion of year-round, full-time workers paid low wages jumped from 12 to 18 percent—nearly one in every
five full-time workers overall, one out of four women workers, one out
of four Black workers and nearly one out of three Latino workers.
Almost half of all young full-time workers, ages 18-24, earn low wages,
up sharply from 1979.[12] (See table 9.) The United States is the only
major industrialized nation where low-wage workers have had large
declines in real earnings.[13]

The U.S. government has encouraged lower wages and wider
income inequality by letting the minimum wage plummet in value. In
1967, a full-time, year-round worker paid minimum wage earned above
the official poverty line for a family of three. The same was true in 1979.
No longer. By 1993, these wage earners were way below the official
poverty line for a family of *two.* "Raised 12 times between 1950 and
1981, the [minimum] wage went through a unique dry spell during the
1980s. As prices rose…Congress held the wage constant at $3.35,"
report William Spriggs and Bruce Klein. The minimum wage was
increased in 1990 to $3.80 and, in 1991, to $4.25. But the 1993 value of
the minimum wage, adjusting for inflation, was 25 percent less than it
was in 1979. President Clinton's belated proposal to raise the minimum
wage to $5.15 by 1997 is financially too little and politically too late.

The falling real minimum wage has had an impact well beyond
those actually earning the minimum, and an especially hard impact on

TABLE 10

Real Hourly Wage and Share of Workforce
by Education, 1973-93

in 1993 dollars

	High School Dropout	High School Graduate	Some College	College Graduate	College and 2+ Years
Hourly Wages					
1973	10.16	11.63	12.86	16.99	20.91
1979	10.06	11.23	12.24	15.52	18.80
1987	8.74	10.49	11.96	15.98	19.77
1989	8.44	10.21	11.82	15.90	20.36
1990	8.21	10.04	11.81	15.99	20.29
1993	7.87	9.92	11.37	15.71	19.93
% Change					
1973-79	−1.1	−3.5	−4.8	−8.6	−10.1
1979-89	−16.1	−9.1	−3.5	+2.4	+8.3
1989-93	− 6.7	−2.8	−3.8	−1.2	−2.1
1973-93	−22.5	−14.7	−11.6	−7.5	−4.7
% Share of Workforce					
1973	28.5	41.8	15.1	8.8	3.6
1989	13.7	40.5	22.3	14.0	6.9
Men's Wages					
1973	11.85	14.02	14.73	19.41	22.20
1979	11.58	13.49	14.29	18.10	20.31
1990	9.23	11.54	13.45	18.16	22.35
1993	8.64	11.19	12.70	17.62	21.71
% Change					
1973-79	−2.3	−3.8	−2.9	−6.7	−8.5
1973-93	−27.1	−20.2	−13.8	−9.2	−2.2
Women's Wages					
1973	7.16	8.79	9.89	13.35	17.36
1979	7.44	8.81	9.67	11.79	15.35
1990	6.59	8.50	10.20	13.52	17.20
1993	6.56	8.57	10.19	13.57	17.69
% Change					
1973-79	+3.9	+0.2	−2.3	−11.6	−11.6
1973-93	−8.4	−2.4	+3.1	+1.7	+1.9

(table continued on next page)

Table 10 (continued)
Share of Workforce by Highest Degree Attained, 1993

	Less than High School	High School or GED	Assoc. College	College Bachelor	Masters	Ph.D., law degree, etc.	At least High School degree	At least College Bachelor
Total	11.1	56.1	8.0	16.9	5.9	2.0	88.9	24.8
Men	13.1	54.5	7.2	16.8	5.8	2.6	86.9	25.2
Women	9.0	57.8	8.9	17.0	6.0	1.3	91.0	24.3

Note: Workforce ages 18 and over. 1993 education data different because in 1992 the Census Bureau Current Population Survey changed how it measures educational attainment.
Source: Mishel and Bernstein, *The State of Working America 1994-95*, Tables 3.18-3.21

women, people of color and rural workers. As Spriggs and Klein put it, "The minimum wage, often dismissed by policy makers and economists as the social safety net of teenagers and part-time workers, is in fact a key determinant of wages for a significant segment of the U.S. work force—high-school educated workers starting out in the job market." Workers close to the minimum—disproportionately women and people of color—tend to receive raises when the minimum wage goes up. Most minimum wage earners are adults, not teenagers, and more than a third are their families' sole breadwinners. Nearly two out of three workers who earn minimum wage are women. "Many policy analysts predicted that the 1990 and 1991 changes in the minimum wage would have disastrous effects," say Spriggs and Klein, "but economists studying these changes have not found the expected negative trade-off between employment levels and increases in the minimum."[14]

LOWER WAGES AND HIGHER EDUCATION

A college degree is increasingly necessary, but not sufficient to earn a decent income. College graduates are also experiencing the wage rollback. The real hourly wages for high school graduates dropped 15 percent between 1973 and 1993. Since 1990, college graduates "have been losing ground at the same rate as workers with less education," reports the Economic Policy Institute's *The State of Working America 1994-95*. By 1993, the real wages of college-educated workers were

7.5 percent below their 1973 level. "In other words, although college-educated workers had a wage advantage in the 1980s, the growth in their wage premium during that time reflects not a 'bidding up' of their wages but rather the driving down of the wages of non-college-educated workers." In short, "rather than a 'skill deficit,' working Americans are confronting a 'wage deficit.'"[15] A growing wage deficit. (See table 10.)

The State of Working America predicts that if current trends persist, over the next ten years "the median male wage will fall another 10.4% (from $11.24 to $10.07) and the median woman's wage will rise another 4.7% (from $8.79 to $9.21). Entry-level wages for high school graduates [the majority of the workforce], in this scenario, could be expected to fall another 24% among young men (from $6.68 to $5.50) and another 13% among young women (from $6.15 to $5.34)."[16] Note that women's wages are predicted to remain lower than men's.

What about all those supposedly high-paid jobs in high-tech industries requiring higher education? It's important not to confuse the occupations with *high growth rates* with occupations creating the *largest number of jobs*. (See table 11.) Over half of the total job growth projected over the 1992-2005 period will be in occupations that don't require more than a high school education. According to a 1992 Labor Department study, 30 percent of each new class of college "graduates between now and 2005 will march straight into the ranks of the jobless or the underemployed."[17]

White-collar and college-educated workers are also going through a process called 'proletarianization,'" writes journalist John Judis. "Initially seen as professionals or as part of management, these workers are now finding their work regulated in the same manner as wage workers in factories and offices. Doctors and nurses have become employees of HMOs; computer programmers have become piece workers for giant software firms. As they have lost the prerogatives of management or the protections of a craft guild, their wages have begun to fall like everyone else's."[18]

Despite the evidence to the contrary, the Clinton administration promotes the skills-mismatch rationale for low wages and high unemployment. Their mantra is retraining and more retraining for reemployment, ostensibly in high-paid, high-tech jobs. In reality, a Labor Department study "found that laid-off workers who underwent training under the Trade Adjustment Assistance Act failed to raise their wages. More than three-quarters of the workers, the study found, 'earned less

TABLE 11
Projected Jobs 1992-2005
moderate growth scenario
in descending order

Fastest growing occupations by growth rate	Occupations producing the most new jobs
home health aides	retail salespersons
human services workers	registered nurses
personal and home care aides	cashiers
computer engineers and scientists	general office clerks
systems analysts	truck drivers
physical and corrective therapy assistants and aides	waiters and waitresses
physical therapists	nursing aides, orderlies and attendants
paralegals	janitors and cleaners
special education teachers	food preparation workers
medical assistants	systems analysts
private detectives	home health aides
correction officers	secondary school teachers
child care workers	child care workers
travel agents	guards
radiologic technologists and technicians	marketing and sales worker supervisors

Sources: U.S. Department of Labor, Bureau of Labor Statistics, *The American Workforce: 1992-2005* (April 1994), pp. 72-73. Also see *1993 Green Book*, p. 539.

in their new job three years after their initial unemployment insurance claim than they did in their pre-layoff job.'"[19]

Corporations may be talking about training, but they aren't doing much of it. As *Business Week* notes, "at 1.4% of payroll, U.S. employers are spending relatively little on training. *Training* magazine says formal staff development spending by U.S. companies with more than 100 employees, at $50.6 billion [in 1994], will be up just 11% from 1990—less than inflation."[20]

UNION-FREE LABOR

Few American managers have ever accepted the right of unions to exist, even though that's guaranteed by the 1935 Wagner Act. Over the past dozen years, in fact, U.S. industry has conducted one of the most successful antiunion wars ever, illegally firing thousands of workers for exercising their rights to organize.

Business Week, May 23, 1994.

Let there be no doubt: a revitalization of the labor movement would help reverse the erosion of the middle class.

Secretary of Labor Robert Reich, *New York Times*, August 31, 1994.

Union jobs provide better wages and benefits than their nonunion counterparts, but they are fast disappearing. Full-time workers who were union members earned median weekly wages of $592 in 1994 compared to $432 for nonunion workers—a wage differential of $8,320 over 52 weeks.[21] Looking at total compensation, including average wages and benefits, "the union advantage runs a little more than $14,000 a year," reports the *American Labor Yearbook*. "The average union differential has remained in the 30%-35% range for the past decade." Unions have the greatest effect in raising the wages of lower-wage workers.[22]

Since the mid-1970s, employers have won a majority of National Labor Relations Board (NLRB) elections. "A number of studies indicate that management opposition to unions, particularly illegal campaign tactics, is a major, if not the major, determinant of NLRB election results."[23]

President Reagan sent a clear union-busting signal to employers when he fired striking air traffic controllers early in his administration. According to an analysis of NLRB figures by University of Chicago professors Robert LaLonde and Bernard Meltzer, cited in *Business Week*, "employers illegally fired 1 of every 36 union supporters during organizing drives in the late 1980s, vs. 1 in 110 in the late '70s and 1 in 209 in the late '60s...Unlawful firings occurred in one-third of all representation elections in the late '80s, vs. 8% in the late '60s...'Even more significant than the numbers is the perception of risk among workers, who think they'll be fired in an organizing campaign,' says Harvard law professor Paul C. Weiler. Indeed, when managements obey the law, they don't defeat unions nearly as often."[24] Strike activity has reached record lows. In 1992, there were only 35 strikes involving 1,000 or more workers versus a peak of 424 such strikes in 1974.[25]

Union votes were important to Bill Clinton's election as president, but he has delivered little on his campaign promises. The passage of NAFTA, which unions opposed, was followed by the defeat of legislation banning permanent striker replacements, which unions supported. Referring to the striker replacement ban, conservative commentator George Will observed, "Even with a Democratic president, organized labor's highest priority was flicked away like a nettlesome gnat."[26] Congress would like to reverse the watered-down executive order banning some striker replacements that Clinton issued after the midterm election.

The unionized share of the workforce has declined from a peak of 35.5 percent in 1945 to 15.5 percent in 1994. Seventeen percent of full-time workers are union members compared to only eight percent of part-time workers.[27] While public sector unionization has grown to nearly 37 percent, the Labor Research Association predicts that private sector unionization, 11.5 percent in 1992, "will sink to 5% by the end of the decade unless labor laws are reformed and unions commit more

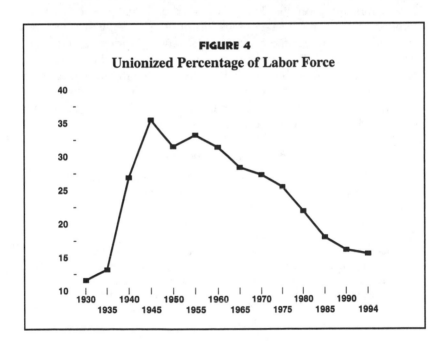

FIGURE 4
Unionized Percentage of Labor Force

resources to organizing."[28] Privatization of government services is often a means of deunionization.

In an article supporting corporatist-style unions, *Business Week* acknowledges the link between declining union membership on the one hand, and lower wages and benefits and widening income disparities on the other: "The resulting drag on pay for millions of people accounts for at least 20% of the widening gap between rich and poor," and weakening unions are "a key reason for the six-percentage-point slide in the 1980s in the share of employees with company pension plans, for the seven-point decline in those with employer health plans, and for a 125-fold explosion in unlawful-discharge suits now that fewer employees have a union to stick up for them."

"Unions are often blamed for more trouble than they've caused," *Business Week* adds. "In the 1970s, for instance, many executives believed that unions inflated prices by lifting wages above some presumed market level. Since then, however, more than 50 quantitative studies have concluded that the higher productivity of unionized companies offsets most of their higher costs."[29]

American workers are working longer for less than their more unionized counterparts in other major industrialized countries. As the U.S. Commission on the Future of Worker-Management Relations acknowledges, "The U.S. earnings distribution among workers has widened greatly and is the most unequal among" industrialized countries. Meanwhile, U.S. workers put in about 200 more hours per year than West European workers. A major cause is the difference in vacation time. "Americans with sufficient seniority typically get two weeks of vacation, though some get more and others less. By contrast, Europeans typically obtain 4-5 week vacations, often legally mandated, from the first year hired."[30]

In the words of the *American Labor Yearbook*:

> With the possible exception of Hong Kong and South Korea, the U.S. provides workers with less legal protection than any other industrialized country...[It] has the smallest proportion of workers covered by collective bargaining agreements.
>
> The U.S. has become a cheap labor haven for global capital looking for low wage and benefit costs, high productivity, and a nonunion environment...For example, German firms such as BMW, Adidas, Siemens, and Mercedes are moving into the Carolinas, where huge tax breaks are available and the unionization rate is below 5%.[31]

DISPOSABLE WORKERS

> Mobility. Empowerment. Teams. Cross-training. Virtual of-
> fices. Telecommuting. Reengineering. Restructuring. Delayering.
> Outsourcing. Contingency. If the buzzwords don't sound familiar,
> they should: They are changing your life. The last decade, perhaps
> more than any other time since the advent of mass production,
> has witnessed a profound redefinition of the way we work...
> More than likely, you are working longer and harder, and
> making less money than did someone in comparable work a
> decade ago...The corporate terrain is shaky, with near continuous
> downsizing and reorganization.
>
> *Business Week*, October 17, 1994. [32]

The jobs of today and tomorrow not only pay less than the
disappearing unionized jobs; they are much more exploitative and
precarious. More workers are going back to the future of sweatshops
and migrant labor. Corporations are rapidly replacing full-time jobs with
variations on day labor and piece work. It's a global trend hurting
workers around the world.

This is "the age of the contingent or temporary worker, of the
consultant and subcontractor, of the just-in-time workforce—fluid,
flexible, disposable," writes Lance Morrow in *Time* magazine. "Companies are portable, workers are throwaway."[33] It is the age of the "flex
force." The age of "McJobs."

As the *American Labor Yearbook* sums it up, "The dominant trend
in the corporate world is the modular corporation—companies that
focus all their energy on a few core activities and outsource everything
else. Companies are shedding plants and workers and operating with
a network of suppliers held together by temporary agreements. A 'core'
group of permanent employees handle the core activities, and contractors or contingent workers are used to manage surges in demand or to
handle special projects or noncore needs. An important part of the
modular style is to stay union-free to avoid any restrictive work rules
or job security arrangements."[34]

Contingent workers are temporary workers, contract workers,
"leased" employees and part-time workers, a growing share of them
involuntary part-timers wanting permanent full-time work. Contingent
workers made up a third of the U.S. workforce in 1993, up sharply from
one-fourth in 1988. Some full-time workers are finding themselves fired
and then "leased" back at a large discount by the same companies.[35]

The Milwaukee-based temporary agency, Manpower Inc., has become the largest private employer in the United States—with about 600,000 people on its payroll. Manpower's CEO estimates that two-thirds of his workforce would rather be working in permanent positions. In 1993, the Michigan electronics manufacturer Robertshaw Controls opened a factory staffed entirely with Manpower temps.[36]

Contingent workers are expected to *outnumber* permanent full-time employees in the United States by the end of the decade. While some professional consultants will thrive, many more people will be working harder for less—permanently juggling long hours at multiple, changing jobs, if they can find them, just to make ends meet.

More than three-quarters of all the new net jobs during 1979-89 were in the low-paying retail trade and services industries (business, personnel, health), which employ a large share of part-timers. Between March 1991, the official end of the last recession, and July 1993, more than a quarter of the new jobs were provided by temporary help agencies and another quarter were part-time jobs, three-quarters of those filled by involuntary part-timers. Between January and July 1993, 20 percent "of the new jobs were people becoming self-employed—a category that includes underemployed people making do with make-shift work as well as budding entrepreneurs."[37] More people were laid off in the first half of 1993 than in the comparable months of 1992 or 1991.[38] The number of involuntary part-timers almost tripled between 1970 and 1993.[39]

The growth in contingent work is a global trend. In 1991, 32 percent of Spain's workers were temporary workers, as were 20 percent in Australia, 17 percent in Portugal, 15 percent in Greece, 13 percent in Finland and 10 percent in France, Germany and Japan. "In Spain, Portugal, Greece, Belgium and the Netherlands, more than 60% of workers in temporary jobs accepted them because they could not find full-time employment."[40] Oei Hong Leong, chairman of Strategic Investment Ltd., which has restructured 100 state-owned firms in China, a top destination for foreign corporate investment, says that "the flood of 100 million rural residents into the cities will ensure urban wages remain competitive internationally. 'Our ventures have stopped hiring long-term workers,' he said. 'We only hire these rural workers on contract. Coming from the countryside, they are happy to work without health insurance or other social benefits.'"[41]

Growing numbers of workers will have little hope of promotion and plenty of fear about falling living standards and unemployment. In the United States, male part-timers earned 41 percent less *per hour* than full-time workers in 1989. Women part-timers earned 24 percent less in wages per hour than women working full time. The compensation difference was even greater in terms of health insurance and other benefits. The average weekly income of full-time workers in 1992 was $445 while it was $259 for temporary workers and $132 for part-time workers, growing numbers of whom are only working part-time or temporary jobs, and earning so little, because they can't find full-time jobs.[42]

Besides lower wages, scarcer benefits and poorer prospects for promotion, contingent workers are excluded or penalized by current labor law, Social Security, disability and unemployment compensation. For example, the majority of states exclude part-time workers and independent contractors from the unemployment insurance program. Contingent workers are also much more vulnerable to discrimination, harassment, and health and safety violations. In the words of *Forbes* magazine, "You can shed a temp if he or she doesn't work out; hiring and firing a regular employee is a lot trickier, thanks to a growing list of antidiscrimination laws."[43]

As *Time* summed it up:

> Long-term commitments of all kinds are anathema to the modern corporation. For the growing ranks of contingent workers, that means no more pensions, health insurance or paid vacations. No more promises or promotions or costly training programs. No more lawsuits for wrongful termination or other such hassles for the boss…Being a short-timer can mean doing hazardous work without essential training, or putting up with sexual and racial harassment. Placement officers report client requests for "blond bombshells" or people without accents. Says an agency counselor: "One client called and asked us not to send any black people, and we didn't. We do whatever the clients want, whether it's right or not."[44]

Even the rosier view, which rejects the idea that a majority of the workforce will become contingent, is not very rosy. It is a world, at best, of serial full-time employment, in which workers somehow get by as they regularly "retool." *Fortune* comments:

> At some point corporate America's drive for flexibility and cost cutting runs head-on into another key imperative: the growing belief that competitive advantage hinges upon retaining a workforce that is motivated, creative, and independent—empowered, in the current jargon. That goal will never be achieved by companies operating with a largely disposable workforce, which is yet another reason to believe that in the

future, most of us, most of the time, will be holding down permanent jobs. What has changed is that we will likely hold five, six, or more full-time posts in our careers, rather than one or two. And as we retool during those transitions, the odds are good that a growing number of us will be forced to find temporary shelter in the uncertain world of contingent work.[45]

Manpower CEO Mitchell Fromstein predicts that the average worker will hold up to 15 different positions by retirement time.[46] Career adviser Carol Kleiman asserts, "The Bureau of Labor's statistics project that we will change careers three times over our lifetimes and that we will change jobs six times, but I think it will be much more than that. [Much] of this will be because we're fired and replaced with somebody cheaper, fired and replaced by nobody or because a computer can do our work."[47]

In a *Washington Post* story on the "growing minimum wage culture," Sheldon Danzinger, professor of public policy at the University of Michigan, observes, "Where you used to have six people in the [secretarial] pool earning $14,000 apiece, today you have one desktop publishing expert making $24,000 and five former secretaries earning $9,000 at Kmart."[48] If they're not unemployed.

3

COMPETING FOR GLOBAL CORPORATIONS

Workers will have to realize that they are now competing for jobs against people who ride to work every day on bicycles, own only one pair of shabby sandals, and are prepared [sic] to live with their families crammed into tiny apartments.

Robert Brusca, chief economist, Nikko Securities (New York).[1]

Like their colonial predecessors, global corporations see the world as their farm, factory, mine, market and playground.[2] As far back as the 1600s, "the Dutch and English sailed the oceans of the world as agents for commercial concerns, the great East India Companies. For these companies the profit motive was preeminent; they did not encourage exploration for its own sake or for reasons of glory or religion."[3] In the 1960s, George Ball, an investment banker and former U.S. government official, applauded the growing number of "cosmocorps," which are "engaged in taking the raw materials produced in one group of countries, transforming these into manufacturing goods with the labor and plant facilities of another group, and selling the products in still a third group...[all] with the benefit of instant communications, quick transport, computers, and modern management techniques." Such corporations, he asserted, are "the best means yet devised for utilizing world resources according to the criterion of profit: an objective [sic] standard of efficiency."[4]

MAKING THE WORLD SAFE FOR PROFITEERING

General Smedley Butler is a Marine Corps legend. He earned two Congressional Medals of Honor, the nation's highest military award for bravery. "As a soldier," said Butler, "I long suspected that war was a racket; not until I retired to civil life did I fully realize it."

"It may seem odd for me, a military man, to adopt such a comparison," Butler wrote in 1935. "Truthfulness compels me to. I spent 33 years and 4 months in active service as a member of our country's most agile military force—the Marine Corps...And during that period I spent most of my time being a high-class muscle man for Big Business, for Wall Street and for the bankers. In short, I was a racketeer for capitalism...

"Thus I helped make Mexico...safe for American oil interests in 1914. I helped make Haiti and Cuba a decent place for the National City Bank boys to collect revenues in. I helped in the raping of half a dozen Central American republics for the benefit of Wall Street. The record of racketeering is long. I helped purify Nicaragua for the international banking house of Brown Brothers in 1909-12. I brought light to the Dominican Republic for American sugar interests in 1916. I helped make Honduras 'right' for American fruit companies in 1903. In China in 1927 I helped see to it that Standard Oil went its way unmolested.

"During those years, I had, as the boys in the back room would say, a swell racket. I was rewarded with honors, medals, promotion. Looking back on it, I feel I might have given Al Capone a few hints. The best *he* could do was to operate his racket in three city districts. We Marines operated on three *continents*."[5] (Italics in original.)

The yearly sales of the leading global corporations dwarf the GNPs of most nations (Gross National Product, GNP, is a nation's total output of goods and services). The top *Fortune* 500 industrial corporation, General Motors, had 1993 sales of $133.6 billion, about the GNP of Denmark and bigger than the GNPs of Saudi Arabia, South Africa, Thailand and Indonesia.

GLOBAL WEBS

Global corporations (also known as multinational and transnational corporations) control more than 70 percent of world trade. The World Bank estimates that a third or more of world trade consists of transfers *within* the 350 largest global corporations. "By 1991 more than half of all U.S. exports and imports were transfers of components and services within the same global corporation, most of them flying the American flag."[6]

According to the *World Investment Report:* "The universe of TNCs [transnational corporations] in the early 1990s was composed of at least 37,000 parent firms that controlled over 200,000 foreign affiliates worldwide, not counting numerous non-equity links. Two-thirds of these parent firms—26,000—were from 14 major home developed countries, an increase of 19,000 since the end of the 1960s…The influence of the largest TNCs on output, employment, demand patterns, technology and industrial relations should not be underestimated: the world's largest 100 TNCs [not counting those in banking and finance], ranked by foreign assets, held $3.4 trillion in global assets in 1992, of which about 40 percent were assets located outside their home countries. The top 100 control about one-third of the world FDI [foreign direct investment] stock."[7] (See tables 12 and 13.)

The top 100 global corporations are all based in the industrialized North. Their industries are mostly chemical and pharmaceutical, electronics and computer, motor vehicle, and mining and petroleum. Ranked by total assets, they are led by General Electric, General Motors, Ford, Royal Dutch/Shell, IBM, Exxon, Toyota and Matsushita Electric.[8] *Business Week* reports that "in 1993, U.S. businesses invested $58 billion in foreign operations, double the level of just two years earlier. So far in 1994, investment overseas is running at a rate that would top $65 billion."[9] At the same time, the United States is the leading destination for direct foreign investment—$32 billion in 1993. China is second, with $26 billion in 1993.[10]

China, where wages are miserly and human rights violations plentiful, accounted for 55 percent of the increase in foreign direct investment flows into Third World countries in 1992. (See table 14.) China now has over 50,000 foreign affiliates in operation. It ranks as the 11th largest exporter in the world and 2nd largest in the Third World. The export share of foreign affiliates in China's total national exports increased dramatically from 13 percent in 1990 to 28 percent in 1993.[11]

As professor of political economy Bennett Harrison describes it, corporations are seeking "concentration without centralization." They are dividing their operations and workers into core and periphery; forging strategic alliances with firms (frequently competitors, e.g. the IBM-Apple alliance) within and across national borders; and creating

TABLE 12

Countries with the Most Companies in the Fortune 500 World's Largest Industrial Corporations, 1993

	Number	Change Since 1992
United States	159	−2
Japan	135	+7
Britain	41	+1
Germany	32	no change
France	26	−4
South Korea	12	no change
Sweden	12	−2
Australia	10	+1
Switzerland	9	no change

Source: *Fortune*, July 25, 1994, p. 138.

TABLE 13

Home Countries of Top 100 Global Corporations, 1992

Ranked by foreign assets, not including banking and finance

Home Country	Number of Companies
United States	29
Japan	16
France	12
Germany	9
United Kingdom-Netherlands	2
Switzerland	6
United Kingdom	9
Italy	2
Sweden	4
Netherlands	2
Canada	3
Belgium	2
Other countries	4

Source: UNCTAD, *World Investment Report 1994*, Figure I.1, p. 8.

TABLE 14

Top Third World Countries for Foreign Direct Investment, 1981-92, and Human Development Rankings

Host Country	1981	1991	1992	1981-92	Human Develop. Index rank*	Income share of lowest 40% households 1980-91	Military expend. as % of education & health 1990-91	Debt service ratio**
		in $billions						
China		4.4	11.2	33.8	94	17.4	114	12.1
Singapore	1.7	4.4	5.6	33.0	43	15.0	129	n.a.
Mexico	2.8	4.8	5.4	29.0	52	11.9	5	30.9
Malaysia	1.3	4.0	4.5	18.8	57	12.9	38	8.3
Brazil	2.5		1.5	17.8	63	7.0	23	30.0
Hong Kong	1.1		1.9	14.7	24	16.2	10	n.a.
Argentina	.8	2.4	4.2	12.2	37	n.a.	51	48.4
Thailand		2.0	2.1	10.2	54	15.5	71	13.1
Egypt	.8			7.8	110	n.a.	52	16.7
Taiwan		1.3		6.5	n.a.	n.a.	n.a.	n.a.
Nigeria	.5		.9	5.2	139	n.a.	33	25.2
Indonesia		1.5	1.8	4.3	105	20.8	49	32.7

Note: In 1992, the top ten host countries had 76 percent of the total foreign direct investment in Third World countries.

*The Human Development Index measures life expectancy, adult literacy, schooling and standard of living reflecting local purchasing power. The highest ranked countries (out of 173) from 1 to 10 are: Canada, Switzerland, Japan, Sweden, Norway, France, Australia, United States, Netherlands, United Kingdom.

**Debt service as a percent of exports of goods and services.

Sources: UNCTAD, *World Investment Report 1994*, Table I.5 and United Nations Development Program, *Human Development Report 1994*, Human Development Indicator Tables.

networks of smaller suppliers and subcontractors in an emerging form of flexible, networked production made possible by computerized manufacturing and information technology. "In many cases, the legally independent small firms from which the big companies purchase parts, components, and services may not be all that independent, after all, but should rather be treated as de facto branch plants belonging to the big firms. *Production* may be decentralized into a wider and more geographically far-flung number of work sites, but *power, finance,* [distribution], and *control* remain concentrated in the hands of the managers of the largest companies in the global economy."[12] (Italics in original.)

Harrison calls Nike's global division of labor an exemplar of the principle of concentration without centralization. "Although Nike is legally registered as an American corporation, not one of the 40 million pairs of running shoes that Nike produces annually is manufactured within the United States: *everything* is subcontracted from elsewhere." Nike's "first tier" of manufacturers is divided this way:

> "Developed partners" located mainly in Taiwan and South Korea work closely with the R&D personnel in Oregon to make the firm's most expensive, high-end footwear (by *partners*, Nike managers mean contractors and suppliers who share some joint responsibility with the core firm, for design or for evaluation of production methods). The Asian partners contract out most of the work to local low-wage subcontractors.
>
> "Volume producers" are considerably larger, more vertically integrated companies with their own leather tanneries and rubber factories that manufacture more standardized products and sell to several buyers, of whom Nike is only one. Production and sales are highly variable from one month to the next.
>
> Finally within this tier, Nike has created what it calls "developing sources"—producers located in Thailand, Indonesia, Malaysia, and China. These are the lowest-wage, low- and semiskilled operations that Nike is gradually upgrading...
>
> Nike managers explicitly acknowledge the advantages of this spatial division of labor within the first tier. Apart from "hedg[ing] against currency fluctuations, tariffs, and duties [and] political climate change...in the long run [this arrangement] keeps pressure on the first tier producers to keep production costs low as developing sources mature into full-blown developed partners."[13]

[With headquarters in Beaverton, Oregon] Nike is the number-one maker of sport shoes in the world...

Virtually 100 percent of Nike's shoe assembly is in Asia. In the last five years the company has closed down twenty production sites in South Korea and Taiwan as wages have risen and opened up thirty-five new ones in China, Indonesia, and Thailand, where wages are rock bottom. The company has a global payroll of over 8,000, virtually all in management, sales, promotion, and advertising. The actual production is in the hands of about 75,000 Asian contractors.

...Nikes made in Indonesia cost $5.60 to produce, and sell on the average in North America and Europe for $73 and as much as $135. The Indonesian girls who sew them can earn as little as fifteen cents an hour. (A 1991 survey of Nike-licensed plants reported in *Indonesia Today* put the average wage for an experienced female worker at $.82 a day.) Overtime is often mandatory, and after an eleven-hour day that begins at 7:30 A.M., the girls return to the company barracks at 9:15 P.M. to collapse into bed, having earned as much as $2.00 if they are lucky.

Richard Barnet and John Cavanagh, *Global Dreams: Imperial Corporations and the New World Order* (1994).

"RACE TO THE BOTTOM"

By the logic of the global corporation, the role of national and international government is to regulate the movement of labor, not capital. Noncitizen immigrants may be treated as "aliens"—denied government services and deported—but not foreign corporations. By the logic of the global corporation, governments should subsidize the profits and socialize the costs of business. By corporate logic, national bans on cancer-causing chemicals, for example, may be banned internationally as unfair trade practices. By corporate logic, government should enforce corporate freedom, not the rights of workers or consumers, through international "free trade" agreements, finance and "development" agencies, and political, police and military intervention.

Cities, states and nations compete with each other in a no-win "race to the bottom" for corporate favor—offering tax subsidies, infrastructure, financing and other enticements. There is no assurance that subsidized corporations will stay. Many do not. For example, Digital Equipment Corporation located a plant in Boston's Roxbury neighborhood, in the government-supported Crosstown Industrial Park, which was founded in 1980 with the promise of jobs for the inner city. Digital shut down the plant in 1993. Then Mayor Ray Flynn was among those protesting the closure, accusing Digital of "an unwarranted disinvestment in a city which has invested millions of dollars in the company's success," citing bond financing, tax incentives, free rent and other subsidies. "In the final analysis, the company got what they could get from the city and from the neighborhood and then decided to get out." Roxbury's official unemployment rate was an estimated 22 percent in early 1993.[14]

According to a study by the Louisiana Coalition for Tax Justice: "To get a small handful of new jobs and corporations, Louisiana gave away $2.5 billion dollars [between 1980 and 1989]...The taxpayer cost per full-time job created was $41,806. Tax breaks granted to six of the state's major polluters cost taxpayers more than $500,000 dollars for each new permanent job created."[15]

As author Robert Goodman puts it, "This kind of public entrepreneuring...[has left] government in the role of competitor and business as welfare recipient. It is a process in which the public takes enormous financial risks, while business surveys the willing suitors and moves freely to where the public risk-taking is greatest."[16] Here's how New Mexico beat California recently in a bid for Intel Corporation's new computer-chip factory:

> New Mexico...could do what California couldn't: slash red tape, offer attractive tax breaks and present a reformed, lower cost worker's compensation system. But despite losing out to Rio Rancho, N.M., California still got something valuable out of its losing effort: a blunt lesson showing what must be done to compete more forcefully next time around...
>
> The New Mexico package gave Intel $114 million worth of incentives: $57 million in property-tax abatements, $36 million in waived new-equipment sales taxes, $20 million in manufacturing tax credits and $1 million in job-training funds. That amounts to $114,000 in concessions for each job Intel creates...
>
> But complicating any potential change in California is a politically charged question: Should a state running an $8.6 billion budget deficit offer incentives to a company like Intel that doesn't need, but expects them?
>
> Intel, after all, earned better than $1 billion last year on sales of $5.8 billion, mostly from its wildly popular microprocessors, the brains inside nearly 100 million personal computers. That makes Intel one of the most profitable companies in the world...

"We're going to build where Intel gets the best deal," said Intel's [Robert] Perlman. "California has to remember it doesn't do much good to have taxes on the books that it doesn't collect because companies don't build there."[17]

The Stride Rite Corporation, long renowned for its day care facilities and philanthropy, is a cofounder of Businesses for Social Responsibility. However, as the *Wall Street Journal* reports, over the last decade Stride Rite has "prospered partly by closing 15 factories, mostly in the Northeast and several in depressed areas and moving most of its production to various low-cost Asian countries." There, "Stride Rite continues its quest for labor bargains. In recent years, it has switched from factories in South Korea as pay rose there to lower-wage Indonesia and China." A Stride Rite director says, "It has become sort of Holy Grail for us." In China, says the *Wall Street Journal*, skilled workers "earn $100 to $150 a month, working 50 to 65 hours a week. Unskilled workers—packers and sorters—get $50 to $70 a month."

Stride Rite closed its U.S. distribution facilities in Roxbury and New Bedford, Massachusetts (a city seeking casino gambling to compensate for declining industry and fishing) and shifted them to Louisville, Kentucky. "It was a difficult decision," said then Stride Rite CEO Ervin Shames. "Our hearts said, 'Stay,' but our heads said, 'Move.'" According to the *Wall Street Journal*, "Kentucky won mainly because of a $24 million tax break over 10 years, vs a $3 million offer from Massachusetts. Lower wage rates also played a role." The United Food and Commercial Workers Union represented the workers in Massachusetts. The Kentucky plant is nonunion.[18] But the move didn't work out the way Stride Rite planned. The high-tech Kentucky warehouse was plagued with "software problems and bad management decisions," the *Boston Globe* reported. The resulting distribution disaster led to lost sales and earnings. Stride Rite's vice president for finance said the problems would cost $20 million to $25 million in lost profits.[19]

Of course, Stride Rite is not alone in combining social rights and wrongs. The "socially-responsible" Esprit clothing company, for example, uses San Francisco garment contractors that pay below-minimum sweatshop wages with no overtime pay.[20]

FREE TRADING ON CHEAP LABOR

> Gaining access to cheaper labor was the most important factor in
> U.S. companies' decisions to invest in [Caribbean] Basin assembly
> plants.
>
> U.S. General Accounting Office, *U.S. Support for Caribbean
> Basin Assembly Industries*, December 1993.

> "Just as with the move of manufacturing overseas, you're going to
> see an increasing flux of technical jobs out of the U.S.," predicts
> Intel Corp. Chief Operating Officer Craig R. Barrett. "We don't have
> any protected domains anymore."
>
> "High-Tech Jobs All Over the Map,"
> *Business Week/21st Century Capitalism*, 1994.

Corporate strategies maximize the ability of corporations to
rapidly invest and *disinvest*, regardless of the impact on workers or
communities—whether in Michigan, Puerto Rico or Ireland; California,
Mexico, Russia or China. Corporations are aggressively automating and
"downsizing" their workforces and shifting operations in a continual
search for greater public subsidies and higher private profits, lower
taxes, less regulation and cheaper labor.

"Cheap labor" does not mean low-skill. Corporations are already
switching to lower-paid, high-skilled industrial and service sector
employees such as computer programmers and engineers. As *Business
Week* put it in an article on the "push East" by European companies,
"Western Europe's backyard has both Philippine-level industrial wages
and well-trained engineers."[21] Bob Funk, president of the Oklahoma
City-based Express Personnel Services, which staffed Moscow's first
McDonald's, says Express has a roster of 65,000 Russian applicants,
mostly college-educated, "who will work for 38 cents an hour." *The
Daily Oklahoman* tells of a manufacturing firm that paid Oklahoma
workers $10 an hour before moving to Poland, where it pays $1.37.[22]

Software programming and computer engineering are increasingly
"outsourced" to Third World countries where, in the words of *Computer
Dealer News*, "the skills of highly educated computer professionals can
be obtained at incredibly low cost. India and China, in particular, are
being viewed as treasure troves of programming talent." As *Business
Week* puts it, "What makes Third World brainpower so attractive is
price...In India or China, you can get top-level [computer engineering]
talent, probably with a PhD, for less than $10,000."[23] More than 100

CORPORATE FREEDOM IN GUATEMALA

ED RABEL, CBS Reporter: The whole country of Guatemala was once virtually a branch office of the United Fruit Company. In the 1950s, it held two-thirds of the usable farm land and monopolized the nation's railroad in its multi-million-dollar banana empire. When a democratically-elected president named Jacobo Arbenz tried to institute a land reform program in 1954 so that poor farmers could have land of their own...the CIA stepped in and overthrew the Guatemalan leader...From that day to this, Guatemalans have lived under nearly constant Government harassment... [Rabel interviewed Fred Sherwood, former head of the U.S. Chamber of Commerce in Guatemala.]

RABEL: Sherwood's own personal holdings are considerable: a rubber plantation, a cement factory, and part of a textile mill which he manages. It's an ideal place to invest, he says, because profits are high, costs are low. Sherwood pays workers at his textile mill about four dollars and fifty cents a day...

RABEL: Is the government pretty cooperative?

SHERWOOD: Oh, yes. They're very cooperative. We don't have restrictions as to environmental things and there's just no restrictions or rules at all, so that makes it nice.

RABEL: Are the people here oppressed in any way?

SHERWOOD:...I have lived here for 36 years...and I don't know of anybody being impressed [sic]. No one forces them to do anything. And I think this is just something that some reporters have thought up.

RABEL:...I want to ask you...about something a [Christian Democrat] politician here in this country told me. And he said that more than 120 of his party's leaders had been assassinated in about an 18-month period. I'm just wondering what you make of...that kind of statement.

SHERWOOD: Well, first place, I'd very much question it, because I don't think there's been a hundred and twenty people of all types assassinated here in the...last year. I mean, I'm not counting the peasants or the—I mean men of that category. No, I think that's probably exaggerated to a great extent. There were a couple of politicians assassinated a couple of years ago, but believe me, they were way out in left field and well, these people are, I think, our enemies...And maybe assassination is not the right word for it, but I don't think they should be—continue allowed to run free to try to destroy our form of government, our way of life, in other words.

Source: "Guatemala, CBS Reports," broadcast September 1, 1982.
Note: Since the 1954 coup, some 200,000 Guatemalans have been killed or "disappeared," according to human rights organizations.

companies, including Hewlett-Packard and Motorola, have set up operations in India's high-tech center in Bangalore. According to the International Labor Organization, the typical programmer in India makes approximately $2,400 a year.[24] "Since the late 1970s, American computer companies have been coming to India to take advantage of well-trained but relatively low-paid computer engineers. At Motorola, for instance, a mid-level engineer makes $800 a month, a fraction of what would be earned in the United States, Europe or Japan."[25]

In the words of a *Business Week* cover story on Mexico and NAFTA, Mexican workers are "smart, motivated, cheap."[26] A 1992 *Wall Street Journal* survey of business executives found that a quarter said that they were "likely" to use NAFTA as leverage to bargain down wages in their U.S. operations.[27] NAFTA boosters pretend that Mexican wages will rise along with productivity, but between 1980 and 1993, the Mexican minimum wage fell 56 percent, adjusting for inflation, while factory productivity rose 41 percent.[28] Mexico's drastic 1994 *peso* devaluation and subsequent austerity measures mean even lower real wages and harder times for Mexican workers.

Global corporations often operate in "free trade zones" (also called "export processing zones"). Repression is used to keep free trade zones free of labor unions as well as health and safety regulations. The typical free trade zone factory worker is a poorly paid young woman. Sexual harassment by male supervisors is common. So is exposure to toxic chemicals.[29]

About 4 million workers are employed in 173 export processing zones around the world, many of them in textiles and electronics. As the *World Investment Report* observes, "The process of evolution of export processing zones partly reflects the changing labor cost advantages of developing countries for TNCs. A distinction can be made between the first generation of zones (i.e., those in the 1970s or early 1980s) that are now reaching maturity, and the second generation, including export processing zones that have experienced considerable expansion throughout the late 1980s and early 1990s." The report explains:

> The former category includes "mature" zones in countries or areas like Mauritius, the Philippines, [and South Korea and Taiwan]. These zones have gone through the full life cycle of a typical export processing zone. Initially, employment in the zones expanded rapidly thanks to sustained FDI [foreign direct investment] in labor-intensive operations. As wages and working conditions improved and restrictions on union activities became less severe, capital-intensive production gradually

Quality, Industriousness and Reliability Is What El Salvador Offers You!

Rosa Martinez produces apparel for U.S. markets on her sewing machine in El Salvador. <u>You</u> can hire her for 33-cents an hour*.

Rosa is more than just colorful. She and her co-workers are known for their industriousness, reliability and quick learning. They make El Salvador one of the best buys.

In addition, El Salvador has excellent road and sea transportation (including Central America's most modern airport) . . . **and** there are **no** quotas.

Find out more about **sourcing** in El Salvador. Contact **FUSADES**, the private, non-profit and non-partisan organization promoting social and economic development in El Salvador. Miami telephone: **305/529-2233** **Fax: 305/529-9449**

*Does not include fringe benefits; exact amount may vary slightly depending on daily exchange rate.

| Visit us in Bobbin Contexpo Booth 700 | Circle #49 on Reader Service Card | Bobbin, March 1991 73 |

replaced labor-intensive activities, and there was a decline in FDI inflows that triggered a fall in employment as labor-intensive production was relocated to more convenient locations.

The second category includes zones in countries like China, the Dominican Republic, Guatemala, Mexico, Sri Lanka and Tunisia. These registered a considerable expansion in the late 1980s, partly as a result of the relocation of investment in simple, labor-intensive manufacturing production from the newly industrializing economies of Asia.[30]

UNCLE SAM'S HELPING HAND

The National Labor Committee in Support of Worker and Human Rights in Central America has exposed how U.S. tax dollars have been used to promote runaway plants by supporting, among other things, advertisements like the 1991 ad on the previous page promoting El Salvador as "one of the best buys." When revolution swept El Salvador during the 1980s, the U.S. government backed the Salvadoran ruling families and military, their death squads and their political front men to make sure El Salvador stayed a "best buy" for corporations.

Similarly U.S. aid has supported corporate freedom at the expense of human rights in Honduras. Posing as the owners of New Age Textiles, National Labor Committee investigators were hosted in Honduras by the U.S.-supported Honduran Foundation for Investment and Development (FIDE). At various U.S.-supported free trade zones, they were told how labor organizing is prevented with computerized blacklists. One zone manager "explained that the blacklist includes all the names of people dismissed for whatever reason from any zone in the country. This way New Age Textiles would be able to present a list of job applicants to the zone management and 'we check it out and will…tell you, okay, you have to get rid of this one or you have to get rid of that one.'"[31]

The National Labor Committee reported how the U.S. Commerce Department, the U.S. Agency for International Development (AID) and the World Bank lured corporations to the Caribbean with promises of tax giveaways, cheap labor and no unions. The Commerce Department sent the following 1991 letter to over 1,000 U.S. businesses:

> The Informational Industries Mission to Barbados and Jamaica will allow a select dozen U.S. firms to evaluate and take advantage of pre-screened business opportunities in the developing world's two leading offshore centers for information processing…

Barbados and Jamaica offer a unique combination of educated, low-cost workers; highly developed telecommunications services; and geographic proximity; which together equal profitability and productivity for U.S. information companies.

Over the past ten years many of your colleagues and competitors have expanded into the Caribbean, creating a growing pool of experienced workers and managers...With labor rates that range from just $1.00-$3.00 per hour, you can imagine the types of margins which these firms are enjoying.

For the reasons cited, you owe it to your company to consider expanding in the Caribbean. This Mission offers the perfect opportunity, because it puts to work for you some 20 U.S. and Caribbean government and business officials.[32]

Candidates Bill Clinton and Al Gore blasted the Bush administration for promoting corporate flight, but the Clinton administration's corporate stance is symbolized by the decision to officially de-link human rights from economic relations with China. U.S. officials boast of "commercial diplomacy" and "commercial engagement." As Commerce Secretary Ron Brown put it on a 1994 trip to China, "We intend to compete in this market, and we intend to win."[33]

HAITI: THE PAST IS PROLOGUE

U.S. officials who know Haiti predict matter-of-factly that after the U.S.-managed "democratization" the same classes will be in charge. "Who are we going to go back to save?" [Major Louis Kernisan, a former U.S. Defense Intelligence Agency attaché in Haiti] asks rhetorically. "You're going to end up dealing with the same folks as before, the five families that run the country, the military and the bourgeoisie. They're the same folks that are supposed to be the bad guys now, but the bottom line is you know that you're going to always end up dealing with them because they speak your language, they understand your system, they've been educated in your country. It's not going to be the slum guy from Cité Soleil. The best thing he can hope for is probably 'Oh, I'll help you offload your cargo truck.' Because that's all he has the capacity to do."

Allan Nairn, "Occupation Haiti," *The Nation*, October 3, 1994.

GLOBAL LOAN SHARKS

To "develop" their countries as cash-crop plantations and export platforms for global corporations, Western-backed Third World regimes—many of them autocratic—went into heavy debt with multinational banks and agencies such as the International Monetary Fund (IMF) and World Bank. Like international loan sharks, the bankers encourage them to rob their people to service the debt. Far from benefitting the general population, the debt was typically used to enrich local and foreign elites, among them dictatorial "kleptocrats" like Mobutu of Zaire, the Somozas of Nicaragua, the Duvaliers of Haiti, and Ferdinand and Imelda Marcos of the Philippines.[34]

This so-called development financing has been politically, economically, socially and ecologically disastrous. Governments attempting to better serve their poor majorities have been punished with lending blockades or forced to accept IMF and World Bank "adjustment" programs. Such programs demand local currency devaluations, encouragement of foreign investment, reduced government spending on social services, curtailment of food and other basic necessity subsidies, higher interest rates and taxes, lower wages, deregulation and privatization. In Haiti, for example, President Aristide's post-exile economic policies are much more acceptable to the IMF, global corporations and the United States than were the economic justice goals he had pursued before being ousted in a military coup.

Women are disproportionately hurt by structural adjustment programs. Even AID acknowledges this. "Women have been forced to act as 'shock absorbers' for structural adjustment." They have disproportionately experienced public sector layoffs and cutbacks in health care, education and so on. "Many women now work 60 to 90 hours per week just to maintain the marginal standard of living they possessed a decade ago."[35]

In *The State of the World's Children 1989*, UNICEF observed: "Throughout most of Africa and much of Latin America, average incomes have fallen by 10% to 25% in the 1980s. In the 37 poorest nations, spending per head on health has been reduced by 50%, and on education by 25%." Taking into account aid, repayments of interest and capital, and the unequal terms of trade between the North's manufactured goods and the South's raw materials, "then the annual flow from the poor to the rich might be as much as $60 billion each year."[36]

In UNICEF's words, "Hundreds of thousands of the developing world's children have given their lives to pay their countries debts, and many millions more are still paying the interest with their malnourished minds and bodies." UNICEF estimates that about 500,000 children die yearly from austerity measures mandated because of debt.[37] Children are also exploited as workers.

CHILD LABORERS

Children are the cheapest laborers on the global assembly line and in the global plantation. Child labor is on the rise in the United States and around the world—along with adult unemployment. The International Labor Organization estimates there may be as many as 200 million child laborers worldwide.[38] They include children kidnapped from their homes to weave carpets in India, and children stitching garments in sweatshops in New York and the free trade zones of Honduras.[39]

"Bangladesh, for example, has become one of the top ten apparel exporters to the U.S. by the widespread use of child labor," writes Richard Rothstein. "The NBC-TV program *Dateline* accused the Wal-Mart retail chain of contracting for the production of garments in a Bangladesh factory where over 60 percent of the 500 workers were children under the age of 13, working up to 20 hours a day and sleeping on the factory floor, earning as little as $7.50 a month."[40] In the United States, the rapidly growing nonunion Wal-Mart pays discount wages of generally $5 to $9 an hour. Meanwhile, the family of the late Sam Walton, founder of Wal-Mart, has a net worth of nearly $22 billion, as noted earlier.

The U.S. General Accounting Office reported in 1992 that in the United States, the number of illegally employed minors—children under age 14—had nearly tripled since 1983. William Halperin, then associate director for surveillance at the National Institute for Occupational Safety and Health, called the findings "astounding," yet probably only "the tip of an iceberg."[41]

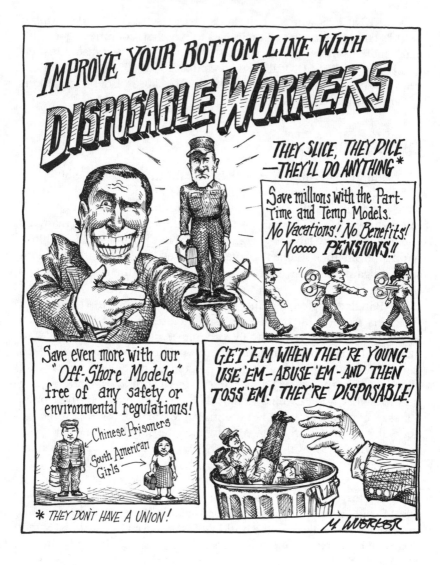

4

FULL OF UNEMPLOYMENT

We never meant to quit our jobs. They quit on us.

> Former Rath Meatpacking employee from Waterloo, Iowa.[1]

There are 35 million people unemployed in OECD countries [includes the United States, Canada, European Union countries, Japan, Australia and New Zealand]. Perhaps another 15 million have either given up looking for work or unwillingly accepted a part-time job. As many as a third of young workers in some OECD countries have no job.

> Organization for Economic Cooperation and Development, *The OECD Jobs Study,* 1994.

According to the International Labor Office, at the beginning of 1994 there were at least 120 million registered unemployed worldwide. Although this figure is by itself alarming, it does not include those who never registered as unemployed or those who stopped looking for a job because they regarded further search as futile. In addition, there were about 700 million workers that were underemployed, i.e., engaged in an economic activity that did not permit them to reach a minimum standard of living.

> United Nations Conference on Trade and Development, *World Investment Report 1994.*

While some workers have "jobs with no futures," others have "futures without jobs." The official U.S. unemployment rate averaged 4.5 percent in the 1950s and 4.8 percent in the 1960s. It climbed in the next decades, averaging 6.2 percent in the 1970s and 7.3 percent in the 1980s—not counting the growing numbers of "discouraged" and other jobless and involuntary part-time workers, discussed below.[2] The 1990s began with another official recession followed by a so-called "jobless recovery." That's like declaring recovery for a patient resuscitated into a coma.

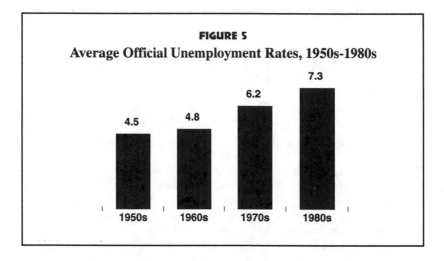

FIGURE 5
Average Official Unemployment Rates, 1950s-1980s

The prevailing definition of "full employment" has become steadily less full of employment and more full of unemployment. The national "full employment" unemployment target of about 3 percent lasted from the mid-1940s until the 1970s, when it moved to 4 percent under the Humphrey-Hawkins bill. Economic movers and shakers believe today's structural or "natural rate" of unemployment is 6 to 6.5 percent. Corporate America does not want real full employment because workers would then be freer to reject jobs with low wages and poor working conditions. They would have more leverage to push for higher wages. Business leaders say they don't want the "wage inflation" of wages outpacing productivity but, as we have seen, wages are falling behind both productivity and price inflation. Wage deflation is the nation's real problem.

The Federal Reserve has helped maintain high unemployment by raising interest rates in order to slow down the economy and keep inflation extremely low—cheering the now famous bond market investors. Edward Herman, professor of finance at the Wharton School of the University of Pennsylvania, says that "the more recent shift to an almost pathological fear of inflation reflects the growth in power of the financial community of brokers, bankers and investors." He explains:

> In earlier years, before the rise of the global bond market and NRU [Natural Rate of Unemployment] theorizing, inflation was seen as a menace, but only in its extreme forms. Even conservative economists often argued that a gently rising price level was possibly ideal, as it would provide small entrepreneurial profit windfalls at the expense of coupon clippers (bond holders), would soften wage struggles by making it easier to raise money wages, and would serve as a general economic stimulus. The idea that inflation, once started, would necessarily get worse, was not a great concern, and is not supported by history. The historic U.S. inflations have never fit the NRU model of acceleration based on a policy of too rigorous efforts to reduce unemployment; they have been rooted in excess demand and speculation resulting from war spending, the release of pent-up war demand, and accumulated high liquidity (1945-48), or fear of war and its effects (Korea, 1950-52). The inflationary spurt in the late 1960s and 1970s was linked to Vietnam war deficits and the oil cartel's price increases of 1973 and 1979. Only external shocks have driven inflation levels over 5 percent in modern U.S. experience.[3]

The economist who President Clinton appointed as vice chair of the Federal Reserve, Alan Blinder, was branded radically "soft" on inflation when he said that the Federal Reserve should be concerned about high unemployment as well as high inflation. However, Blinder believes that today's so-called "nonaccelerating inflation rate of unemployment" is in the 5.7 to 6 percent range.[4] That range used to be considered unacceptable. The Federal Reserve continues its war on inflation, which is low, at the expense of employment. That's not a policy serving most Americans. As Max Sawicky of the Economic Policy Institute puts it, "A commitment to full employment, at the cost of a marginally higher level of inflation, benefits most of the poor and the middle class."[5]

LEANER AND MEANER

Corporations have been steadily "downsizing" their workforces. Information technology is making middle managers expendable along with clerical and assembly workers. Between 1979 and 1992, the total worldwide employment of the *Fortune* 500 dropped from 16.2 million to 11.8 million.[6] In 1993, the *Fortune* 500 had profits of $62.6 billion.

> Downsizing and other "trends have created an 'industrial reserve
> army'—to borrow a term from Karl Marx—so large that a quite extraor-
> dinary and prolonged surge in output would be required to put all its
> members to full-time, well-paid work. Two indications of the yawning
> chasm between job supply and demand, in Detroit alone: in October,
> the Detroit Post Office handed out 20,000 applications for such jobs as
> clerk, sorter and letter carrier, even though it announced it would have
> at most a few hundred openings and that some of them would not be
> filled for three to five years. Last week Detroit was again the scene of a
> sort of job panic: thousands of unemployed workers began lining up at
> 7 a.m. to apply for jobs that might never exist in a gambling casino that"
> might never be built.
>
> *Time*, November 22, 1993.

Fortune says what makes that year's profits "even more impressive is
that sales growth in 1993 was virtually stagnant. So by all means, join
in with Maureen Allyn, chief economist of Scudder Stevens & Clark,
who declares, 'Hats off to America's industrial heartland.'"

"Employees, though, might well voice a few loud gripes," adds
Fortune. "Total employment among the 500 fell for the ninth straight
year [to 11.5 million]...while median employment dropped 5.3%, to
10,136. Often the jobs that remained were far less lucrative. Caterpillar,
for example, forced the United Auto Workers to accept a two-tier wage
system...Scudder's Maureen Allyn: 'U.S. industry needed to get lean
and mean, but we probably went overboard.'"[7]

"Hot Damn! They Did It Again," *Business Week* declared as profits
for the 900 U.S. companies in their Corporate Scoreboard matched "the
staggering 45% profit gain of the second quarter" of 1994 by jumping
45 percent in the third quarter, as corporate sales rose 10 percent. The
leading industries with the biggest gains between 1993 and 1994 were
forest products (+927%), gas utilities (+782%), cars and trucks (+382%),
savings and loan (+333%), railroads (+259%) and publishing (+183%).
How did earnings rise so much faster than sales? Here's what *Business
Week* says:

> What's making companies so profitable? It's a simple matter of
> productivity and its brake on labor costs...Unit labor costs, the wages
> and benefits that go into producing a good or service, are growing by
> less than 1%—a pace not seen since the early 1960s. Among
> manufacturers, unit labor costs fell 2.7% in the third quarter [of 1994].

By contrast, the price of goods and services climbed 2.8% in the same period.

And fortunately for Corporate America, those fundamentals won't change appreciably next year...The spread may diminish, but as long as prices are rising faster than costs, margins will continue to widen.

Restructuring has also helped pump up margins. By slashing payrolls, investing in technology, or simply overhauling assembly lines, companies are making more efficient use of fewer workers...

The huge pool of labor has a lot to do with the prevailing wage restraint. True, the jobless rate has fallen to 5.9%, from 7.3% a year ago. But that's only part of the story. The unemployment statistics don't count the roughly 4 million part-time workers who are eager for full-time jobs. In addition, the explosive increase in the number of temporary workers gives few employees much leverage in negotiating pay raises.[8]

Corporations are betting that the rising disposable incomes of "winners" in the global economy will compensate for falling incomes among disposable workers. It's a short-sighted bet. It's more likely all this job-eliminating downsizing will be equivalent to farmers selling their seed corn. Short-term profit for long-term disaster. Some call it "corporate anorexia."

Though applauded by Wall Street, the evidence about downsizing's impact on company performance to date is mixed. According to the 1994 American Management Association survey—whose respondents are mostly major companies, nearly half of them in manufacturing—"51% of companies reporting workforce reductions since January 1989 reported an increase in operating profits after the cuts; 20% said operating profits declined...Productivity gains have been even more elusive. Among all firms reporting reductions, only a third said productivity increased; nearly as many (30%) said it had declined...The surest after-effect of downsizing is a negative impact on employee morale, which suffered in 86% of all firms reporting cuts any time since January 1989." According to the survey, "workforce reductions begin to show more positive effects some three years after the most recent round of cuts—although time does little to heal the...negative impact on employee morale."[9]

In *Business Week's* words, "This is the bleak underside of the new workplace: For every empowered employee, there's at least another cowering in his office, putting in longer hours to keep up with a job that used to keep two people busy. For every highly skilled worker moving up the ladder, there's another, marginalized, struggling to make ends meet."[10]

Corporations are demanding that employees cooperate in corporate restructuring—through worker-management teams, quality circles and so on—without sharing in the benefits of increased productivity and profit. As *Business Week* puts it, "We increasingly demand that our workers take on responsibility and risk, yet their pay is falling. Will $8-an-hour machinists do high-performance work?" *Business Week* quotes MIT professor Paul Osterman: "You can't expect workers to keep contributing their ideas when they don't get rewarded for them."[11]

The main supposed inducement for worker cooperation is continued employment at a time of high unemployment, but often that is not the case. Take Romie Manan's testimony to the Commission on the Future of Worker-Management Relations about his experience at National Semiconductor's plant in Santa Clara, California:

> Manan explained how National had told workers that they had to team up with management in order to beat Japanese competition. Fearing for their jobs, he said, workers agreed. "Increasing the company's profitability, they said, would increase our job security," Manan testified. "That was the purpose of the teams—to make us more efficient and productive...We became more efficient...Then the company took the ideas contributed by the experienced workforce in Santa Clara...and used them to organize new fabs [fabrication lines] with inexperienced workers in Arlington, Texas, where wages are much lower. Then the experienced workers lost their jobs."[12]

OVERTIME FOR SOME, NO TIME FOR OTHERS

Between 1979 and 1992, U.S. manufacturing output rose 13 percent, while the workforce declined by 15 percent.[13] The Bureau of Labor Statistics predicts that between 1990 and 2005, "the value of goods manufactured in the United States will climb 41 percent. But the number of people employed to make those goods will fall 3 percent."[14] Rather than hire additional workers, many employers are automating and overworking their remaining employees.

According to the 1994 American Management Association survey, "policies intended to 'share the pain' and lessen job loss by reducing pay or hours or spreading the work are generally in decline. Rather than *share* work to save jobs, many companies do the opposite, *expanding* the work day for those still employed. Half of the firms that have downsized since 1988 say they have extended working hours and/or overtime as an alternative to new hiring."[15]

Compared to the late 1960s, "the average worker is working about an extra month of work per year," writes Juliet Schor, author of *The Overworked American*. "Factory overtime has now reached its highest recorded level...In the automobile industry, where tens of thousands of workers have been laid off, daily overtime has become standard...The UAW estimates that 59,000 automobile jobs would be created if the plants were on a 40-hour week."[16] In May 1994, the average U.S. worker at auto and supplier plants logged a record 7.9 hours a week of overtime.[17] Overtime is combined with speed-up to squeeze out extra production from the workers left after layoffs. In July 1994, General Motors increased assembly line speeds at Buick in Flint, Michigan from 70 to 76 vehicles per hour. "Greedy employers," asserts UAW President Owen Bieber, are "trying to produce far too much product with far too few people."[18]

Instead of constructively addressing the harmful link between overtime for some and unemployment for others, President Clinton and Labor Secretary Robert Reich have chided workers for complaining about record overtime. As Secretary Reich put it in a November 1994 press briefing touting the administration's economic progress: "The factory work week has edged up to 42.1 hours; that is a level not seen since the end of World War II. Throughout the industrial Midwest—in fact, I've heard complaints from workers who say that they don't want to work as much overtime as they are getting—and that's certainly a problem if workers don't want to work overtime, but it's a far better problem than not having a job." The next day, President Clinton addressed the National Association of Realtors convention and told them that the big gripe among Michigan autoworkers is too much overtime. He said, "That, folks, is a high-class problem."[19]

Actually, it's a health problem for the workers, a social problem for their children and communities, and an unemployment problem for the nation. In fall 1994, more than 11,000 auto workers went on a three-day strike at Buick City in Flint, Michigan, with the demand that General Motors hire more workers, rather than continue its practice of forced overtime, which was robbing the workers of health, leisure and time for family and other responsibilities. Workers "were averaging 10 hours a day on the job, routinely worked one weekend day and, at times, were forced to put in seven days a week on the factory floor."[20] Injuries were increasing. That strike was settled when GM agreed to hire hundreds of additional workers and settle plentiful health and safety grievances, among other demands.[21] However, more strikes against forced overtime and layoff-induced understaffing have followed.

The problem of burnout is widespread. A middle manager at a large high-tech company undergoing reengineering told *Business Week*: "This year, I had to downsize my area by 25%. Nothing has changed in terms of the workload. It's very emotionally draining. I find myself not wanting to go in to work, because I'm going to have to push people to do more, and I look at their eyes and they're sinking in to the back of their heads. [People] numbing. But they're not going to complain, because they don't want to be the next 25%."[22]

BEHIND THE UNEMPLOYMENT RATE

The U.S. government downsizes the unemployment rate, but not the reality, much as it does poverty. There's a large gap between the number of people wanting jobs and the number included in the unemployment rate. The official rate doesn't include would-be workers who have searched for work in the past year, or even the last five weeks—but not in the past *four* weeks. The official rate leaves out people defined as "discouraged workers," people with child-care problems and millions of others without jobs. It doesn't include involuntary part-timers. (See table 15.)

Business Week observes, "Increasingly the labor market is filled with surplus workers who are not being counted as unemployed. The rate of labor force participation—those working or looking for work—has dropped sharply for men since 1989. Estimated conservatively, some 1.1 million prime-age male workers are out of the labor force compared with five years ago...And there are at least 500,000 more workers with some college who have jobs but are underemployed compared to 5 years ago."[23]

Alternative unemployment and underemployment measures, such as the Urban League's "Hidden Unemployment Index," have typically adjusted the official rate by adding in "discouraged workers" and involuntary part-timers ("part-time for economic reasons")—two categories that the Labor Department made more restrictive beginning in 1994, resulting in lower official numbers. David Dembo and Ward Morehouse advocate a more complete alternative "jobless rate" which reflects the larger pool of jobless workers (including "discouraged") and adjusts for involuntary part-time employment using a full-time equivalence formula. Their 1993 jobless rate was 13.8 percent. Dembo and Morehouse observe:

> The Jobless Rate—about twice the official Unemployment Rate—rises and falls with the official rate. However, as more people are forced to work part time and as increasing numbers have dropped out of the official labor force altogether, the Jobless Rate tends to diverge even more from the official rate. During cyclical downturns (recessions)…the Jobless Rate increases more than does the Unemployment Rate as record numbers of Americans give up looking for work and more and more people work part time for economic reasons…With each succeeding recovery period, the Jobless Rate has fallen less and less.[24]

In Europe too, unemployment is racheting upward. "After each cyclical downturn, [joblessness] locks in even higher," notes *International Management*. "Many who lose jobs never work again." Over half of Europe's 400 largest firms planned major layoffs for 1995.[25]

The U.S. Labor Department acknowledged in late 1993 that the government had been substantially underestimating unemployment among women. Blatant sexism biased the unemployment surveying.

U.S. DEPARTMENT OF LABOR DEFINITIONS OF EMPLOYED AND UNEMPLOYED PERSONS

Employed persons: All persons who, during the [survey] reference week, did any work at all as paid employees in their own business, profession, or on their own farm; or who worked 15 hours or more as unpaid workers in an enterprise operated by a member of the family; and all those who were not working but who had jobs or businesses from which they were temporarily absent because of vacation, illness, bad weather, child-care problems, maternity or paternity leave, labor-management dispute, job training, or other family or personal reasons, whether or not they were paid for the time off or were seeking other jobs.

Unemployed persons: All persons who had no employment during the reference week; were available for work, except for temporary illness, and had made specific efforts to find employment some time during the 4-week period ending with the reference week. Persons who were waiting to be recalled to a job from which they had been laid off need not have been looking for work to be classified as unemployed.

TABLE 15
Unemployment and Underemployment, 1994

Official Unemployment Rates, 1994

All Workers	White	Black	Latino	Men	Women	Teenagers
6.1	5.3	11.5	9.9	6.2	6.0	17.6

Joblessness and Involuntary Part-time Work, 1994
numbers in thousands

	Total	Men	Women
Official Unemployed	7,996	4,367	3,629
Not Included in Unemployment Rate			
Persons who want a job	6,218	2,449	3,769
Searched for work in previous year	2,630	1,138	1,492
Available to work now	1,807	830	977
Reason not currently looking			
Discouragement over job prospects*	500	296	204
Reasons other than discouragement	1,307	534	772
Family responsibilities	213	31	183
In school or training	267	137	129
Ill health or disability	150	69	81
Other**	677	298	379
Involuntary Part-time Workers*** (Part-time for Economic Reasons)	4,625		

*"Includes believes no work available, could not find work, lacks necessary schooling or training, employer thinks too young or old, and other types of discrimination."

**"Includes those who did not actively look for work in the prior four weeks for such reasons as child care and transportation problems, as well as a small number for which reason for nonparticipation was not ascertained."

***The categories for "discouraged workers" and for those working "part-time for economic reasons" (involuntary part-timers) were narrowed significantly beginning in 1994, leading to a large reduction in the numbers of people counted. Discouraged workers were excluded from the unemployment rate in 1967.

Sources: Bureau of Labor Statistics, *Employment and Earnings*, January 1995; *How the Government Measures Unemployment*, March 1994.

As more women worked outside the home, government interviewers continued to begin their survey this way: When men responded the interviewer typically asked, "What were you doing most of last week, working or something else?" Women were typically asked whether they were "keeping house or something else?" If they answered keeping house, the interviewer didn't bother to find out if they were laid off or looking for work, so even if they were, the government counted them as homemakers, not unemployed members of the workforce. When the government refigured the overall official unemployment rate for the 12 months through August 1993 it was 7.6 percent, not 7.1 percent.[26] Women's unemployment rate would be even higher if the government included "discouraged workers" and people not currently looking for work because of child-care problems, for example.

Official Black unemployment is more than double the White rate; the Latino rate is almost double the White rate. (See table 15.) As *The State of Working America* reports, "Even at the peak of the last business cycle in 1989, the 11.4% unemployment among black workers was higher than the average unemployment reached in any post-war *recession*." (Italics in original.) The official Black unemployment rate averaged 14.1 percent between 1976 and 1993.[27] As the official unemployment rates for Black and White workers dropped in 1994, diverging even further from the real jobless rates, the Federal Reserve stepped up its efforts to slow down the economy.

People with disabilities are especially hard hit in a high-unemployment economy. According to Patricia Kirkpatrick, author of a report on the status of people with disabilities, "Statistics in this area are not current or complete, but they indicate that as many as 66% of all working-age Americans with disabilities [and over 77 percent of working-age Blacks with disabilities] are unemployed. The major causes have to do with exclusionary practices and attitudes of employers, inaccessible work environments and inadequate levels of education."[28] (Educational attainment may also reflect discrimination.) Looking at persons 21 to 64 years old, the Census Bureau report, *Americans With Disabilities: 1991-92*, found that 80.5 percent of those with no disability were employed and only 52 percent of those with a disability were employed. The respective figures for men are 88.8 percent and 59.1 percent; for women, 72.6 percent and 45.2 percent. The employment rate is much lower for those categorized as having a "severe disability," defined, for example, as using a wheelchair, or being a long-term user of canes or crutches, or having developmental disabilities. Only 23.2

percent of persons 21 to 64 years old with a severe disability were employed. Other government reports measure by "work disability" status. But as *Americans With Disabilities* explains, "the work disability question implies that the only factor affecting the ability to work is the condition of the person. This is clearly not the case. Under one set of environmental factors, a given condition may hinder or prevent work, but if physical and/or social barriers are removed, the same condition may have no effect on the ability to work."[29]

To make matters worse for all the unemployed, unemployment insurance is not ensuring. Less than half of all officially unemployed workers receive any unemployment benefits. And unemployment benefits have fallen behind inflation. Low-wage workers and contingent workers—disproportionately women and people of color—are less likely than others to qualify for unemployment benefits (they may not meet work time or earnings requirements). When they do qualify, their temporary payments are only a fraction of their meager wages. The average unemployment benefit is only 37 percent of the average wage.[30] And unemployment compensation has been taxed since 1978. Eligibility varies by state and benefits typically last only a maximum of 26 weeks whether or not you've found a job.

"Studies in several states have found that a substantial proportion of new AFDC (Aid to Families with Dependent Children) families are headed by individuals who have recently lost their jobs," the Center on Budget and Policy Priorities reported in 1992. "For unemployed people who do not have children, little or no cash assistance may be available if they fail to receive unemployment benefits."[31] In other words, there is no "safety net" for many people thrown out of work.

TECHNOLOGICAL UNEMPLOYMENT

Today, the power of a personal-computer microchip doubles every 18 months.

Business Week, October 17, 1994.[32]

As bad as unemployment and underemployment are now, the situation is going to get much worse in the future, without a major change in policies. Trends analyst Jeremy Rifkin predicts that within a few decades hundreds of millions of people working globally in manufacturing, services and agriculture could be displaced through automation, artificial intelligence and biotechnology. "We are fast moving into a world where there will be factories without workers and agricultural production without farms or farmers," warns Rifkin.[33]

In the past, farmers and farmworkers displaced by the mechanization of agriculture were absorbed in large numbers by manufacturing. Many workers displaced by the earlier wave of manufacturing automation were absorbed by the service sector. There is no new industry capable of absorbing the millions of workers being displaced by automation and reengineering in the contemporary era of "thinking machines." Biotechnology, for example, is a low-employment industry. "The high-technology revolution is not normally associated with farming," writes Rifkin, but "technological changes in the production of food are leading to a world without farmers, with untold consequences for the 2.4 billion [people worldwide] who rely on the land for their survival."[34]

President Clinton has rejected trickle down economics, warns Rifkin, only to embrace the similarly damaging myth of "trickle down technology." Rifkin observes:

> In the high-tech electronic culture of the 21st century envisioned by the Clinton Administration, "virtual" communities increasingly will replace "traditional" ones as millions of people carry on the business of day-to-day life—from shopping to medical checkups—electronically over the computer transom, bypassing face-to-face exchanges in the marketplace. Over an extended period of time, millions of traditional service-sector jobs will be eliminated in the wake of the revolutionary advances in electronic communications technology.
>
> Automated tellers and cashiers, self-service gasoline pumps, and computerized reservations handling and shopping merely are the first wave of the new displacement technologies. Voice and signature recognition, robotics, virtual reality technologies, and artificial intelligence are about to transform the concept of work in ways never before imaginable, providing a near complete substitute for human labor in the execution of untold numbers of tasks...
>
> If the Clinton high-tech vision succeeds, millions of American workers in the service and white-collar sectors will be replaced in the coming decades, without the prospect of further employment somewhere else. Unlike the past, no new mass employment sectors are emerging to absorb the millions of labor refugees that are likely to result from the automation of service and white-collar jobs...
>
> Even if re-education and retraining were possible, not enough high-tech jobs will be available in the automated economy of the 21st century to absorb the legions of dislocated workers.[35]

John Maynard Keynes warned of "technological unemployment" during the 1930s in *The General Theory of Employment, Interest and Money*. In the late 1940s, Norbert Wiener, the MIT mathematician who established the science of cybernetics—the study of communications and control systems involving living organisms and machines—was alarmed at the danger of widespread and permanent technological unemployment from automation. As Rifkin recounts, Wiener "became so fearful of the high-tech future he and his colleagues were creating that he wrote an extraordinary [1949] letter to Walter Reuther, president of the United Auto Workers...He warned Reuther that the cybernetic revolution 'will undoubtedly lead to the factory without employees.' [Wiener] predicted that 'In the hands of the present industrial set-up, the unemployment produced by such plants can only be disastrous,'" and he urged organized labor to address the issue.[36]

In the face of mass unemployment during the Great Depression, the American Federation of Labor (AFL) called for a 30-hour week in 1932. In 1933, the U.S. Senate passed a bill introduced by Senator Hugo Black of Alabama mandating a 30-hour week for all businesses engaged in interstate and foreign commerce. A survey of business executives by the Industrial Conference Board found that more than half had reduced the number of hours worked to save jobs and promote consumer spending. Unfortunately, President Roosevelt—who later came to regret it—joined with business leaders to kill the 30-hour legislation.[37]

The Kellogg Company had switched to a 6-hour day in 1930. As Harvard economist Juliet Schor tells it, "They were searching for a strategy to cope with the unemployment of the Depression. To their surprise, they found that workers were more productive, on the order of 3 percent to 4 percent...According to W. K. Kellogg, 'the efficiency and morale of our employees [are] so increased, the accident and insurance rates are so improved, and the unit cost of production is so lowered that we can afford to pay as much for six hours as we formerly paid for eight.'"[38]

In the 1950s and beyond, however, the AFL-CIO largely capitulated to management on the issue of automation, explains Rifkin. Rather than renew the demand for shorter hours, for example, labor counted on retraining to shift displaced workers into higher-skilled, technical jobs. Though some unions strongly resisted, such as the longshoremen's and printers' unions, in general, labor "failed to come to grips with the central dynamic of the automation revolution—management's single-minded determination to replace workers with machines wherever possible, and, by so doing, reduce labor costs, increase control over production, and improve profit margins."[39]

In 1963, a committee of prominent scientists, economists and academics such as J. Robert Oppenheimer, Robert Theobald and W. H. Ferry called attention to *The Triple Revolution*: the cybernation revolution, the weaponry revolution and the human rights revolution. They warned: "A new era of production has begun. Its principles of organization are as different as those of the industrial era were different from the agricultural. The cybernation revolution has been brought about by the combination of the computer and the automated self-regulating machine. This results in a system of almost unlimited productive capacity which requires progressively less human labor." As Rifkin points out, "The committee acknowledged that 'The Negroes are the hardest hit of the many groups being exiled from the economy by cybernation,' but predicted that, in time, the new computer revolution would take over more and more of the productive tasks in the economy, leaving millions of workers jobless. The committee urged the President and Congress to consider guaranteeing every citizen 'an adequate income as a matter of right.'"[40]

President Johnson established a National Commission on Guaranteed Incomes in 1967. In supporting a guaranteed annual income, the Commission's report stated, "Unemployment or underemployment among the poor are often due to forces that cannot be controlled by the poor themselves. For many of the poor, the desire to work is strong but the opportunities are not...Even if the existing welfare and related programs are improved, they are incapable of assuring that all Americans receive an adequate income."[41] President Nixon's proposal for a small guaranteed annual income through the 1969 Family Assistance Plan satisfied no one.

Today, terms like cyberspace and virtual reality have become commonplace, and so has high unemployment and falling incomes. Yet proposals for a "guaranteed annual income" and a 30-hour week to "share the work" have not returned to the fore of public debate, much less been embraced by the U.S. government.

As computerization and just-in-time production is shaking up the manufacturing sector, so too "just-in-time retailing" will shake up that large part of the service sector. As *Forbes* puts it, "More Americans are shopping by computer, television or telephone, buying what they want quickly and efficiently. And therein lies a very serious threat to the country's traditional retail industry and to the 19 million people it employs."[42] A shrinking number of workers and managers will be needed to sell discount goods at discount wages. The evidence is already coming in. A Census Bureau survey of retail establishments in Washington, DC, Maryland and Virginia shows that although the number of stores increased between 1987 and 1992, the number of employees fell.[43]

In Mexico, where numerous U.S. and other corporations have set up shop to take advantage of cheaper labor, there are already signs of technological unemployment. At Panasonic's TV factory in Chalco, employment fell in 1994 while sales and production rose. Edgardo Leyva, personnel manager at the Panasonic factory, told a reporter, "'Maybe in the Far East wages are low enough to assemble by hand, but here it's still cheaper to bring in machines.'...Machines don't need costly job training, don't quit and don't get paid vacations, he said."[44]

Today, U.S. and other corporations are shifting computer programming to countries like China and India. "Skeptics wonder whether offshore programmers will be needed at all in the years to come. For an increasingly large percentage of applications that aren't complex, most of the code may soon be generated by CASE (computer-aided software engineering) tools."[45]

"Let us remember," cybernetics founder Norbert Wiener warned in a 1950 book, "that the automatic machine...is the precise economic equivalent of slave labor. Any labor which competes with slave labor must accept the economic consequences of slave labor."[46]

"I've called the family together to announce that, because of inflation, I'm going to have to let two of you go."

5
_____

THE DYING AMERICAN DREAM AND THE SNAKE OIL OF SCAPEGOATING

impoverish
1. to make poor 2. to deprive of strength, resources, etc.

poor
1. having little or no means of support; needy 2. lacking in some quality; specif., a) inadequate b) inferior or worthless c) contemptible 3. worthy of pity; unfortunate

Webster's New World Dictionary.

"Since 1973," reports the Children's Defense Fund, "most of the fastest increases in poverty rates occurred among young white families with children, those headed by married couples, and those headed by high school graduates. For all three groups, *poverty rates more than doubled in a single generation*, reaching levels that most Americans commonly assume afflict only minority and single-parent families."[1] (Italics in original.) The same was true for college graduates, as middle class incomes became harder to achieve. The poverty rates for children in young families headed by college graduates have also more than doubled since 1973. (See tables 8 and 10.)

As the American Dream has become more impossible for more people, a variety of local and national leaders are using scapegoating to deflect blame from the economic system and channel anger to support reactionary political causes. Talk-show demagogues have built their careers on a rising volume of hate.

Scapegoating labels like "underclass" and myths like the "culture of poverty" mask undermining and impoverishing economics. Racist and sexist scapegoating makes it easier to forget that the majority of poor people are White, and encourages White males to blame falling incomes on mythical "reverse discrimination." Scapegoating makes it easier to treat inner city neighborhoods like outsider cities—separate, unequal and disposable. Scapegoating encourages people to think of "the poor" as the "Other America," Them and not Us. That makes it easier to divide people who should be working together to transform harmful social and economic policies. Makes it easier to write off more and more Americans as Untouchables. Makes it easier to leave unjust economic practices untouched.

Setting the poverty line too low makes the Them versus Us distinction easier. The more people there are who are officially considered *not* poor, the easier it is to blame poverty on personal failings rather than systemic failings. Schwarz and Volgy recall that in 1980 (when official unemployment was over 7 percent) "in the public's mind, the foremost causes of poverty were that the poor weren't thrifty, that they did not put in the needed effort, and that they lacked ability or talent. Popular majorities did not consider any other factor to be a very important cause of poverty—not low wages, or a scarcity of jobs, or discrimination, or even sickness."[2]

In 1990, the *Boston Globe* investigated birth in the "death zones," illuminating the link between poverty, racism, inadequate health care and infant mortality through the stories of Black and Latina women. An editorial contrasted reader responses with reaction to news that a dolphin was about to be dispatched from Boston's aquarium to the U.S. Navy: "Urgent appeals to save the dolphin are pouring in. The dolphin's innocence and dependency upon human kindness are noted. Money is no object to assuring it tender, loving care." For "the babies, most of them black and Hispanic," the typical reaction was not compassionate, but cruel. The majority of letters and phone calls "are ugly and racist. The mothers are termed 'moral-less' and 'irresponsible pigs.' The babies are described as 'inferior' and 'leeches.' They are degraded as 'trash that begets trash.'"[3]

"The poor are less obviously deserving today than they used to be," wrote an editor of the neoliberal *Washington Monthly* in 1993.

"Steinbeck's Joads [in *The Grapes of Wrath*] weren't criminals or drug addicts...Victims of the Depression or the sharecroppers who flooded the North after World War II could justifiably be portrayed as victims of upheaval. But today, some serious measure of responsibility for the poor and their sorrows clearly lies with the poor. Housing projects become nightmares; inner city schools become war zones; the drug trade becomes the small business of choice."[4] "The old issues were economic and structural," asserts conservative political scientist Lawrence Mead. "The new ones are social and personal." Scapegoaters don't let reality get in their way.

In reality, as *The State of Working America* observes, looking at the 1979-92 period, "the major forces driving the increase in poverty rates were nondemographic factors, primarily wages and benefits." In addition, the system of government taxation and income support had become less effective in reducing poverty.[5] The government slashed public investment and social programs as unemployment rose and wages fell. Focusing on urban America, author Mike Davis observes:

> The national urban programs that have suffered the most savage retrenchment [during 1980-92] have been subsidized housing (82 percent), economic development assistance (78 percent) and job training (63 percent). Again, as ideologically designed, federal aid has been cut off from cities precisely as they have confronted the most wrenching restructuring since the industrial revolution. Like the Irish tenantry during the Famine of the 1840s, the contemporary American urban poor have been doomed by the state's fanatical adherence to laissez-faire dogma. The decline in housing subsidies, for example, has helped put more urban Americans out of work than did the Great Depression, while the evaporation of job training funds and the termination of the Comprehensive Employment Training Act (CETA) have consigned myriads more to the underground drug economy. The United States is the only major industrial nation to respond to the international competitive regime of the 1980s by ruthlessly eliminating structural adjustment assistance to workers and cities.[6]

As Herbert Gans reminds us, "When Gunnar Myrdal invented or reinvented the term underclass in his 1962 book *Challenge to Affluence*, he used the word as a purely economic concept, to describe the chronically unemployed, underemployed, and underemployables being created by what we now call the post-industrial economy. He was thinking of people being driven to the margins, or entirely out, of the modern economy, here and elsewhere; but his intellectual and policy concern was with reforming the economy, not with changing or punishing the people who were its victims."[7]

Once California belonged to Mexico and its land to Mexicans; and a horde of tattered feverish Americans poured in. And such was their hunger for land that they took the land...and they guarded with guns, the land they had stolen...

Then, with time, the squatters were no longer squatters, but owners...And as time went on...the farms grew larger, but there were fewer of them.

Now farming became industry, and the owners...imported slaves, although they did not call them slaves: Chinese, Japanese, Mexicans, Filipinos. They live on rice and beans, the business men said. They don't need much...And if they get funny—deport them.

And all the time the farms grew larger and the owners fewer...

And then the dispossessed were drawn west—from Kansas, Oklahoma, Texas, New Mexico; from Nevada and Arkansas families, tribes, dusted out, tractored out...

...

In the West there was panic when the migrants multiplied on the highways. Men of property were terrified for their property...And the men of the towns and of the soft suburban country gathered to defend themselves; and they reassured themselves that they were good and the invaders bad, as a man must do before he fights. They said, These goddamned Okies are dirty and ignorant. They're degenerate, sexual maniacs. These goddamned Okies are thieves.

John Steinbeck, *The Grapes of Wrath,* chapters 19 and 21 (1939).

THE REGRESSION CURVE

Scapegoating makes racism politically correct. A nationwide 1990 survey by the National Opinion Research Center at the University of Chicago—in which most respondents were White—found an abundance of racist stereotypes: 78 percent of the non-Black respondents said Blacks are more likely than Whites to "prefer to live off welfare" and less likely to "prefer to be self-supporting." In addition, 62 percent said Blacks are more likely to be lazy; 56 percent said Blacks are violence-prone; and 53 percent said Blacks are less intelligent. Among non-Latino respondents, 74 percent said Hispanics are more likely to prefer to live off welfare; 56 percent said they are more lazy; 50 percent thought them more violence-prone; and 55 percent said Hispanics are less intelligent.[8]

How many more people will believe that Blacks are less intelligent, and that's why they are poorer, and that's preordained by their genes, after reading or hearing about the widely-featured book, *The Bell Curve*? It is the latest in a long history of regressive attempts to legitimize racism with pseudo-science.

Looking back on the old eugenics, biologist Ruth Hubbard and coauthor Elijah Wald write in *Exploding the Gene Myth*: "Hereditarianism produced beautifully self-fulfilling prophecies. Anyone who succeeded was, ipso facto, a superior person. Since the children of the wealthy and educated usually turn out to be wealthy and educated, while the children of the poor tend to remain poor, it was quite clear to hereditarians that talent ran in the family."[9]

Eugenicists (the actual term eugenics was coined in the 1880s) used "bad heredity" to explain all sorts of conditions, including "pauperism," "criminalism," "shiftlessness" and "feeblemindedness." "Drapetomania" was supposedly "a hereditary mental disease said to be prevalent among black slaves in the South, which manifested itself in an irresistible urge to run away from their masters."[10]

Eugenics shaped the Immigration Restriction Act of 1924, which was designed to decrease immigration to the United States by people from southern and eastern Europe—among them Jews fleeing pogroms in Russia—who were then seen as more likely to have "hereditary defects" than people of British and northern European descent. With the support of eugenicists, the U.S. government maintained the restrictions during the 1930s and 1940s and blocked Jews from immigrating and escaping the genocidal Nazis.[11]

Eugenics also shaped compulsory sterilization laws. As Hubbard and Wald recount: "By 1931, some thirty states had compulsory sterilization laws on their books, aimed mostly at the 'insane' and 'feebleminded.' These categories were loosely defined to include many recent immigrants and others who were functionally illiterate or knew little or no English and who therefore did poorly on IQ tests. The laws also were often extended to so-called sexual perverts, drug fiends, drunkards, epileptics, and others deemed ill or degenerate. Although most of these laws were not enforced, by January 1935 some twenty thousand people in the United States had been forcibly sterilized, most

of them in California. The California law was not repealed until 1979."
A 1972 survey of obstetricians found that "although only 6 percent
favored sterilization for their private patients, 14 percent favored it for
their welfare patients. For welfare mothers who had borne illegitimate
[sic] children, 97 percent...favored sterilization."[12]

As Hubbard and Wald remind us, "The old eugenics reached its
ultimate extreme in the Nazi extermination programs. Initially, these
were directed against the same sorts of people eugenicists had targeted
in Great Britain and the United States—people labeled as having
physical or mental disabilities." [13] The Nazis' anti-Semitic scapegoating
of Jews as a "parasitic race," which helped win them popular support,
was systematically escalated into the genocidal extermination of six
million Jewish people. Gypsies and homosexuals were also scapegoated as "dysgenic," and targeted for death.

The Pioneer Fund has long financed leading eugenicists, including Arthur Jensen of U.C. Berkeley and J. Philippe Rushton of the
University of Western Ontario whose work is part of the "evidence" in
The Bell Curve. The Pioneer Fund's 1937 founders included Frederick
Osborn, who served as president of the American Eugenics Society and
described Nazi eugenic policy as the "most important experiment which
has ever been tried." The Pioneer Fund was financed originally by
"textile tycoon Wickliffe Draper, whose other projects included paying
for the translation of eugenics texts from German into English" and who
"supported Senator Joseph McCarthy, opposed federal civil rights laws
and favored the 'repatriation' of black Americans to Africa."

The Pioneer Fund has also funded eugenics advocate Roger
Pearson.[14] Pearson is a white supremacist and neoNazi who, as
chairman of the World Anti-Communist League, "was responsible for
flooding the European League chapters with Nazi sympathizers and
former officers of the Nazi SS."[15] Pioneer Fund treasurer John B. Trevor
Jr. "was a longtime official of the Coalition of Patriotic Societies, which
in 1942 was named in a U.S. Justice Department sedition indictment for
pro-Nazi activities. Trevor was the [Coalition's] treasurer in 1962 when
it called for the release of all Nazi war criminals and announced its
support for South Africa's 'well-reasoned racial policy.'"[16]

The Pioneer Fund has provided strong financial backing for the
anti-immigrant Federation for American Immigration Reform. The federation was behind California's 1994 "Save Our State (SOS)" Proposition
187, coauthored by former Immigration and Naturalization Service
Commissioner Alan Nelson. Proposition 187 denies public education,

nonemergency medical care and social services to undocumented immigrants and requires teachers, doctors, social service providers and police to report suspected illegal immigrants to immigration and other authorities.[17] In the words of a critical report, "It will create a nation of informers."[18]

It is no accident that growing anti-immigrant sentiment and action targets Latinos and other immigrants of color rather than Canadian, Italian, Irish, Polish and other White immigrants, documented or undocumented. Immigrants of color are blamed for sapping California's economy and the nation's. Never mind that the economy depends in part on immigrant labor and recent studies confirm that immigrants actually create more jobs than they fill and pay significantly more in taxes than the cost of the public services they receive.[19]

Though at this writing Proposition 187 is not technically in force while its constitutionality is contested in the courts, it is already taking a toll on Latinos in California—citizens and legal residents along with the undocumented. *Time* reported about a Mexican American mother who called the Coalition for Humane Immigrant Rights of Los Angeles "to say her sick two-year-old had been left waiting five hours, then was turned away with only cursory examinations on two successive nights at the Kaiser Foundation Hospital in Hayward, California, 30 miles from San Francisco. Limp, dehydrated and near death, the child was finally admitted on the third day—and immediately attached to an IV. Then, as she sat by her child's bed, the mother, a legal resident, was asked for her immigration papers." Among the other callers whose experiences were noted by *Time* was a nurse from Woodland Hills. She "was pelted with rocks and anti-Hispanic epithets at a high school she has walked by for 10 years without incident."[20]

Unfortunately, California is going down a path it has been down before. In February 1942, President Franklin Roosevelt signed an executive order giving the army the power to arrest all Japanese American men, women and children on the West Coast. Without warrants or court hearings, 110,000 people were forcibly taken from their homes to internment camps where they were imprisoned for over three years. Many permanently lost their homes and property. Racism was apparent in the fact that while Japanese Americans were suspected en masse as spies and saboteurs, German Americans were not rounded up.

In reviewing *The Bell Curve*, Harvard scientist Stephen Jay Gould exposes the book's false premises and suspect statistics. Gould challenged similar arguments in his 1981 book, *The Mismeasure of Man*. He writes that *The Bell Curve*, "with its claims and supposed documentation that race and class differences are largely caused by genetic factors and are therefore essentially immutable, contains no new arguments and presents no compelling data to support its anachronistic social Darwinism, so I can only conclude that its success in winning attention must reflect the depressing temper of our time…when a mood for slashing social programs can be powerfully abetted by an argument that beneficiaries cannot be helped, owing to inborn cognitive limits expressed as low I.Q. scores."[21]

At the same time *The Bell Curve's* ravings were echoing around the nation, *Discover* magazine had an unheralded special issue on race, which noted that many scientists don't even consider race to be a biological category, much less a significant one. *Discover* editor Paul Hoffman writes, "The genetic differences between the so-called races are minute. On average there's 0.2 percent difference in genetic material between any two randomly chosen people on Earth…Skin color may only be skin deep. Surgeons, thankfully, understand this: in organ transplants a black donor can be a better match for a white patient than another white person might be. Would that the rest of us understood that too."[22] Moreover, as Lawrence Wright put it in *The New Yorker,* "Whatever the word 'race' may mean elsewhere in the world, or to the world of science, it is clear that in America the [racial] categories are arbitrary, confused, and hopelessly intermingled."[23]

The message from *The Bell Curve* coauthor Charles Murray, a leading advocate of abolishing welfare and affirmative action, is that Blacks are intellectually inferior, but they shouldn't feel bad about it—hey they're good at sports and music. Murray and his late coauthor Richard Herrnstein call for "wise ethnocentrism" (a concept as unwise, reactionary and dangerous as the anti-environmental "wise use," a so-called "free market environmentalism," which advocates the abolition of existing environmental laws and deregulation of industry). "It is possible," they say, "to look ahead to a world in which the glorious hodgepodge of inequalities of ethnic groups—genetic and environmental, permanent and temporary—can be not only accepted but celebrated."[24]

In the words of *Business Week* reviewer John Carey, *The Bell Curve* is atrocious science and "a house of cards constructed to promote a political agenda." He writes:

Even if we suspend reason and accept the book's belief in IQ, *The Bell Curve* founders on contradictions. Social scientists agree that IQ scores of all groups have risen some 15 points in the last 40 years—and the gap between whites and blacks has narrowed. So how can Murray and Herrnstein argue that growing social ills are partly caused by an increase in dumb folks [sic]?...How can they say coaching doesn't raise scores over the long-term, then dismiss a big long-term increase in a Milwaukee program as merely a product of coaching? And how can they denigrate the college degrees earned by blacks who matriculate despite lower SAT scores without saying that whites with the same SAT scores—the disadvantaged perhaps, or children of alumni—are equally undeserving?[25]

Hubbard and Wald explain that "I.Q. tests, which were designed to pinpoint those areas in which a child needed special attention, have come to be used as measures of 'intelligence,' marking people with a single number that is supposed to represent not only their current but their 'potential' abilities."[26] As Richard Lacayo pointed out in *Time*, "Craig Ramey, a researcher at the University of Alabama at Birmingham, studied poor children who were enrolled as infants in a multiyear program that provided them and their mothers with health care and a stimulating learning environment. Many of them developed and sustained normal [sic] IQs of around 100, while those in a control group were as much as 20 points lower. *The Bell Curve* describes Ramey's Abecedarian Project as provocative but inconclusive and leaves it at that."[27]

The racist, elitist, reactionary agenda of *The Bell Curve* is trumpeted in the publisher's words on the book jacket. They are worth quoting, for they reveal the extent to which many in this society are readopting, now under the false guise of science, some of the worst attitudes from the past:

> In our time, the ability to use and manipulate information has become the single most important element of success, no matter how you measure it: financial security, power or status...In such an era, high intelligence is an increasingly precious raw material for success. But despite decades of fashionable denial, the overriding and insistent truth about intellectual ability is that it is endowed unequally, for reasons that government policies can do little to change...
>
> Herrnstein and Murray break new ground in exploring the ways that low intelligence, independent of social, economic, or ethnic background lies at the root of many of our social problems. The authors also demonstrate the truth of another taboo fact: that intelligence levels differ among ethnic groups...

With relentless and unassailable thoroughness, Herrnstein and Murray for the first time show that for a wide range of intractable social problems, the decisive correlation is between a high incidence of the problem and low intelligence of those who suffer from it: this holds for school dropouts, unemployment, work-related injury, out of wedlock births, crime, and many other social problems.[28]

The authors of *The Bell Curve*, their publicists and apologists are adept in the use, misuse and manipulation of information. Whites who take solace in *The Bell Curve* should make no mistake. Those who are manipulating information to justify the higher unemployment, greater poverty and lower wages of Blacks are those who likewise blame White workers without advanced degrees (the majority) for their lower wages in comparison with so-called knowledge workers. It's easy to jump from the skills-mismatch thesis to the brains-mismatch one: The CEO is a millionaire or billionaire because *he's* smarter. The losers in downsizing are losers because they have downsized intelligence. Already, as the American Dream excludes more and more Whites, there's growing talk of a pathological "White underclass."[29]

As Charles Murray told an interviewer on a liquor-filled first-class flight to Aspen, Colorado, in the past "people were poor because of bad luck or social barriers. 'Now,' he says, 'what's holding them back is that they're not bright enough to be a physician.'" In Murray's words, the White kids who drop out of school are the low IQ, low income "White trash."[30]

The evils most fostered by slavery and oppression are precisely those which slaveholders and oppressors would transfer from their system to the inherent character of their victims. Thus the very crimes of slavery become slavery's best defense...For, let it be once granted that the human race are of multitudinous origin, naturally different in their moral, physical, and intellectual capacities, and at once you make a plausible demand for classes, grades and conditions, for different methods of culture, different moral, political, and religious institutions, and a chance is left for slavery, as a necessary institution.

Frederick Douglass, 1854.[31]

THE RAW DEAL

Stereotypes reinforce the supposed behavioral explanations of persistent poverty which provide cover for economies that persistently impoverish. Boston's 19th-century Irish immigrants, for example, were portrayed as having a culture of poverty and violence a century before Oscar Lewis famously applied the term "culture of poverty" to Mexicans, Puerto Ricans and African Americans. The "famine Irish" (who had fled Ireland's potato famine and massive land evictions) were economically exploited and socially stereotyped as immoral, drunkards and criminals—hence the term "Paddy wagon" for police wagons. Alcoholism was once recorded in the Massachusetts registry as a cause of death for Irish immigrants, not for Protestant Anglo-Saxons. In the late 19th and early 20th centuries, when large numbers of Italians, Greeks, Russian Jews and others came to Boston and elsewhere, they were also labeled as "dangerous and undesirable elements" and "inferior."[32] A *Denver Post* columnist called New York City "a cesspool" of "immigrant trash."[33] As White immigrants and especially their children were assimilated, racism against African Americans—who, unlike Whites, were systematically, violently enslaved and segregated—remained virulent.

The U.S. Constitution once counted Black slaves as worth three-fifths of Whites. Today, Black per capita income is three-fifths of Whites'. That's an economic measure of racism. The Latino-White ratio is even worse.[34]

Since the time of slavery, Blacks have been systematically dispossessed of the fruits of their labor and denied government benefits which helped many White Americans prosper. After emancipation came American apartheid. The North's Jim Crow segregation laws were adopted and adapted in the post-Civil War South. Black Codes made criminal offenses of such things as "insulting" language and gestures and "vagrancy," which included leaving the old plantations and being unemployed while searching for work elsewhere, or being in particular localities without special permission. The Black Codes mandated involuntary plantation labor as a form of punishment. They allowed judges to provide planters with the slave labor of minors who had become separated from their parents, or whose parents were dead or deemed unable to support them—with preference going to the former owner of the children. The Black Codes enforced near-slave contract labor by "servants" for "masters," sharecropping peonage and convict leasing. From the end of the Civil War in 1865 to 1890, Blacks were over 95 percent of the inmate populations in most southern state penal systems and Black state convicts were leased out to work on plantations and railroads, and in mines and factories. Lynching and "capital punishment" were the ultimate weapons.[35] In northern cities Black men and women were largely restricted to domestic service, manual labor and the lowest paid manufacturing jobs, whatever their skill and schooling.[36]

When the New Deal-era Social Security and unemployment compensation programs were established, President Roosevelt acceded to southern demands to exclude from coverage the occupations then heavily employing Blacks, as well as women: private domestic workers and agricultural laborers. (In 1937, only 8 percent of Black men and 4 percent of Black women worked in jobs covered by the original Old Age Insurance program.)[37] They got a raw deal lasting generations.* Jill Quadagno reviews this important chapter in American history in her book, *The Color of Welfare:*

> Roosevelt sought to stabilize his unwieldy coalition of northern workers and white southerners by refusing to back legislation abolishing lynching or poll taxes and by weaving racial inequality into his new welfare state. This was accomplished by excluding agricultural workers and domestic servants from both old-age insurance and unemployment compensation and by failing to provide national standards for unemployment compensation...
>
> [The South's] economy was driven by cotton production, which flourished through a sharecropping system that locked tenants—both black and white—to the land...Sharecropping operated without cash.

---

* Domestic workers became entitled to Social Security pensions in 1951, but received virtually no unemployment protection until 1978, when federal law required coverage of certain farm workers and some private, household workers. As seen early in Clinton's presidency, most household employers did not pay Social Security taxes for their housekeepers, nannies and other employees. In 1994, Clinton signed new legislation, the so-called Zoe Baird bill, which actually made things worse in the guise of improvement. As Marc Linder and Larry Norton explain: "Under the old law, both employers and household workers had to pay a tax, now set at 7.65 percent each, when workers earned $50 or more a quarter...By raising excluded income to $1,000 a year, the new law deprives household workers of Social Security's protections for all lesser sums...In the future, it will be adjusted for inflation in $100 increments...[Moreover] while the law calculates the $1,000 separately for each employer, tens of thousands of full-time employees work only one day every two weeks, or a half-day every week, for the same family. With workers commonly earning $4.25 to $5 an hour, many will fall short of the $1,000 threshold for each of several or many employers. As far as the Social Security Administration is concerned, all that hard work and income will have disappeared." Marc Linder and Larry Norton, "Nanny Tax Lets Poor Pay, Rich Profit," *New York Times*, November 13, 1994.

Planters loaned money to croppers for seeds, equipment, food, and rent...Debt kept sharecroppers nearly enslaved...

Although Roosevelt's electoral victory did not hinge on southern support, he needed southern Congressmen to move his programs past the key House and Senate committees. They opposed any program that would grant cash directly to black workers...In 1935 more than three-quarters of African Americans still lived in the South. Most sharecropped. Those not sharecropping worked as day laborers when planters needed extra hands at picking time...Outside the cotton fields black women worked as maids, earning perhaps $2.50 a week. Federal old-age insurance paid directly to retired black men and women, even at the meager sum of $15 monthly, would provide more cash than a cropper family might see in a year.

Because of southern opposition, agricultural workers and domestic servants—most black men and women—were left out of the core programs of the Social Security Act. Instead they were relegated to the social-assistance programs, where local welfare authorities could determine benefit levels and set eligibility rules.

Quadagno adds, "The New Deal also encouraged farmers to replace workers with machines through farm subsidies and other benefits to agriculture...Farm subsidies were thus passed on to black sharecroppers in the form of evictions."[38]

With the mechanization of southern agriculture and mining, millions of Blacks moved north in the 1940s and 1950s. They and their children would be undercut again as manufacturing relocated outside the cities (and abroad) and automation reduced the blue-collar jobs that had provided some Blacks with decent incomes. While Whites were benefiting from government policies that subsidized segregated suburbanization, Blacks were being hurt by redlining and disinvestment in the urban neighborhoods where they had homes, jobs and businesses.[39]

The Federal Housing Administration (FHA) was created in 1934 to provide guaranteed mortgages for new construction. The "G.I. Bill" of 1944 provided Veterans Administration (VA) loan guarantees to subsidize home mortgages for returning veterans, almost all in suburbia—where most new wartime industrial capacity was also located. The FHA and VA programs insured about one-third of all homes purchased in the 1950s. The FHA and the real estate industry promoted racial segregation as the key to neighborhood stability and housing values. A report prepared for the FHA in the 1930s ranked 15 racial and ethnic groups according to the impact of their presence on property values— values reflecting prejudice. English, Germans, Scotch, Irish and Scandinavians were classified as having the most favorable impact; Negroes and Mexicans the most detrimental.[40]

"All through the 1930s and 1940s," explains political scientist Dennis Judd, "F.H.A. administrators advised and sometimes required developers of residential projects to draw up restrictive covenants against nonwhites as a condition of obtaining F.H.A.-insured financing. Since areas that were all black were considered even worse credit risks than mixed neighborhoods, the policy closed almost all African-Americans out of the federally insured market and excluded them from the new suburbs altogether."[41] The U.S. Supreme Court ruled that racial covenants could not be enforced in 1948, but de facto segregation continued. "Between 1946 and 1959, less than 2 percent of all the housing financed with the assistance of federal mortgage insurance was made available to blacks," writes Judd. "In 1960, not a single African-American could be counted among the 82,000 residents of Long Island's Levittown [New York]. The situation was typical."[42]

A 1968 National Commission on Urban Problems deplored the "tacit agreement among all groups—lending institutions, fire insurance companies, and FHA"—to redline inner city neighborhoods, denying them credit and insurance. The commission reported that up until the summer of 1967, "FHA almost never insured mortgages on homes in slum districts, and did so very seldom in the 'gray areas' which surrounded them. Even middle-class residential districts in the central cities were suspect, since there was always the prospect that they, too, might 'turn' as Negroes and poor whites" moved in.[43]

Redlining denies residents, however qualified, the mortgages, insurance, home-improvement and home-equity loans so essential for a secure home and retirement. College educations are often financed by the kind of home-equity loans absent in redlined areas. Loans and insurance needed for the start-up, expansion and protection of local businesses are also denied.

As Charles Finn, the author of an important study of mortgage lending for the Boston Redevelopment Authority, put it, "Banks, as an important source of capital, play a pivotal but often invisible role in determining whether a community will thrive or decline...Mortgage and construction lending decisions are often made based upon expectations about neighborhood growth or decline—expectations about risk. Thus, banks' expectations of neighborhood growth or decline often become reality—a 'self-fulfilling prophecy.' Without a steady flow of credit, neighborhoods deteriorate. Economic opportunities for residents of these neighborhoods are reduced, even during periods of economic growth. During periods of economic decline, disinvested neighborhoods suffer disproportionately."[44] The Finn report observed, "The ultimate effects of restricted credit availability on neighborhoods, it was generally agreed, are physical neighborhood decline, reduced housing values, crime, and reduced opportunities for socioeconomic mobility."[45]

Banking and insurance discrimination continues through the present despite legislation such as the 1975 Home Mortgage Disclosure Act, the 1976 Equal Credit Opportunity Act and the 1977 Community Reinvestment Act. Mounting evidence of mortgage discrimination received important confirmation when the Federal Reserve Bank of Boston released an important report on racial disparities in mortgage lending in 1992. The powerful study took into account a full array of financial and employment variables used by lenders, including credit histories, loan-to-value ratios, income-to-debt burdens and other factors. It found that even after controlling for all these variables, Black and Latino mortgage applicants in the Boston metropolitan area were about 60 percent more likely to be turned down than Whites. "In fact," the report states, "high-income minorities in Boston were more likely to be turned down than low-income whites." The Boston Federal Reserve report showed that most mortgage applicants, of any race, do not have perfect credentials and lenders have considerable discretion over how to judge compensating factors in weighing income-to-debt ratios, past credit problems and other factors. "The results of this study suggest that for the same imperfections whites seem to enjoy a general presumption of creditworthiness that black and Hispanic applicants do not, and that lenders seem to be more willing to overlook flaws for white applicants than for minority applicants."[46]

A 1993 congressional hearing documented the continued role of insurance redlining. "Insurance is the invisible key to economic advancement," observed Rep. Joseph Kennedy (D-MA). "The industry has used it to lock tight the door of economic opportunity for millions of consumers. The evidence presented to this Subcommittee clearly suggests a pattern of massive, nationwide discrimination against low-income and minority Americans...The message that insurance companies are sending to low-income and minority consumers is crystal clear: you are irresponsible, you are dangerous, and you don't deserve insurance. Solely because of the color of their skin, the size of their paycheck, and the address of their home, millions of Americans must pay more in premiums for less coverage, take their chances with shadowy unregulated and underfunded companies, or go without any insurance at all and face financial disaster as a daily fact of life."[47]

By 1991, 51 percent of Whites lived in the suburbs and only 26 percent in central cities. The majority of Blacks—56 percent—remained in central cities while only 27 percent lived in suburbs.[48] In 1960, per capita income was 5 percent higher in a sample of cities than in their surrounding suburbs. By 1987, suburban per capita income was 59 percent higher than in the cities.[49] Housing discrimination remains pervasive. According to a 1991 Department of Housing and Urban Development (HUD) report of fair housing testing audits in 25 U.S. cities, Blacks encounter discrimination more than half of the time.[50] Racial bias in employment and education will be discussed in the next chapter.

BLAMING WOMEN FOR ILLEGITIMATE ECONOMICS

The reality is that the U.S. economy is increasingly producing poverty wages and persistently high unemployment. The reality is that most poor Americans are White, many married couples are poor and even if there were no children of color or single mother families, the United States would still have an extraordinarily high poverty rate. The myth of a matriarchal "culture of poverty" hides this reality of an economy of impoverishment and governmental neglect.

Women are scapegoated as producers and reproducers of poverty. Historically, "women have been viewed as the breeders of poverty, criminality and other social problems," observes Mimi Abramovitz, professor of social policy at the Hunter College School of Social Work. "From the 'tenement classes' of the mid-1800s and the 'dangerous classes' of the 1880s, to Social Darwinism and eugenics, to Freudian theories of motherhood, to Moynihan's 'Black matriarchy' and today's 'underclass,' society blames women for the failed policies of business and the state."[51]

In *The Negro Family*, Daniel Patrick Moynihan, then a Labor Department official, embellished sociologist E. Franklin Frazier's thesis of the Black matriarch in whom "neither economic necessity nor tradition had instilled the spirit of subordination to masculine authority." Moynihan claimed in his 1965 report that matriarchal families are at the core of a Black "tangle of pathology"—and this, not racism, was the "fundamental source of the weakness of the Negro Community." The civil rights movement was then struggling to dismantle American apartheid. Moynihan's thesis was the antithesis to the Black liberation movement, feminism and the welfare rights movement. The Johnson White House released the report shortly after the Watts riots. After serving in the Nixon and Ford administrations, Moynihan went on to become a powerful Democratic senator, and his rhetoric is echoed loudly by others.

African American women have been stereotyped since slavery as mammies, matriarchs, welfare mothers and other "controlling images," explains Patricia Hill Collins, a professor of African American studies and sociology. The mammy was "the faithful, obedient domestic servant...the mammy symbolizes the dominant group's perceptions of the ideal Black female relationship to elite White male power...She has accepted her subordination." While "the mammy represents the 'good' Black mother, the matriarch symbolizes the 'bad' Black mother...Spending too much time away from home, these working mothers ostensibly cannot properly supervise their children and are a major contributing factor to their children's school failure. As overly aggressive, unfeminine women, Black matriarchs allegedly emasculate their lovers and husbands." The image of the Black matriarch in the post-World War II era was "a powerful symbol for both Black and White women of what can go wrong if white patriarchal power is challenged. Aggressive, assertive women are penalized—they are abandoned by their men, end up impoverished, and are stigmatized as being unfeminine."[52]

Societal images of women changed quickly to reinforce their role in wartime industry—and changed again to undermine their role in postwar industry and society. As Susan Faludi writes in *Backlash*: "Rosie the Riveter was revered and, in 1941, Wonder Woman was introduced." Women protested for equal pay and expanded day care, and overwhelmingly voiced their intention to keep their jobs in peacetime. When the war ended, so did the supportive images of women workers. Women were abruptly purged from higher-paid industrial jobs, and the government shut down wartime day care centers and eliminated federal funding for day care.

"Employers who had applauded women's work during the war," says Faludi, "now accused working women of incompetence or 'bad attitudes'—and laid them off at rates that were 75 percent higher than men's...The rise in female autonomy and aggressiveness, scholars and government officials agreed, was causing a rise in juvenile delinquency and divorce rates—and would only lead to the collapse of the family. Child-care authorities...demanded that wives stay home."[53]

A study of "schizophrenic" women hospitalized in the San Francisco Bay Area during the 1950s "concludes that institutionalization and sometimes electric shock treatments were used to force women to accept their domestic roles and their husbands' dictates." Male violence against wives and children was not the subject of even a single article in the major journal of American family sociology between 1939 and 1969. Fifties-era psychiatrists "regarded the battered woman as a masochist who provoked her husband into beating her."[54]

"The backlash of the feminine-mystique years did not return working women to the home," says Faludi. "Rather, the culture derided them; employers discriminated against them; government promoted new [discriminatory] employment policies...the proportion of [women] who were relegated to low-paying jobs rose, their pay gap climbed, and occupational segregation increased as their numbers in the higher-paying professions declined." Faludi observes, "Women's contradictory circumstances in the '50s—rising economic participation coupled with an embattled and diminished cultural stature—is the central paradox of women under a backlash."[55] And backlashes hit women of color hardest.

Two decades ago, Senator Russell Long of Louisiana referred to welfare mothers as "brood mares."[56] "Essentially an updated version of the breeder woman image created during slavery," observes Patricia Hill Collins, the welfare mother "image provides an ideological justification for efforts to harness Black women's fertility to the needs of a changing political economy...Slaveowners wanted enslaved Africans to 'breed' because every slave child born represented a valuable unit of property, another unit of labor, and, if female, the prospects for more slaves."[57]

Negroes for sale—a Negro woman, 24 years of age, and her two children, one eight and the other three years old. Said Negroes will be sold separately or together, as desired. The woman is a good seamstress. She will be sold low for cash, or exchange for groceries. For terms apply to Matthew Bliss and Company, 1 Front Levee.

Slavery-era advertisement in the *New Orleans Bee*.[58]

As the percentage of births to unmarried women rose in the post-World War II period—especially among White women—and Aid to Dependent Children was opened to their offspring, both Black and White women were viewed as breeders, observes Ricki Solinger in her book on single motherhood and race. But White unwed mothers "were viewed as socially productive breeders whose babies," if given up for adoption, "could offer infertile couples their only chance to construct proper families." Black women "were viewed as socially unproductive breeders, constrainable only by punitive, legal sanctions. Proponents of school segregation, restrictive public housing, exclusionary welfare policies, and enforced sterilization or birth control all used the issue of relatively high rates of black illegitimacy to support their campaigns." (In 1960, about 94 percent of Black but only 29 percent of White out-of-wedlock babies lived with biological parents or relatives.)

White unwed mothers could be redeemed from their state of "shame" through racially-biased government-supported maternity homes, adoption and subsequent homemaker mom/breadwinner dad marriage—which, though rare for most of American history, was enshrined as traditional with the help of postwar television. Black women, says Solinger, were "simply blamed" for the "population bomb," escalating welfare costs and giving birth "to Black America, with all its 'defects.'"[59] Behind the "population bomb" rhetoric was this reality: Blacks made up a higher percentage of the U.S. population in 1850, during slavery, than in 1950, or anytime in the 20th century.

"The bodies of black women became political terrain on which some proponents of white supremacy mounted their campaigns," writes Solinger, and "the black illegitimate baby became the child white politicians and taxpayers loved to hate."[60] And so it goes today. The slaveowners' control of fertility echoes again in the present economy which wants Black women's reproduction further reduced because Black workers, and therefore Black children, are increasingly considered surplus. Norplant contraceptive implants, which can cause bleeding, strokes, numbing, scarring and other side effects, as well as birth defects, have become—like earlier sterilization abuse—a eugenics weapon for judges and politicians. Thousands of women have joined in class-action suits against the makers of Norplant.[61]

Today, liberals and conservatives alike accuse single mothers, especially Black single mothers, of putting their children and all society at risk.[62] In a widely-publicized 1992 speech at Yale University, in which he slandered single mothers and affirmative action, neoliberal Massachusetts Senator John Kerry recycled Moynihan's false choice between patriarchy and pathology:

> Twenty-seven years ago, my Senate colleague Daniel Patrick Moynihan warned that: "from the wild Irish slums of the 19th century eastern seaboard, to the riot-torn suburbs of Los Angeles, there is one unmistakable lesson in American history: A society that allows a large number of young men to grow up in broken families…never acquiring any stable relationship to…authority, never acquiring any rational expectations about the future—that society asks for and gets chaos. Crime, violence, unrest, disorder—more particularly, the furious, unrestrained lashing out at the whole social structure—that is not only to be expected; it is very near inevitable." (Ellipses Kerry's.)[63]

Imagine labeling married-couple families as pathological breeding grounds of patriarchal domestic violence, or suggesting that women should never marry, because they are more likely to be beaten and killed by a spouse than a stranger. As the *Journal of Trauma* reports, "Domestic violence is the leading cause of injury to women and accounts for more visits to hospital emergency departments than car crashes, muggings, and rapes combined." Nationally, about a third of all murdered women are killed by husbands, boyfriends and ex-partners (less than a tenth are killed by strangers); "men commonly kill their female partners in response to the woman's attempt to leave an abusive relationship."[64] According to the National Crime Victimization Survey, "Women suffering violent victimizations [other than rape] were almost twice as likely to be injured if the offender was an intimate" rather than a stranger.[65]

The term "domestic violence" is as inadequate as the response. Nationally, it is estimated that a woman has between a one-in-five and a one-in-three chance of being physically assaulted by a partner or ex-partner during her lifetime. In the words of a 1992 congressional report, "Every week is a week of terror for at least 21,000 American women" of all backgrounds, whose "domestic assaults, rapes and murders were reported to the police." As many as 3 million more domestic violence crimes may go unreported yearly.[66]

Stephanie Coontz writes in her myth-busting study of families, *The Way We Never Were*, "families whose members are police officers or who serve in the military have much higher rates of divorce, family violence, and substance abuse than do other families, but we seldom accuse them of constituting an 'underclass' with a dysfunctional cul-

> Illegitimacy is the central social problem of our time...
>
> The main reason for scrapping welfare is to reduce the number of babies born to single women...
>
> A major change in the behavior of young women and the adults in their lives will occur only when the prospect of having a child out of wedlock is once again so immediately, tangibly punishing that it overrides everything else—the importuning of the male, the desire for sex, the thoughtlessness of the moment, the anticipated cuddliness of the baby. Such a change will take place only when young people have it drummed into their heads from their earliest memories that having a baby without a husband entails awful consequences. Subtle moral reasoning is not the response that works. "My father would kill me" is the kind of response that works.
>
> Charles Murray, "What To Do About Welfare," *Commentary*,
> December 1994.

ture."[67] More often, the stresses of their jobs are used to rationalize their behavior.

Liberals have joined with conservatives in the crusade to restigmatize motherhood outside marriage. Secretary of Health and Human Services Donna Shalala, former chair of the Children's Defense Fund, told *Newsweek*, "I don't like to put this in moral terms, but I do believe that having children out of wedlock is just wrong." She told the House Ways and Means Committee, "I don't think anyone in public life today ought to condone children born out of wedlock...even if the family is financially able."[68] President Clinton told the National Baptist Convention in September 1994, "I know not everybody is going to be in a stable, traditional family like you see in one of those 1950 sitcoms, but we'd be better off if more people were." He preached, "You shouldn't have a baby when you're not married. You just have to stop it."

The awful labeling of children as "illegitimate" has again been legitimized. Besides meaning born out of wedlock, illegitimate also means illegal, contrary to rules and logic, misbegotten, not genuine, wrong—to be a bastard. Single mothers and their children, especially Black women and children, have become prime scapegoats for illegitimate economics. Once again, to use Solinger's words, "the black illegitimate baby [has become] the child white politicians and taxpayers loved to hate."[69] Never mind that impoverished women don't create poverty any more than slaves created slavery.

Stigma is accompanied by negative expectations and prejudicial treatment. In a study cited by Coontz, "teachers shown a videotape of a child engaging in a variety of actions consistently rate the child much more negatively on a wide range of dimensions when they are told that he or she comes from a divorced family than when they believe the child to come from an intact home."[70]

The typical women behind the rise in never-married mothers in the 1980s, explains the U.S. General Accounting Office, "differed from the stereotype: They were not unemployed teenaged dropouts but rather working women aged 25 to 44 who had completed high school." The percentage of total births to teenage mothers was less in 1990 than 1980. Contrary to image, the *proportion* of Black children born to unmarried mothers—most of them not teenagers—has grown because the birth rates of *married* Black women have fallen so dramatically.[71]

Also contrary to stereotype, single mother families—Black and White—increased at a higher rate in the 1970s than in the 1980s or 1990s. This was true for those headed by never-married women as well as divorced women. And true even though a significant portion of the increase since 1980 is due to changes in Census Bureau survey procedures.[72] It's also important to understand that the term "single-parent" does not necessarily mean that the family does not have two parents living together; it may mean two parents who are not legally married. "It has become increasingly likely that a child born to an unmarried mother is not actually born into a single-parent family." There has been a large rise in the number of families composed of unmarried couples, including same-sex couples, with children.[73]

The proportion of households headed by women has been rising in all regions of the world. Women are reported to be the sole breadwinners in one-fourth to one-third of the world's families. "Studies in many nations show that it is more often women's income that meets the family's basic needs, such as food, clothing, health care, and education."[74] In the words of a congressional report, "Almost all major industrialized countries have experienced large increases in the number of births to unmarried women." As of 1991, the amount of births to unmarried women as a percentage of all live births was 48 percent in Sweden, 47 percent in Denmark, 30 percent in the U.K., 30 percent in France (1990), 30 percent in the United States, 29 percent in Canada and 15 percent in Germany.[75] None of the other countries have U.S. proportions of poverty.

THE WAGES OF DISCRIMINATION

It shouldn't be surprising that in the United States, Black and Latino families—whether one-parent or two-parent families—have higher poverty rates than White families since the wages and job opportunities of people of color reflect educational and employment discrimination. It shouldn't be surprising that single-parent families—male or female-headed—have high rates of poverty since, with the fall in real wages, two or more incomes are increasingly needed to keep families out of poverty. Since single mothers of color experience both race and gender discrimination, their families are the most impoverished. Nationally, 46 percent of all female-headed families with children under 18 were below the official 1993 poverty line as were 23 percent of single father families with children. In other words, single father families have very high rates of poverty, but single mother families have even higher rates. The official 1993 poverty rates for families with children under 18 were 40 percent for those with White single mothers, 20 percent with White single fathers; 58 percent for those with Black single mothers, 32 percent with Black fathers; 61 percent for those with Latina single mothers and 28 percent with Latino fathers.[76]

The fact that many female-headed households are poorer because women are generally paid less than men is taken as a given in much poverty policy discussion, as if pay equity were a pipe dream not even worth mentioning. A 1977 government study found that if working women were paid what similarly qualified men earn, the number of poor families would decrease by half.[77] A 1991 government study found that "many single mothers will remain near or below the poverty line even if they work at full-time jobs. Problems they are likely to face include low earnings; vulnerability to layoffs and other work interruptions; lack of important fringe benefits such as paid sick leave and health insurance; and relatively high expenses for child care."[78]

Despite men's wage losses during 1973-93 and small gains by women with more than a high school degree, male high school graduates still have higher hourly wages than women with some college, and male college graduates have higher wages than women with graduate education. (See table 10.) Women working year-round, full-time in 1993 earned 72 cents for every dollar men earned. Women don't pay 72 cents on a man's dollar for their rent or their college degrees, or 72 percent as much to feed their children.

Looking at the 1990-92 period, the Census Bureau reported that men who left a full-time job or were laid off, and then found another full-time job, saw their paychecks drop from an average of $456 to $312 a week. Women's wages fell from an average of $321 weekly to an even more meager $197. Among the men, an estimated 37 percent had employer-provided health insurance in their old jobs, but only 25 percent did in their new jobs. Among women, only 23 percent had health benefits in their old jobs and only 14 percent had health insurance in their new jobs.[79]

Instead of rooting out discrimination, encouraging adequate wages, promoting full and flexible employment, and implementing the kind of child care and other family supports common in numerous countries, many U.S. policy makers are busily blaming women for their disproportionate poverty. For women, "wage discrimination is worse in the U.S. than in any other major developed country except Japan." The Reagan and Bush administrations cared not. The Equal Employment and Opportunity Commission (EEOC), for example, "filed only two equal pay lawsuits in 1992, compared with 79 in 1980."[80]

Most mothers work outside the home as well as inside. But you wouldn't know that by looking at school hours and the scarcity of after-school programs and affordable day care. More than half of all women with children under age 6, and three-fourths of women with children ages 6 to 17, are in the paid workforce. By 1993, only 10 percent of all families, and only 21 percent of families with children under 18, fit the stereotype fifties family of a breadwinner father and a homemaker mother who cares for the children and does not work outside the home.[81]

Despite the obvious need, subsidized child care is scarce. In Massachusetts, for example, the average cost for professional day care ranges from $5,000 to $8,000 a year, depending on the child's age.[82] The federal tax deduction for child care expenses is capped at an absurdly low amount, and then reduced further, depending on income, resulting in an average taxpayer credit estimated at $435 for 1994—for an estimated total credit of $2.7 billion. By contrast, mortgage interest is fully deductible on acquisition debt of up to $1 million for first and second homes. The 1993 tax revenue loss for the mortgage interest deduction, disproportionately benefiting higher-income families, was $44 billion.[83]

When it comes to child care, women are hit at both ends, paying large sums for care while earning so little as child care teachers that many can't even afford to enroll their own children in the centers where they work. Nationally, child care teaching staff, nearly all women, had average earnings of only $9,363 in 1988, while sanitation workers earned $19,163 and workers in cigarette factories earned $30,590. People who take care of animals in zoos make an average $2,500 more a year than child care teachers.[84]

In the words of a comprehensive study commissioned by the Boston Foundation, after food, housing and taxes, child care is the biggest expense for working parents of all incomes. "For moderate-income families, child care costs can swamp dreams of going back to school, home ownership, or savings for college. For the working poor and for low-income families, subsidized child care can be the key to staying off welfare, to getting an education, a better job, and housing."[85] As a government report put it, "Among the factors that encourage low-income mothers to seek and keep jobs—factors such as more education, training, and transportation—affordable child care is a decisive one."[86]

WELFARE QUEENS AND WORKER BEES

The writers and scholars and politicians who wax most rhapsodic about the need to replace welfare with work make their harsh judgments from the comfortable and supportive environs of offices and libraries and think tanks. If they need to go to the bathroom midsentence, there is no one timing their absence. If they take longer than a half-hour for lunch, there is no one waiting to dock their pay. If their baby sitter gets sick, there is no risk of someone having taken their place at work by the next morning. Yet these are conditions that low-wage women routinely face, which inevitably lead to the cyclical nature of their welfare histories.

Rosemary L. Bray, *New York Times Magazine*, November 8, 1992.

Racist and sexist scapegoating have come together most viciously in the rollback of welfare. Myths crowd out realities, to provide support for terrible social and economic policies, whose harmful consequences ripple throughout society. The demonization of the welfare mother, writes Rosemary Bray, a former editor of the *New York Times Book Review* whose family received welfare when she was a child, reinforces the patriarchal notion "that women and children without a man are fundamentally damaged goods" and allows "for denial about the depth and intransigence of racism."[87] It allows those benefiting from rising economic inequality to shift the blame for the system's failure to produce sufficient jobs and income onto supposed personal failures such as deficient morals and "work ethic."

AFDC (originally called Aid to Dependent Children, ADC) expanded for many reasons, among them population growth; the inclusion of mothers—and not just their children—in recipient counts after 1950; higher rates of female-headed households (e.g., with the rise in divorce rates, decline in women giving up their out-of-wedlock babies for adoption); the reversal of state practices such as denying welfare to "illegitimate" children and kicking recipients off the rolls during cotton-picking season; and the national welfare rights movement beginning in the mid-1960s. The proportion of women of color on AFDC rose in the 1950s and 1960s because of two often-neglected factors: the displacement of Blacks from southern agriculture by mechanization and their migration to northern cities—where jobs and low-cost housing were increasingly lost to automation, plant closures, disinvestment and "urban renewal"—and the lessening of AFDC eligibility discrimination.[88] Discrimination in other government programs continued; for example, as noted earlier, unemployment insurance provided virtually no protection for private domestic workers and farm workers until 1978.

AFDC has not expanded to match the rising pace of people in poverty, especially for children. The number of AFDC child recipients as a percentage of children living below the official poverty line has fallen from a high of 81 percent in 1973 to 63 percent in 1992. The number of all AFDC recipients as a percent of the pre-welfare official poverty population dropped from 55 percent in 1979 to 49 percent in 1991. In 1992 (the latest year of full data), there were 13.6 million AFDC recipients, two-thirds of whom were children (9.2 million).

About 39 percent of families receiving AFDC are White, 37 percent are Black (a lower percentage than 1973), 18 percent are Latino, 3 percent are Asian and 1 percent are Native American. There are disproportionately more people of color on welfare because disproportionately more people of color are poor, unemployed and underemployed, and they have disproportionately less access to other government income support programs such as unemployment, workers compensation and Social Security. The official 1993 unemployment rate for women maintaining families was 7.7 percent for Whites and 13.7 percent for Blacks.[89] The real jobless and underemployment rates are much higher.

Scapegoaters don't care if women turn to AFDC after fleeing violent husbands or after losing their jobs. Some women turn to AFDC to find health care or disability insurance. One study estimated that providing health insurance to all employed single mothers would reduce the AFDC caseload by about 10 percent. Many countries require paid maternity leave. The United States does not. An Ohio study found that a woman on pregnancy leave is ten times more likely to lose her job than one on medical leave for other reasons.[90] The Family and Medical Leave Act, finally enacted in 1993 with much struggle and fanfare, stipulates only unpaid leave and excludes many workers from coverage. In Massachusetts in the year following the Family Leave Act's passage, "few area employees have used the law, saying unpaid time off is a luxury they cannot afford."[91]

In the name of reform, politicians have substituted fighting welfare for fighting poverty. AFDC benefits have been chopped repeatedly as if, once you have too little money, it doesn't matter how little you have. Between 1970 and 1994, the median state's maximum monthly benefit for a family of three was cut nearly in half (47 percent), adjusting for inflation. Until 1979, all families receiving AFDC were eligible for food stamps; today, 13 percent don't receive any food stamps. When food stamps are added to AFDC, the combined median benefit is still only 72 percent of the official poverty line.[92] Contrary to common belief, fewer than one out of four families receiving AFDC live in public housing or receive any rent subsidies. In 40 of 44 metro areas surveyed nationally, the cost of a modest two-bedroom apartment, according to HUD's Fair Market Rent level, is greater than the *entire* AFDC benefit for a family of three with no other income; in 28 metro areas a one-bedroom apartment would cost more than the entire AFDC benefit for a family of three.[93]

A government report assessing poverty trends between 1980 and 1988, "found that the primary reason for the apparent poverty rate increase among women heading single-parent families living alone is the decrease in [AFDC and other] transfer payments, particularly reductions in means-tested assistance and social insurance. The poverty rate increase occurred despite the fact that these women were working more and earning more." According to a congressional report, "In 1979 approximately 30 percent of individuals in single-parent families were removed from poverty as the result of means-tested transfers, food and housing benefits, and Federal tax policy. By 1990, this had declined to 20 percent." Meanwhile, "the percentage of elderly individuals removed from poverty due to social insurance programs increased from 68 percent to 73 percent from 1979 to 1990."[94]

Welfare budget cutters pretend that AFDC is a major drain on public money when, in fact, it is not. AFDC accounted for about 1 percent of federal outlays in 1994 and states spent 2 percent of their revenues on AFDC. The gap between image and reality is vast. For example, a poll of 1994 voters found that one out of five believed that welfare was *the largest* federal government expense, larger even than defense.[95]

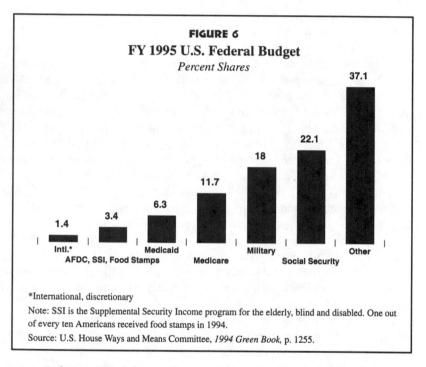

FIGURE 6
FY 1995 U.S. Federal Budget
Percent Shares

*International, discretionary

Note: SSI is the Supplemental Security Income program for the elderly, blind and disabled. One out of every ten Americans received food stamps in 1994.

Source: U.S. House Ways and Means Committee, *1994 Green Book,* p. 1255.

Politicians and the media sow the seeds of hatred with slanderous stereotypes of corrupt and lazy "welfare queens." When California cut its monthly AFDC payment for a mother and two children in 1991—which was already $2,645 below the official annual poverty line—Governor Pete Wilson said it meant "one less six-pack per week."[96]

Contrary to the "welfare as a way of life" stereotype, the typical recipient has one or two children and "is a short-term user" of AFDC. Most families receiving AFDC will be enrolled for less than two years, if single spells are considered, and cumulatively less than four years total, if multiple spells over time are considered.[97] A minority of families become long-term recipients. Those who do become long-term recipients have greater obstacles to getting off welfare such as lacking prior work experience, a high school degree or child care, or having poor health or disabilities, or caring for a child with disabilities.

Also contrary to stereotype, most daughters in families who received welfare do not become welfare recipients as adults.[98] The myth of an intergenerational Black matriarchy of "welfare queens" is particularly disgusting since Black women were enslaved workers for over two centuries and have always had a high labor force participation rate and, because of racism and sexism, a disproportionate share of low wages and poverty.[99]

In the stereotype world, the exceptions make the rule: The stereotypical "welfare mother" is a "baby having babies." For example, in the "Replacing Welfare with Work" chapter of the Democratic Leadership Council's blueprint for the Clinton presidency, the only age reference is to the "15-year-old welfare mother with a new baby." In reality, *0.1 percent* of mothers receiving AFDC are 15 or younger, and *less than 4 percent* are 18 or younger.[100]

A General Accounting Office report reviewing the 1976-92 period observes: "In 1992, never-married women receiving AFDC were less likely to be teenage mothers. They were also older and better educated than never-married women receiving AFDC in 1976. Similar changes occurred among all never-married mothers."[101]

The "babies having babies" stereotype of welfare feeds the welfare backlash and undermines much-needed efforts to actually help young teenage mothers complete school, pursue higher education, secure decent child care and get a job with a living wage in these increasingly difficult economic times. Many of the harshest critics of teenage pregnancy are also adamant opponents of providing sex education and family planning services for teenagers. Advocates of abolishing welfare completely for all unwed mothers under 18 or 21 years old—or even 26 years old—or requiring them to live at home to receive AFDC, ignore these realities: While teen mothers receiving AFDC typically live with relatives, and only a minority live alone with their children, some teen mothers would be endangered living with family members. The Boyer and Fine study funded by the National Center on Child Abuse and Neglect found that in a sample group of young women who had been pregnant as adolescents, 55 percent reported having been molested, and the majority (54 percent) of that group said their molesters were family members.[102]

Being married is neither necessary nor sufficient to avoid poverty. The official 1993 poverty rates for married-couple families with children under 18 were 8 percent for Whites, 14 percent for Blacks and 24 percent for Latinos![103] As seen in a previous chapter, poverty is much greater and rising in younger families. The poverty rate for children in the families of married couples under 30 climbed from 8 percent in 1973 to 17 percent in 1989, and 20 percent in 1990 during the recession. (See table 8.)

Still, a wave of policies under names like "wedfare" and "bridefare" is being enacted—and worse policies being proposed—that reward women who marry and punish unmarried women and their children. It's popular policy now to deny women increased benefits for additional children, with the long-disproven rationale that more benefits beget more children. Remember that existing benefits are already way below what the government considers necessary for subsistence, and the proportion of female-headed households was rising while AFDC benefits were plunging.

Many women leave welfare—though often not poverty—after finding jobs and/or marrying men. Black women have a harder time doing either than White women, not because of a self-perpetuating "cycle of dependency," but a cycle of discrimination and demographics. Some analysts point to a "dearth of marriageable Black men," by which they mean employed men earning above-poverty wages, without mentioning the dearth of Black men, period, as racism-fueled mortality takes its toll. The Black female-male ratio between the ages of 25 and 44, for example, was 100 to 87 in 1989, while it was 100 to 101 for Whites.[104]

ENDING WELFARE INSTEAD OF POVERTY

The welfare system of recent decades did not create poverty, but it did minimize help and maximize humiliation. Theresa Funiciello has known the welfare system as a recipient, organizer, employee, consultant and author. She describes the system this way: "The welfare acted like the women had nothing better or more useful to do than jump to the snap of virtually endless demands to supply papers, evidence of 'proper behavior,' and other time-and soul-consuming documentation of their worthiness. They had no concept of what it was like to scrounge for necessities in every conceivable corner of your life." She explains that all the run-arounds, lost files, long waits in demeaning offices, brutality by guards and unjustified cut-offs were intended to keep the rolls down. "It ensured that only those *in truly desperate need* would subject themselves to the endless red tape and humiliation of the welfare...Since welfare recipients are perceived to be the dregs of society, there is no need to treat them humanely."[105] (Italics in original.)

When Barbara Sobel, then head of the New York City Human Resources Administration, posed as a welfare applicant to experience the system firsthand, she was misdirected, mistreated and so "depersonalized," she says, "I ceased to be." She remained on welfare, with a mandatory part-time job as a clerk in a city office, despite repeated pleas for full-time work, and learned that most recipients desperately want jobs.[106]

Some women turn to AFDC after losing jobs; others combine work and welfare because their earnings are so low. As the Center for Law and Social Policy points out, the data tend to provide a misleading impression of recipients' work histories. The low percentage of women receiving welfare who also have paid jobs "to a great extent, reflects budgeting rules that tend to make a family ineligible for assistance after it enters employment." Data from a number of states suggest that 34 to 40 percent of current AFDC recipients have been employed over the past year.[107] The Institute for Women's Policy Research found that four out of ten recipients work at paid jobs, either by simultaneously combining work and welfare benefits (17 percent) or cycling between work and welfare (22 percent).[108]

State and federal policies have imposed various mandatory work and training programs for welfare recipients. A 1988 federal study estimated that there were only enough "low-skill" job openings nationwide to employ one out of six AFDC recipients who might be expected to work under the Family Support Act of 1988. Most families receiving AFDC have at least one child five years old or younger; 40 percent have a child two years old or younger. In a discriminatory, dangerous move to expand day care for AFDC recipients on the cheap, many states are exempting child care providers from health and safety regulations or loosening them for child care under the Family Support Act.[109]

The widespread pretense that leaving welfare through "workfare" (by whatever name) means leaving poverty and improving the lives of children, undermines efforts to make work fair and supportive of all families with adequate jobs, wages, paid family leave, child care, health care, training, unemployment compensation and so on. It is work*farce*. There are about 4 million adults receiving AFDC. In 1993, nearly 3 million people who worked *full time, year round* were below the official poverty line; over 7 million were at 150 percent of the poverty line, an alternative measure of poverty, which is still inadequate for child care expenses.[110] Many parents with young children cannot work full time inside the home and full time outside it.

Instead of promoting full employment at decent wages—enabling anybody who wants a job to find a job and transition between jobs—welfare removers pretend that there are jobs enough for everyone, if only they have the right "work ethic." Never mind that it is Federal Reserve Board policy to keep millions of people unemployed, and that temporary and part-time jobs are being substituted for full-time ones. By the government's undercounting measure, 8 million people were unemployed in 1994; millions more were working part time involuntarily.

Speaking about his plans to reform welfare, President Clinton told U.S. governors in February 1993: "We will remove the incentive for staying in poverty"; people should not "draw a check for doing nothing when they can do something." We have to reject the notion of work which presumes that a mother raising a child with the help of welfare is getting something for "doing nothing," while someone managing a corporation whose toxic waste is polluting that mother's community is a productive member of society.

Clinton promised to "end welfare as we know it." He opened the door wide for extremists who wanted to end welfare, and knew how to seize their opportunity. Clinton offered a politically doomed package of carrots and sticks. What's left are sticks. Under the Republican *Contract With America*—which is being rapidly implemented at this writing—we are returning to the days when states denied welfare to "illegitimate" children and had the right to be as mean and miserly as they wished. AFDC funding will be capped at reduced levels, despite high unemployment and poverty rates, ensuring a growing gap between the number of people eligible and the number of people actually receiving assistance. Also on the chopping block are Supplemental Security Income (SSI), which provides assistance to elderly, blind and disabled persons; public housing; nutrition programs, including the school lunch program, food stamps and WIC (supplemental nutrition program for pregnant and nursing Women, Infants and Children); education; and employment training. Moreover, leading politicians want to cut off all AFDC, SSI, housing, food stamps and other assistance to noncitizens (except perhaps those over 75), including legal residents who pay taxes.[111]

The ultimate goal of the Right is to abolish welfare altogether and replace it with nothing—except prisons and, perhaps, poorly funded orphanages. No one should doubt that dismantling welfare—without replacing it with the kind of progressive initiatives discussed later—will lead to more hunger, homelessness, crime and, as battered women's advocates are warning, the beating and murder of women and children less able to flee their abusers.

I believe in a social safety net, but I think that it's better done by churches and by synagogues and by volunteers.

Newt Gingrich.[112]

Jackie Gingrich filed court papers during their separation saying Newt was providing only $700 a month for her and the girls, then ages 17 and 14. The papers said she could not pay the basic household bills and was facing imminent cutoff of the utilities. Church members took up a collection to help out.

Newt Gingrich filed papers in response, including an accounting of his monthly expenses, which showed that he was spending $400 on food and dry-cleaning for himself.

Washington Post Weekly, 1995.[113]

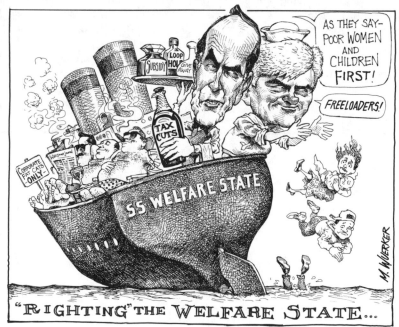

6

CYCLE OF UNEQUAL OPPORTUNITY

He was born on third base and decided that he'd hit a triple.

Jim Hightower, radio talk show host and former Texas Agriculture
commissioner, speaking about George Bush.

We hear a lot about the supposed "underclass cycle of dependency." Not about the upperclass cycle of dependency on unequal opportunity. When it comes to who gets what from government, language helps discriminate. Labor, women and people of color are called "special interests" although together they are the great majority of the population. The private profit-making interest of Corporate America substitutes for the "national interest."

"Welfare" has become synonymous with AFDC—Aid to Families with Dependent Children—and has been transformed from a positive into a negative term. The much greater public subsidies, lucrative government contracts and tax "incentives" for private corporations are not called "Aid For Dependent Corporations."[1] The billions of dollars in "welfare for the well-off" such as much-abused subsidies for "business" meals and travel and mortgage interest deductions on luxury homes are not called food and housing handouts.[2]

Land plundered from Mexico is called Texas, California, New Mexico and Arizona—while undocumented Mexican immigrants are called illegal aliens. When Native Americans were dispossessed of land and life, *they* were called savages. The long trail of broken treaties is camouflaged with terms like "Indian giver." Instead of equal rights, much less reparations, former slaves and their descendants got American apartheid and continued discrimination. Redlining, which siphons the savings and pensions of people of color into investment in whiter, higher-income areas is not called looting. While bankers created the S&L crisis, throwing money at spendthrifts, they rejected qualified applicants of color seeking money for homes and businesses—and then expected everyone to pick up the bailout tab. Discriminatory pay for women and people of color is not called robbery. Knowingly dumping carcinogenic industrial waste is not called premeditated murder.

LEGACIES

Affirmative action has been twisted to slander people of color as subpar beneficiaries of "reverse discrimination." Meanwhile, without stigma, there is de facto affirmative action for White and wealthier alumni offspring who don't otherwise meet college standards despite their more privileged backgrounds. A *Boston Globe* article on so-called "legacy admissions" noted that the acceptance rate for children of Harvard alumni was more than double the rate for all applicants, class of 1992. "Far from being more qualified, or even equally qualified, the average admitted legacy at Harvard between 1981 and 1988 was significantly *less* qualified than the average nonlegacy."[3]

In his book, *The Rage of a Privileged Class*, Ellis Cose recounts a conversation about affirmative action with a White Harvard student who is the brother of a close friend. The student was furiously indignant, saying things like: Why "couldn't they compete like everyone else? Why should hardworking whites like himself be pushed aside for second-rate affirmative action hires?" Cose recalls:

> When the young man paused to catch his breath, I took the occasion to observe that it seemed more than a bit hypocritical of him to rage on about preferential treatment. A person of modest intellect, he had gotten into Harvard largely on the basis of family connections. His first summer internship, with the White House, had been arranged by a family member. His second, with the World Bank, had been similarly arranged. Thanks to his nice internships and Harvard degree, he had been promised a coveted slot in a major company's executive training program. In short, he was already well on his way to a distinguished career—a career made possible by preferential treatment.[4]

A long history of government welfare such as the Homestead Act, segregated housing subsidies and ongoing federal land, mineral and timber giveaways, is rewritten as "pulling yourself up by your own bootstraps." As illustrated by the story of Texas Senator Phil Gramm, a right-wing Republican presidential hopeful, welfare takes many forms: "Born in Georgia in 1942, to a father who was living on a veterans disability pension, Gramm attended a publicly funded university on a grant paid for by the federal War Orphans Act. His graduate work was financed by a National Defense Education Act fellowship, and his first job was at Texas A&M University, a federal land-grant institution."[5]

As *Business Week* put it in a post-1994 election editorial: "Senator Phil Gramm...has also been big on cuts, except when it came to Texas pork such as the Superconducting Super Collider. Western Republican senators hollered about the millions in the crime bill that went to midnight basketball...But they defend the tens of billions that subsidize ranching, mining, and lumbering every year. The hypocrisy on spending must stop."[6] Senators like North Carolina's Jesse Helms are eager to subsidize cancerous tobacco, not nutrition programs. Many of the same politicians dedicated to cutting millions of women and children off welfare staunchly defend an 1872 law that allows giant mining companies to strip minerals from public lands, take the profits, pay next to nothing in return and leave behind plundered lands and environmental hazards. When it comes to ending corporate welfare, there's a little talk and less action.

"For most of the past two decades, American politics have been driven to the right by a crude but powerful assumption: that those 'tax and spend' Democrats have been taking away the taxpayers' hard-earned money and giving it to 'them'—the so-called undeserving poor," observes *Newsweek.* "Roughly half of all American families receive some sort of federal benefit—a social-security check, a farm loan, a tax break, a federally guaranteed scholarship. Only a third of all the money spent on government entitlement programs goes to the poor."[7] Behind the rhetoric, "payments to the poor add up to less than the three largest tax breaks that benefit the middle class and wealthy: deductions for retirement plans, the deduction for home mortgage interest and the exemption of health-insurance premiums that companies pay for their employees."[8]

It is estimated that "since 1960, around 80 percent of social-welfare expenditures have been in programs not focused exclusively on the poor...A continuing measure of the two-tier nature of the income support system lies in the fact that Social Security was indexed for inflation in 1972, while Aid to Families with Dependent Children was not."[9] Social Security payments are based on a worker's wage record in covered employment, which reflects sex and race discrimination.[10] Moreover, because of shorter life expectancies than their White counterparts, Black men and women benefit less from Social Security. As of 1990, "one of every three 45-year-old African American men will die without seeing a single Social Security check; the comparable figure for White men is one in six."[11]

UNLEARNING EXPECTATIONS

Education is often portrayed as the great ladder out of poverty, and sometimes it is. But the school system is heavily rigged in favor of the already-privileged. Children of color and low-income Whites are tracked by race and income into the most deficient and demoralizing schools and classrooms. Democracy is a mockery in a country where education is *increasingly* separate and unequal. The title of Jonathan Kozol's *Savage Inequalities* does not exaggerate.

Today, education is perhaps the most important function of state and local governments...In these days, it is doubtful that any child may reasonably be expected to succeed in life if he is denied the opportunity of an education. Such an opportunity, where the state has undertaken to provide it, is a right which must be made available to all on equal terms.

United States Supreme Court, *Brown v. Board of Education*, 1954.

A cash-strapped school district here has begun selling advertising space in its gymnasiums, in its hallways, on its school buses and in its newsletters.

The district is believed to be the first in the nation to sell ad space. It is using the money to buy books, laboratory equipment and other supplies that the City of Colorado Springs could not provide.

Pupils at one elementary school travel in bright yellow buses painted with the round red spots that sell 7-Up. Burger King ads, designed with the help of students, are painted on other district buses.

New York Times, November 13, 1994.

The so-called public school system is heavily weighted against low-income students because of reliance on property taxes for funding (and, increasingly, on a school's ability to collect activity fees and fundraise). "Typically," writes Kozol, "very poor communities place high priority on education, and they often tax themselves at higher rates than do the very affluent communities," but the higher rates cannot offset the income gaps.[12] And, like the mortgage interest deduction, the property tax deduction on federal taxes subsidizes higher income people the most. The wide variations in local school funding mean that wealthier districts spend two to four to even more times as much per pupil than poorer ones, making the education system more reflective of apartheid than democracy. In Texas during 1991-92, spending ranged from $2,337 per pupil in the poorest district to $56,791 in the wealthiest.[13]

In rich districts kids take well-stocked libraries, laboratories and state-of-the-art computers for granted. In poor schools they are rationing out-of-date textbooks and toilet paper. Rich schools often look like country clubs—with manicured sports fields and swimming pools. Poor schools often look more like jails—with concrete grounds and grated windows. Art, music, physical education, field trips, foreign languages and advanced courses are often considered necessities for the affluent, luxuries for the poor.

Wealthier citizens argue that lack of money isn't the problem in poorer schools—family values are—until proposals are made to make school spending more even. Then money matters greatly for those who already have more. "Research experts want to know what can be done about the values of poor segregated children," writes Kozol. "But they do not ask what can be done about the values of the people who have segregated these communities. There is no academic study of the pathological detachment of the very rich."[14]

Behind the stale rhetoric of equal opportunity is the reality of discrimination. "It doesn't make sense to offer something that most of these urban kids will never use," a Chicago businessman told Kozol. "No one expects these ghetto kids to go to college. Most of them are lucky if they're even literate. If we can teach them some useful skills, get them to stay in school and graduate, and maybe into jobs, we're giving them the most that they can hope for."[15]

Before becoming labor secretary, Robert Reich observed that "the growing inequality in government services has been most apparent in the public schools." He contrasted three predominantly White Boston-area communities:

> Belmont, northwest of Boston, is inhabited mainly by symbolic analysts and their families. In 1988, the average teacher in its public schools earned $36,100. Only 3 percent of Belmont's 18-year-olds dropped out of high school, and more than 80 percent of graduating seniors chose to go on to a four-year college.
>
> Just east of Belmont is Somerville, most of whose residents are low-wage service workers. In 1988, the average Somerville teacher earned $29,400. A third of the town's 18-year-olds did not finish high school, and fewer than a third planned to attend college.
>
> Chelsea, across the Mystic River from Somerville, is the poorest of the three towns. Most of its inhabitants are unskilled, and many are unemployed or only employed part time. The average teacher in Chelsea, facing tougher educational challenges than his or her counterparts in Belmont, earned $26,200 in 1988, almost a third less than the average teacher in the more affluent town just a few miles away. More than half of Chelsea's 18-year-olds did not graduate from high school, and only 10 percent planned to attend college.[16]

In a school system where some kids are tracked for success, others for failure, children of color are hit especially hard. They are tracked by school, within schools and within classrooms. "American children in general—and black children in particular—are rated, sorted, and boxed like so many potatoes moving down a conveyer belt," observes social psychologist Jeff Howard. "There is the 'gifted and talented' or advanced placement track for those few (exceedingly few when it comes to black children) considered highly intelligent. There are the regular programs for those of more modest endowment, and the vocational or special education classes for those considered 'slow.' Only children in the gifted programs can expect the kind of education that will give them access to the challenges and rewards of the 21st century. Placement in vocational or special education programs is tantamount to a sentence of economic marginality at best." Howard points out, "Black students make up 16 percent of public school students, yet make up almost 40 percent of those placed in special education or classified as mentally retarded or disabled. They are even more severely under-represented in the upper end of the placement hierarchy."[17]

Jeannie Oakes, author of *Keeping Track: How Schools Structure Inequality*, found that youngsters of color "were consistently assigned to lower tracks even when they had higher test scores than white youngsters who were placed in the highest tracks."[18]

Too often, poverty and prejudice limit the life expectancies and expectations of children of color. They are often starved of school resources and positive reinforcement. Dr. Deborah Prothrow-Stith, assistant dean of the Harvard School of Public Health, summarizes an Illinois study where "66 student teachers were told to teach a math concept to four pupils—two white and two black. All of the pupils were of equal, average intelligence. The student teachers were told that in each set of four, one white and one black student was intellectually gifted, the others were labelled as average. The student teachers were monitored through a one-way mirror to see how they reinforced their students' efforts. The 'superior' white pupils received two positive reinforcements for every negative one. The 'average' white students received one positive reinforcement for every negative reinforcement. The average black student received one positive reinforcement for every 1.5 negative reinforcement, while the 'superior' black students received one positive response for every 3.5 negative ones." While "superior" intelligence was nurtured in the White students by the young student teachers, it was discouraged in the Black "superior" students.

Prothrow-Stith observes, "Social scientists and educators have proven time and again that children tend to perform academically as they are expected to perform. By and large, children who are expected by their parents and their teachers to work hard and achieve, do just that...Children who are labelled as 'C' students, tend to do 'C' work." The negative reinforcement given many children of color in school is part of a process that Jeff Howard calls "spirit murder."[19] The educational caste system endures despite a mountain of evidence about effective schooling and popular wake-up calls such as Kozol's *Savage Inequalities* and the movie *Stand and Deliver*, the story of Jaime Escalante's success in teaching advanced placement math to Black and Latino kids previously written off by Los Angeles school officials and teachers as too "dumb" to learn difficult subjects and go on to college.[20]

Despite continued discrimination in school resources and expectations, Blacks ages 25-29 (a useful measure of recent educational attainment trends) have almost closed the once-wide gap with Whites on high school graduation rates—the rates are 83 percent for Blacks, 87 percent for Whites—and reduced it for those with at least a college bachelor's degree. Still, the college gap remains wide. Only 13 percent of Blacks ages 25-29 have at least a college bachelor's compared with 25 percent of Whites. The respective rates for Latinos are much lower—61 percent (high school) and 8 percent (college).[21]

RATIONING HIGHER EDUCATION

Higher education, like health care, is rationed by income. Sky-rocketing tuition and educational cutbacks are undermining progress for lower-income students at a time when a college degree is increasingly essential for a shot at decent earnings. "Even as a good education has become the litmus test in the job market," says *Business Week*, "the widening wage chasm has made it harder for lower-income people to get to college. Kids from the top quarter have had no problem: 76% earn bachelor's degrees today, vs. 31% in 1980. But less than 4% of those in bottom-quarter families now finish college, vs. 6% then."

According to a congressionally-mandated commission, "in the 1980s, the cost of attending a private college or university soared 146 percent—a higher rate than medical, home, food and car costs." But between 1980 and 1990, federal financial aid rose only 47 percent, says the independent college association. As reported by *Business Week*, "Tuition at public colleges, where 80% of students go, jumped an inflation-adjusted 49% in the 1980s, to $1,900 a year, according to a study by Harvard University economist Thomas J. Kane. With room and board, the tab will run to $5,400—an amount families should be expected to pay only if they earn $52,000 a year, according to federal guidelines. Meanwhile, Pell grants—the federal program that gives an average of $1,500 a year to more than a quarter of the country's 14 million college students—trailed inflation by 13% in the 1980s."[22]

Today's college students are working longer hours at jobs while in school, and they have more debt when they graduate. They are typically older and take five or six years to graduate because of such factors as job demands and not enough space in courses needed for graduation because of cutbacks. According to Northeastern University's Center for Labor Market Studies, "less than one-third of all college undergraduates complete their education in the four years after high school—compared to 45.4 percent in 1977."[23]

UNREVERSED DISCRIMINATION

Many White men who are "falling down" the economic ladder are being encouraged to believe they are falling because women and people of color are climbing over them to the top or dragging them down from the bottom. That way, they will blame women and people of color rather than the system.

Discrimination is compounded by insult. It's common for people of color to get none of the credit when they succeed—portrayed as undeserving beneficiaries of affirmative action and "reverse discrimination"—and all of the blame when they fail.

For centuries there were virtual quotas of zero for people of color in top universities, higher paid industries and government. As discrimination persists, many Whites are saying that "reverse discrimination" is a larger problem than racism. A study of the views of 15-to-24-year-olds found that 49 percent of Whites believe that it is more likely that "qualified whites lose out on scholarships, jobs, and promotions because minorities get special preferences" than "qualified minorities are denied scholarships, jobs, and promotions because of racial prejudice." Only 34 percent believed that minorities are more likely to lose out. Many Whites voiced racist stereotypes.[24]

It is common for White males today to talk of racial and gender discrimination as relics of the past and claim that when society isn't color-blind there is reverse discrimination. Pollster Geoffrey Garin, who conducted focus groups exploring the views of young Whites on behalf of People for the American Way, says a theme especially strong among working-class Whites is: "Whatever prejudice whites feel to blacks is provoked by things that blacks do, and whatever prejudice blacks might feel to whites is provoked by something that happened long ago."[25]

An ABC News *PrimeTime Live* report illuminated the routine and wide-ranging nature of today's racial discrimination. *PrimeTime* went to the Leadership Council for Open Metropolitan Communities in Chicago, a group that tests for fair housing, to find two testers—one White, one Black—trained in presenting themselves the same way. The testers were two friends, both from Midwestern, middle class families and graduates of Big Ten universities. *PrimeTime's* hidden cameras watched as John Kuhnen, White, and Glenn Brewer, Black, moved temporarily to St. Louis, Missouri and walked around, shopped and looked for work and housing in White and racially mixed neighborhoods. "At times the two men were treated equally, at times there was ambiguity," *PrimeTime* reported, "but tonight we're going to show you some of the ways in which they were treated differently because this didn't happen just once or twice, it happened every single day."

John gets quick service from salespeople while Glenn is ignored or tailed. At a car dealer Glenn is quoted a higher price, downpayment and interest rates for the same car as John. Both sign up and pay a fee at a storefront job service. "John is told pleasantly it's against the rules to share a confidential job listing with a friend. But when Glenn gets that information, it's a lecture, complete with a little warning about laziness." A dry cleaning business advertising for help tells Glenn that the positions are filled and then encourages John to apply. On a nighttime walk downtown, "one just ahead of the other," a police car passes by John and then the officer stops to lean out the window and inspect Glenn. Another night, when they are walking on a residential street in White South St. Louis, a truck slows down and the driver tells Glenn, "A little far south, ain't it?" When they look for housing, John gets welcoming information. Glenn gets warned about obeying rules by a manager who tells him that "he wanted to keep his building clean 'because it was not a ghetto.'" Elsewhere, John is told an apartment is available immediately. When he leaves without making any commitment, Glenn walks in and the manager tells him a woman paid a deposit on the last available apartment early that morning.

After the investigation ended, Glenn Brewer commented, "You walk down with a suit and tie and it doesn't matter. You carry yourself in a very respectful manner, it doesn't matter. Someone still makes determinations about you, determinations that affect the quality of your life, and the only basis is the one thing that will not change about

TABLE 16

Official Youth Unemployment Rates, 1994

	All Races	White	Black	Latino
Ages 16-19	17.6	15.1	35.2	24.5
Male	19.0	16.3	37.6	26.3
Female	16.2	13.8	32.6	22.2
Ages 20-24	9.7	8.1	19.5	11.8
Male	10.2	8.8	19.4	10.8
Female	9.2	7.4	19.6	13.5

Note: Remember these rates only count people who have searched for work within the last four weeks.

Source: Bureau of Labor Statistics, *Employment and Earnings*, January 1995, Tables 3-4, pp. 164-67.

you...I'm going to be black forever." *PrimeTime's* Diane Sawyer noted, "We chose St. Louis for this report, but we think it could have been any city and the national studies on discrimination bear this out."[26]

In 1992, the Massachusetts Commission Against Discrimination became the nation's first state-sponsored program to use testers to assess employment discrimination. As reported in the *Boston Globe*, "Although they were strangers, Quinn O'Brien and Darryl Vance had much in common. Both were handsome, articulate undergraduates with ambition. Vance had his eye on medical school; O'Brien was prelaw." They were among six students trained as employment testers. The Canadian O'Brien, who is White, was a junior at Boston College. Vance, who is Black, was a junior at Northeastern University. Vance was given better educational and employment credentials for the testing. O'Brien received many job offers while Vance's offers were scarcer and for less money and fewer benefits.[27]

The State of Working America reports that a Black worker with less than nine years experience earned 16.4 percent less in 1989 than an equivalent White worker (in terms of experience, education, region and so on). The gap has widened greatly since 1973, when Blacks earned 10.3 percent less, and 1979, when Blacks earned 10.9 percent less. "In terms of education, the greatest increase in the black-white earnings gap was among college graduates, with a small 2.5% differential in 1979 exploding to 15.5% in 1989."[28]

While official uncmployment rates are high for White young people, they are much higher for Blacks and Latinos. (See table 16.)

Using carefully matched and trained pairs of White and Black young men applying for entry-level jobs, the Urban Institute documented in a 1991 study that discrimination against Black job seekers is "entrenched and widespread." An earlier study documented discrimination against Latinos.[29]

During the official recession of July 1990-March 1991, Blacks were hit hardest. According to the *Wall Street Journal*, Black workers "lost a disproportionately high share of jobs in companies that cut staff, but also gained a disproportionately low share of positions added during the recession." Many lost their jobs despite having seniority. At Digital Equipment Corporation, for example, Blacks made up under 7 percent of the workforce in 1990 and bore 11 percent of the layoffs by 1991. At BankAmerica, Blacks were under 8 percent of the workforce and bore 28 percent of the job losses.[30] The General Accounting Office also studied racial differences in 1990-91 layoffs. It found that among private sector workers over 20 years old, Blacks made up about 9 percent of the sample, but experienced over 10 percent of the layoffs. Latinos made up over 7 percent of the sample, but 9 percent of the layoffs. Compared with Whites and Latinos, Blacks experienced the longest spells of unemployment among displaced workers who found jobs and showed the largest loss in wages in their new jobs. Blacks were also disproportionately affected by layoffs in prior periods when the economy was growing.[31]

The federal government has also been "downsizing," with discriminatory impact on Blacks. During 1992 the federal government fired Black workers at more than twice the rate of Whites. The *San Jose Mercury News* editorialized, "It's not that they have less education, experience or seniority. The difference has nothing to do with job performance. A new federally sponsored study shows that blacks are fired more often because of their skin color." Blacks, who were 17 percent of the executive branch workforce in 1992, were 39 percent of those dismissed. Whites were 72 percent of the workforce and only 48 percent of those fired. (Latinos and Asians were fired at roughly the same rates as Whites.) "Rank didn't help. Black senior managers went out the door as often as black clerks...It gets worse. The deck is stacked against fired minority workers with legitimate grounds for reinstatement, the study shows. They win only one in every 100 appeals."

The *Mercury News* observed, "That racial discrimination against blacks persists is not surprising. But it is when it happens at such an obscene level in federal employment. The feds wrote the book on equal opportunity and employment. If they can't apply the rules at home, how can they enforce them elsewhere?"[32] The *Philadelphia Inquirer* has also commented on federal employment racism: "Add to these findings numerous other studies that show the same, disturbing trends in both the public and private sector and it is clear that something is seriously amiss with race relations in the American workplace."[33]

The top rungs of Corporate America are almost exclusively White and male—fictional advertisement and TV diversity notwithstanding. According to a 1995 government report, White males make up only 29 percent of the workforce, but they hold 95 percent of senior management positions (vice president and above).[34] A national survey of senior executives found that in the 1980s, women increased their minuscule share of top corporate positions from .5 to 3 percent, while Blacks (men and women) inched from .2 to .6 percent and Latino/as from .1 to .4 percent.[35] Only about 6 percent of those on the boards of directors of *Fortune* 500 companies are women, and they are even more underrepresented on the more powerful board committees.[36]

Discrimination against women is pervasive from the bottom to the top of the pay scale, and not because women are on the "mommy track." *Fortune* observes that "at the same level of management, the

---

TABLE 17

Median Household Income and Official Poverty Rates 1989 and 1993

income in 1993 dollars

	All		White		Black		Latino	
	Median Income	Poverty Rate	Median Income	Poverty Rate	Median Income	Poverty Rate	Median Income	Poverty Rate
1989	$33,585	13.1%	$35,329	10.2%	$21,232	30.8%	$25,382	26.3%
1993	$31,241	15.1%	$32,960	12.2%	$19,532	33.1%	$22,886	30.6%
% Change 1989-93								
	−7.0	+2.0	−6.7	+2.0	−8.0	+2.3	−9.8	+4.3

Source: U.S. Census Bureau, *Income, Poverty, and Health Insurance: 1993* (October 1994).

typical woman's pay is lower than her male colleague's—even when she has the exact same qualifications, works just as many years, relocates just as often, provides the main financial support for her family, takes no time off for personal reasons, and wins the same number of promotions to comparable jobs."[37]

Susan Faludi reports, "In a 1990 national poll of chief executives at Fortune 1000 companies, more than 80 percent acknowledged that discrimination impedes female employees' progress—yet, less than 1 percent of these same companies regarded *remedying* sex discrimination as a goal that their personnel departments should pursue."[38]

The media is part of the problem. In 1993, according to the American Society of Newspaper Editors (ASNE), an estimated 10 percent of newsroom employees were people of color—approximately 5 percent Black, 3 percent Latino and 2 percent Asian (the United States is nearly 13 percent Black, 9 percent Latino and 4 percent Asian). Many of them are employed in metropolitan areas with large communities of color. Nearly half of U.S. newspapers have all-White newsrooms. Women were an estimated 38 percent of the newsroom in 1993. Top management is even more heavily White and male. ASNE reports that 96 percent of newsroom executives are White and 85 percent are male.[39]

DIVIDE AND CONQUER

The false charge of "reverse discrimination" provides scapegoats, rather than solutions, for the economic distress being felt by more men and women of all races. Elites don't want men and women to come together across racial lines to change a system that is redistributing wealth upward. They want them turning instead on each other—divided and conquered.

The reverse discrimination myth allows Whites to make the generic assumption that Blacks are unqualified and Whites are qualified. If Blacks *are* hired on the job or admitted to the university, it's affirmative action. If Whites *aren't* hired or admitted, it's reverse discrimination. Instead of challenging that racist attitude, liberal politicians are increasingly joining with conservatives in using it as a rationale for ending affirmative action and making the point moot. If, with affirmative action's removal, Blacks and other people of color and women are even less represented in better jobs and academia, then that will be taken to show they never deserved to be there to begin with, rather than as a sign of continued discrimination.

"It's still a statistical piece of cake being a white man," chided *Newsweek* following release of the movie *Falling Down*. "They dominate just about everything but NOW and the NAACP; even in the NBA, most of the head coaches and general managers are white guys. So now they want underdog status, too?" A companion piece asks, "So why would white men feel they are being pushed to the wall when they hold most of the top jobs? One clue was offered by a Black female executive on a large newspaper who said that her employer routinely told unqualified white male applicants that they could not be hired because the next slot had been promised to a black, a Latino or a woman."[40]

Susan Faludi also noted the tendency of media "personnel officers to use affirmative action as the all-purpose alibi when rejecting white male applicants. 'I've seen them send out these rejection letters saying, "Sorry, but we had to hire a black or a woman," when the real reason they didn't hire the guy was that he's unqualified,' says an editor who witnessed this practice firsthand at the *New York Times*."[41] For White males, the messages are: It's not your fault you didn't get the job or promotion. It's not the economy's fault you are losing the job. It's the fault of women and people of color.

A 1994 Times-Mirror poll underscored the polarizing impact of years of top-down scapegoating during hard economic times. "Voter attitudes are punctuated by indifference to the problems of blacks and poor people. And resentment toward immigrants is widespread...An early 1990s trend toward growing public support for social welfare programs has been reversed. The percentage of Americans thinking the government should take care of needy people fell by 12 percentage points between 1992 and 1994 [from 69 percent to 57 percent]." For the first time in seven years of Times-Mirror polling, a majority of Whites, 51 percent, say they agree that equal rights have been pushed too far—up from 42 percent in 1992.[42]

7

LOCKING UP "SURPLUS" LABOR

It costs about $25,000 a year to keep a kid in prison [not counting costly prison construction]. That's more than the Job Corps, or college.*

New York Times, May 7, 1992.

Even before the prison expansion and harsher sentences endorsed in the 1994 Crime Bill, the United States led all nations but one—Russia—in locking people up. With the world's second highest imprisonment rate, some 1.3 million people are incarcerated in the United States at a yearly cost of nearly $27 billion.[1] The federal and state prison populations swelled 188 percent between 1980 and 1993—though, contrary to common belief, the crime rate generally went down in that period.[2]

---

* *Americans Behind Bars,* a 1993 report by the Edna McConnell Clark Foundation, found that the cost of prison construction averaged $54,209 per bed for state facilities and $78,000 per bed for federal facilities, not counting all the costs of financing and debt servicing. For example, New York State opened 27 new prisons between 1983 and 1990. The state issued $1.6 billion in bonds for their construction. "When interest rates are factored in, the total cost to taxpayers over the next 30 years will be $180,000 per bed, or $5.4 billion, according to the Correctional Association of New York."

The federal prison population is over half Black and Latino. The state prison population was 35 percent White, 46 percent Black and 17 percent Latino as of 1991. Between 1988 and 1992, the number of Blacks entering state prison increased 42 percent, twice the rate of Whites.[3] The racially biased "War on Drugs" is increasingly responsible.

In an unusual editorial shortly after the 1992 Los Angeles riots, the *New York Times* quoted a 1990 report by the Correctional Association of New York and the New York State Coalition for Criminal Justice: "It is no accident that our correctional facilities are filled with African-American and Latino youths out of all proportion...Prisons are now the last stop along a continuum of injustice for these youths that literally starts before birth." The *Times* concluded, "There's nothing inherently criminal in young black men of the 1990's any more than there was in young immigrant men of the 1890's. What is criminal is to write them off, fearfully, blind to the knowledge that thousands can be saved, from lives of crime and for lives of dignity."[4]

ROUND UP THE USUAL SUSPECTS

> The fact that the legal order not only countenanced but sustained slavery, segregation, and discrimination for most of our Nation's history—and the fact that the police were bound to uphold that order—set a pattern for police behavior and attitudes toward minority communities that has persisted until the present day. That pattern includes the idea that minorities have fewer civil rights, that the task of the police is to keep them under control, and that the police have little responsibility for protecting them from crime within their communities.
>
> "The Evolving Strategy of Police: A Minority View,"[5]
> U.S. Department of Justice, 1990.

The United States imprisons Black males at a rate more than four times higher than South Africa under apartheid. The number of Black males in prisons and jails in the United States (583,000) is greater than the number of Black males enrolled in higher education (537,000). Their annual incarceration cost, an estimated $11.6 billion, is about the same as the combined federal 1994 budget for all low-income employment programs, community development grants and Head Start.

The Washington-based Sentencing Project found that on an average day in 1989 one out of four Black men in their twenties was in prison or jail, on probation or on parole. The comparable figure for Latino males was one in ten, and for White males, one in sixteen. Women's rates were much lower, but the racial disproportions were parallel.[6] Other studies found that on an average day in 1991, 42 percent of Black males ages 18-35 living in Washington, DC and 56 percent of those living in Baltimore, were either in jail or prison, on probation or parole, out on bond awaiting disposition of criminal charges or being sought on an arrest warrant. The great majority of arrests were not for violent crimes. If present policies continue, some three out of four Black males in the nation's capital will be arrested and imprisoned at least once between the ages of 18 and 35.[7] A hard search for a job becomes an even harder one after you have a criminal record on your life résumé.

Shortly after the Rodney King case in Los Angeles, the *Boston Globe* ran an article titled, "GUILTY...of being black: Black men say success doesn't save them from being suspected, harassed and detained." The article began, "They are among Boston's most accomplished citizens. They each have a story to tell about being viewed suspiciously by salespeople, bank clerks or police...The incidents are frighteningly common." Boston Celtics basketball player Dee Brown was forced to the pavement by suburban police with drawn guns who mistook him for a bank robber; never mind that he didn't fit the description and was simply looking through mail with his fiancee outside the Wellesley post office. Ron Homer, chairman of the Boston Bank of Commerce, says he "has been mistaken for a waiter and a doorman and has had trouble cashing checks." Homer, who lives in the wealthy, predominantly White suburb of Lexington, hesitates to shop in neighboring suburbs where suspicious shopkeepers don't know him.

Harvard Law School Professor Charles Ogletree has been stopped by police numerous times and sometimes frisked. He worries about his son. "It scares the hell out of me when I think that there is little I can do to ensure his safety, because the police don't see him as a person. They see him as a statistic, one they equate with crime."[8]

The police equation of youth of color and crime was spotlighted in spring 1989 when the Boston Police Department formalized a "search on sight," "stop and frisk" policy against Black and Latino youths—especially in the Roxbury neighborhood—ostensibly directed at gang members. A September 1989 Suffolk Superior Court ruling found that the announcement of the policy by Deputy Superintendent William Celester "was, in effect, a proclamation of martial law in Roxbury for a narrow class of people, young blacks, suspected of membership in a gang or perceived by the police to be in the company of someone thought to be a member." Justice Cortland Mathers said, "I have taken and credit testimony from blacks in the Egleston Square area that they, as individuals and in groups, are forced to open their mouths, placed spread eagle against walls, required to drop their trousers in public places and subjected to underclothing examinations. Deputy Celester stated to a reporter for the *Boston Herald* that his policy has resulted in 'hundreds of searches but few arrests.' The Court finds a tacit understanding exists in the Boston Police Department that constitutionally impermissible searches will not only be countenanced but applauded in the Roxbury area."[9]

Police misconduct reached new heights in October 1989, when a White furrier from the suburbs named Charles Stuart killed his pregnant wife Carol after a birthing class in Boston's racially mixed Mission Hill neighborhood. He blamed the crime on a Black male assailant, setting off a racist police and media dragnet for the inner city destroyer of the "Camelot couple" from the suburbs. The dragnet yielded a suspect sharing the same first name with Willie Horton, the 1988 presidential election's Black symbol of White fear, and the frame-up didn't end until Charles Stuart committed suicide when his brother provided incriminating information to authorities in January 1990. As John Demeter and I wrote at the time:

> Two Charles Stuarts have been portrayed in the media and both are tinged with racism: the heroic white victim assaulted by a Black "urban savage" and the postmortem Charles Stuart with the "dark side" of a sociopath. The "dark" Charles Stuart was showcased on the cover of *Time* magazine (January 22 [1990]). His diabolical eyes stare out from a face that is black on top, white on the bottom. In the *Time* still, taken from TV footage the night of Carol Stuart's murder, a shadow created by the rearview mirror of the Stuarts' car becomes "The Shadow" described in the *Boston Globe* article, "Shadows Loom in the Stuart Case" (January 16).
>
> The *Globe* feature used racially coded language to explain psychoanalyst Carl Jung's theory of "a dark part of the self" called "The Shadow." In the words of one Jungian analyst, "When we finally dare to become aware of the shadows within ourselves, we find black sheep neither we nor anyone in our families has wanted to acknowledge, and we find the shadiest aspects of our communities and nation, too." The article is illustrated on the front page of the Living/Arts section with Jung's drawing of "The Shadow," which is not Caucasian like himself, but a person of color. Without reference to the racist implications of the

drawing, the article later acknowledges on an inside page that there are no Black Jungian analysts and notes that Jung himself was accused of racism and sexism.

Charles Stuart projected his crime onto a Black man and the media in its pack soul-searching used racial language to recast Stuart's image. As WBZ-TV's Bill Shields commented on January 17, "very few people knew he [Stuart] had a dark side, a diabolical side, one he kept hidden from his friends."...

Dark is variously defined in dictionaries as without light, black, the opposite of white, evil, sinister, ignorant, unenlightened, shady, shadowy, gloomy, concealed, having unfavorable prospects. African-Americans were contemptuously called "darkies."...

White, in contrast, is defined as light, cleansed, morally or spiritually pure, spotless, Caucasian, opposite to black, innocent, honest, harmless, snow-white. In Hollywood, the good-guys wear white hats, the bad-guys wear black hats.[10]

Glen Pierce of Northeastern University's Center of Applied Science calculated that the likelihood of a White woman in Massachusetts being shot to death by a Black man she did not know is one in four million—the same risk she runs of being hit by lightning. Pierce "believes that consciously or unconsciously, reporters used the deaths of Carol Stuart and her unborn child to increase ratings and boost sales...He believes that by misrepresenting the crime problem, reporters are frightening the electorate and driving them to the right," making White voters with exaggerated fears more punitive in their politics and blind to the reality that poor communities and poor people of color are most often the victims of crime.[11]

The Charles Stuart case was recalled in 1994, when Susan Smith of South Carolina said a Black man in his late twenties or early thirties had forced her out of her car and took off with her children in the back, setting off a nine-day manhunt complete with composite drawings of the alleged kidnapper. This nightmare drama with a fictional Black villain ended when Smith confessed to drowning her two young sons. Fred Smith (no relation) was one of many Black men questioned by authorities. He said townspeople threatened him. "They said I was a child molester," Smith said. "We Blacks have got to say, 'Quit using the black man as a scapegoat.'"[12]

Stereotypes can influence perception of even unambiguous events. In one study, "subjects were shown pictures of a white man holding a razor during an argument with a black man. When the pictures were described to others, the white subjects recalled the black man as wielding the razor!"[13]

There is a national pattern of racial persecution under the guise of policing and prosecution. Former Los Angeles Police Department Chief Daryl Gates has acknowledged, "I think people believe that the only strategy we have is to put a lot of police officers on the street and harass people and make arrests for inconsequential things. Well, that's part of the strategy, no question about it."[14]

The ABC News show *20/20* did their own hidden-camera investigation in Los Angeles to see if Black men are "being singled out by police, pulled over even when they're doing nothing wrong." The show's conclusion? "They can be future doctors and Olympic stars, but many police still see them as suspects, drug dealers. They weren't in our case. *20/20* rented expensive cars and put our own staffers, black and white, behind the wheel. The difference will disturb you. One group was stopped, questioned, harassed time after time. Lynn Sherr's investigation lets you see for yourself. Young black men are often 'Presumed Guilty.'"

20/20 talked to Olympic gold medalist Al Joyner. He was stopped by a group of police officers, with guns drawn, who allegedly suspected him of driving a stolen car. They let him go, then a few minutes later pulled him over again saying, recalls Joyner, "'You're a suspect. Your car—you are a suspect in a hit-and-run: a burgundy RX7; a black man with a baseball cap.' I didn't have an RX7, but I am black with a baseball cap." He worried police would have shot him if he "slipped coming out of that car." Willie Williams succeeded Daryl Gates as chief of the L.A. Police Department after the 1992 riots. Williams says, "I understand what Al Joyner has said. My son, at 19, was driving my seven-year-old Lincoln, in Philadelphia, was stopped three times in a seven-hour period...He was a young man in a nice-looking car...And he was black." Williams was a Philadelphia police captain at the time.[15]

Studies have found that people of color experience overcharges at arrest and disproportionately high bail even for minor offenses. The high bail makes it harder to get out of jail before trial, and "detainees are more likely to be indicted, convicted, and sentenced more harshly than released defendants."[16] A study of California, Michigan and Texas found that controlling "for relevant variables influential in sentenc-ing...blacks and Hispanics were more likely to be sentenced to prison, with longer sentences, and less likely to be accorded probation than white felony offenders."[17] A Department of Justice study of sentences under federal sentencing guidelines found that when convicted for federal weapons offenses, "blacks and Hispanics were both sentenced to prison more frequently than whites and for longer periods of time." The study also found that Blacks received longer sentences for bank robbery and drug offenses, a subject to which we shall return.[18]

Racism also affects application of the ultimate punishment, the death penalty. In the words of retired Supreme Court Justice Harry Blackmun, "the death penalty remains fraught with arbitrariness, discrimination, caprice, and mistake."[19] The motto of the current Supreme Court majority appears to be: Better to execute the innocent then allow for a lengthy appeals process. According to a 1994 congressional report, "Throughout American history, the death penalty has fallen disproportionately on racial minorities. For example, since 1930 nearly 90% of those executed for the crime of rape...were African-Americans." The report also observes: "Analysis of prosecutions under the federal death penalty provisions of the Anti-Drug Abuse Act of 1988 reveals that 89% of the defendants selected for capital prosecution have been either African-American or Mexican-American. Moreover, the number of prosecutions under this Act has been increasing over the past two years with no decline in the racial disparities. All ten of the recently approved federal capital prosecutions have been against black defendants."[20]

COLORING THE DRUG WAR

The typical cocaine user is white, male, a high school graduate employed full time and living in a small metropolitan area or suburb.

William Bennett, former national drug policy director.[21]

There's as much cocaine in the Sears Tower or in the stock exchange as there is in the black community. But those guys are harder to catch.

Commander Charles Ramsey, supervisor of the
Chicago Police Department's narcotics division.[22]

It's insanity...We're putting young people in prison for 10 years on their first [drug] offense without possibility of parole, a longer sentence than is served in many states for murder.

Former Federal Judge J. Lawrence Irving, now a private mediator.[23]

It is impossible to understand why so many people of color, particularly Blacks, have a record—and why so many more will get a

record—without understanding the racially biased "War on Drugs." The
share of those convicted of a drug offense in the federal prison system
skyrocketed from 16 percent of inmates in 1970 to 25 percent in 1980,
38 percent in 1986 and 61 percent in 1993—and is expected to reach
72 percent by 1997. The percentage of drug offenders in state prisons
rose from 6 percent in 1979 to 9 percent in 1986 to 22 percent in 1992.
Among women state prisoners, a third are serving time for drug
offenses. Many of those serving time for drug charges are nonviolent,
low-level offenders with no prior criminal records.

More than three out of four drug users are White (non-Hispanic),
but Blacks are much more likely to be arrested and convicted for drug
offenses and receive harsher sentences. The overall arrest rate for drug
possession is more than twice as high as for sale and/or manufacturing.
In 1993, 39 percent of those arrested on illicit drug charges were
Black—up from 30 percent in 1984.[24] In New York City, an astounding
92 percent of people arrested for drug offenses in 1989 were Black or
Latino.[25]

As the Los Angeles Times reported, law officers and judges say,
"Although it is clear that whites sell most of the nation's cocaine and
account for 80% of its consumers, it is blacks and other minorities who
continue to fill up America's courtrooms and jails, largely because, in
a political climate that demands that something be done, they are the
easiest people to arrest."[26] They are also the easiest to scapegoat. If the
"drug war" were prosecuted and portrayed without racism we would
see a lot more handcuffed White politicians, movie stars, suburban
teenagers, doctors, stockbrokers, athletes and law enforcement officers
on the TV news and "entertainment" shows.

Earlier "drug wars" were also racially biased. "The first drug
prohibition law was an 1875 San Francisco ordinance prohibiting opium
and aimed at Chinese workers, who were no longer needed to bring
the railroad west and who were blamed for taking jobs of whites during
a depression," Diana Gordon writes in her book, The Return of the
Dangerous Classes. "Themes of racism and nativism, as well as methods
of elite manipulation of social conflict, run through the subsequent
history of drug policy and reinforce its prohibitionist tendency. Marijuana became a concern only when associated with 'degenerate'
Mexicans working on farms (and therefore taking scarce jobs from
Americans) during the Great Depression in the Southwest. Cocaine, a
medical blessing when used as an anesthetic in the Civil War, came to
be viewed as a dangerous stimulant when associated with blacks in the

first two decades of the [20th] century, despite contemporary evidence that African-Americans were rarely users."

"The war on drugs thus signals the return of the dangerous classes," Gordon observes. The idea of dangerous classes arose in the United States in the second half of the 19th century, "spurred by migration and immigration—the flow into cities of people displaced from farms by agricultural mechanization and from far-off lands by poverty and pogrom."[27] The current drug war begun in the 1980s, says Gordon, is not only "a rearguard action against full equality for racial minorities," but an instrument for "whipping young people (and often cultural liberals) back into line."[28]

A *USA Today* special report found that Blacks were four times more likely than Whites to be arrested on drug charges in 1991.

> The war on drugs has, in many places, been fought mainly against blacks.
>
> In every part of the country—from densely packed urban neighborhoods to sprawling new suburbs, amid racial turmoil and racial calm—blacks are arrested at rates sometimes wildly disproportionate to those of whites...
>
> Tens of thousands of arrests—mostly in the inner-city—resulted from dragnets with paramilitary names. Operation Pressure Point in New York City. Operation Thunderbolt in Memphis. Operation Hammer in Los Angeles.
>
> But largely lost in law enforcement's anti-drug fervor, critics say, is the fact that most drug users are white...
>
> [Police officials] say Blacks are arrested more frequently because drug use often is easier to spot in the Black community, with dealing on urban street corners...rather than behind closed doors.
>
> And, the police officials say, it's cheaper to target in the black community.
>
> "We don't have whites on corners selling drugs...They're in houses and offices," says police chief John Dale of Albany, N.Y., where blacks are eight times as likely as whites to be arrested for drugs..."We're locking up kids who are scrambling for crumbs, not the people who make big money."[29]

While many of the easily spotted street corner buyers are White, as well as the big money traffickers and money launderers, you don't have to be dealing or buying on street corners to feel the racial bias of the "drug war." A study in the *New England Journal of Medicine* found both racial and economic bias in the reporting of pregnant women to authorities for drug or alcohol abuse, under a mandatory reporting law. The study found that substance abuse rates were slightly higher for pregnant White women than pregnant Black women, but Black women were about ten times more likely to be reported to authorities. The bias was evident whether the women received their prenatal care from private doctors or public health clinics. Poor women were also more likely to be reported to authorities.[30] Though mothers are increasingly losing custody and being prosecuted for drug use during pregnancy, the doors of most drug treatment centers remain closed to pregnant women. Less than 14 percent of women needing drug treatment receive it.[31]

Youth of color *don't* use drugs at higher rates than Whites, but they are much more likely to be arrested, and the disproportionate arrests feed the false stereotypes that stigmatize all youth of color. In May 1992, then Health and Human Services Secretary Louis Sullivan "announced a national media campaign aimed at dispelling misconceptions about alcohol and other drug use among African-American youth and at reinforcing the strengths and positive activities among these youths." Sullivan said, "Our studies show that contrary to many misconceptions, these youngsters are less likely to use alcohol and other drugs than are kids from other ethnic groups."[32]

Former Director of National Drug Control Policy Bob Martínez has acknowledged the misleading impression left by account after account of Blacks being arrested. It is "one of the big tragedies in the whole news coverage of the drug war...You will never know it by virtue of the way that the drug war is covered, by virtue of the way that police engage in sweeps, and that's wrong, because I'm telling you that when kids come out of sometimes difficult conditions and remain drug-free, are not abusing alcohol, are not using tobacco, somebody's doing some kind of a job in that neighborhood, and that does not get out."[33]

In a Los Angeles crackdown on drug dealing around schools, nearly all those charged were Black and Latino. The results were predictable. "Officers were placed at predominantly minority schools," reports the *Los Angeles Times*, "despite the federal studies showing more drug use among white youths."[34]

The American Bar Association (ABA) found that between 1986 and 1991, drug arrests skyrocketed by 78 percent for juveniles of color, while *decreasing* by a third for other juveniles.[35] "The decision of whether to charge a youth with possession is a highly subjective process," reports the National Center on Institutions and Alternatives. "Being labeled a seller as opposed to a user often determines whether the youth is held in detention, dealt with by juvenile justice agencies, prosecuted as an adult, or released to his family." In Baltimore in 1981, before the "drug war" heated up, 15 White juveniles and 86 African American juveniles were arrested for sale of drugs. Look at the numbers gap a decade later: In 1991, 13 White juveniles and 1,304 African American juveniles were arrested for sale of drugs; 159 White juveniles and 470 African American juveniles were arrested for possession.[36] Nationally, the arrest rate for White juveniles on heroin/cocaine charges rose from about 19 per 100,000 in 1980 to 42 in 1985 to 68 in 1990. The Black juvenile arrest rate skyrocketed in the same period from 31 per 100,000 to 121 to 766 per 100,000.[37]

"When a white middle-class youth is arrested for a non-violent offense," writes former Judge Lois Forer, "the juvenile court usually 'adjusts' the offense. The boy has no record. In the inner city, youths are routinely adjudicated delinquent. Later this record counts heavily against them."[38]

The "drug war" has been used to justify the erosion of constitutional protections against unwarranted stops, searches and seizures, and the rollback of other civil liberties. In the words of the *Los Angeles Times*: "As police have moved en masse into poor minority communities...their presence has meant that innocent citizens have been swept up along with the guilty...Across the nation, blacks—and some Latinos—complain that their neighborhoods are barricaded, that roadblocks are set up for identification checks, that they are rousted from their apartments without warrants, that police target them with 'stop on sight' policies and that they are disproportionately arrested in 'sweep' operations for minor misdemeanors and traffic violations that have nothing to do with the drug war."[39]

Racist self-fulfilling prophecy is evident in the use of racial characteristics in drug suspect profiles, which guide who is stopped and searched. As summed up by Steven Duke and Albert Gross in their book, *America's Longest War*, "Hispanics and 'hippie types' bear the major brunt of the profiles near our southern border, but young African-Americans suffer from it wherever they go. An African-American who drives a car with an out-of-state license plate is likely to be stopped almost anywhere he goes in America. A survey of car stoppings on the New Jersey turnpike revealed that although only 4.7 percent of the cars were driven by blacks with out-of-state plates, 80 percent of the drug arrests were of such people. The *Pittsburgh Press* examined 121 cases in which travelers were searched and no drugs were found. Seventy-seven percent of the people were black, Hispanic or Asian. In Memphis, about 75 percent of the air travelers stopped by drug police in 1989 were black, yet only 4 percent of the flying public is black."[40]

MANDATORY DISCRIMINATION

Beginning in the mid-1980s, Congress has enacted a growing number of harsh mandatory minimum sentences; New York led a state wave of extreme mandatory minimums with the Rockefeller drug laws implemented in the 1970s. The racial bias of the "drug war" is epitomized by the much harsher federal and state mandatory minimums for crack cocaine, for which mostly Blacks are arrested, than powder cocaine, for which mostly Whites are arrested.

The federal mandatory minimum of five years applies to distribution of 500 grams of powder cocaine, but as little as 5 grams of crack cocaine. Nine out of ten persons sentenced for federal crack offenses in 1992 were Black. (In 1990, 500 grams of powder cocaine was worth about $50,000; 5 grams of crack, about $125). There is also a five-year mandatory minimum for simple possession of more than 5 grams of crack (the same minimum, for example, as a second offense for the sexual exploitation of children). In 1991, the Minnesota Supreme Court declared unconstitutional state statutes that mandated a sentence of four years in prison for a first-time conviction for possession of 3 grams of crack, but probation for first-time possession of 3 grams of powder cocaine. The evidence showed that in 1988, over 92 percent of all persons convicted of crack possession were Black while 85 percent of those convicted of powder cocaine possession were White. The court found there is no rational basis for distinguishing between crack cocaine and powder cocaine.[41]

A report to Congress by the United States Sentencing Commission found that most federal mandatory minimum penalties were never or rarely used with the most glaring exception of drug violations. Of those convicted with mandatory sentences, 64 percent were Black or Latino. The Commission concluded, "The disparate application of mandatory minimum sentences in cases in which available data strongly suggest that a mandatory minimum is applicable appears to be related to the race of the defendant, where whites are more likely than non-whites to be sentenced below the applicable mandatory minimum."[42] Half the federal offenders convicted under mandatory minimum statutes in fiscal year 1992 had zero criminal history points.[43]

Looking at cases where mandatory minimums apply for drug offenses, a report published by the Federal Judicial Center found that "there has always been a tendency for the sentences of whites to be lower than the sentences of non-whites, a difference that, unfortunately, has become larger over time." According to the report, the average sentence for Blacks was 28 percent higher in 1984 than that for Whites. After narrowing to a difference of 11 percent in 1986, the gap steadily increased. By 1990, the average sentence for Blacks was 49 percent higher than for Whites.[44]

A U.S. Sentencing Commission survey found that judges, defense attorneys and probation officers responded negatively to mandatory minimum sentencing laws, with the most frequent response being that they are too harsh.[45] A growing number of judges are bluntly speaking out against mandatory minimums and, in some cases, such as Lois Forer, resigning their positions rather than imposing sentences they consider unconscionably unjust. Forer, a trial judge in Philadelphia for 16 years, wrote *A Rage to Punish*, condemning mandatory minimums for, among other things, violating "the principle of proportionality, that the punishment should not exceed the gravity of the offense," and because "the crimes to which the mandatory law applied were arbitrarily selected and bore no rational relationship to public safety, dangerousness, culpability, law enforcement, or deterrence of crime."[46]

New York Judge Jack Weinstein announced that he would no longer hear low-level drug cases prosecuted under mandatory minimums, explaining, "I simply cannot sentence another impoverished person whose destruction has no discernible effect on the drug trade."[47] As Judge J. Spencer Letts of California put it, "Under the statutory minimum, it can make no difference whether [the defendant] is a lifetime criminal or a first-time offender. Indeed, under this sledgehammer approach, it could make no difference if the day before making this one slip in an otherwise unblemished life, defendant had rescued fifteen children from a burning building, or had won the Congressional Medal of Honor while defending his country."[48]

Mandatory minimum statutes transfer sentencing discretion from theoretically neutral judges, who rule publicly, to prosecutors, who are by definition not neutral and who exercise their control secretly. The prosecutor decides whether to impose charges for which mandatory minimums apply and whether the harshest possible charges will be imposed. The prosecutor controls who will be able to benefit from providing incriminating information and other assistance to the prosecution. As Forer writes, "The public does not know what 'deal' has been made or the basis for the decision. It is a secret process not unlike that of the hated Star Chamber that was abolished in England in 1641."[49] One obscene result is that low-level offenders are often treated more harshly than high-level offenders because the low-level offenders can't provide the kind of information and other assistance the prosecutor wants in exchange for a reduced sentence.[50]

The courts, juvenile facilities, jails and prisons are jammed. "The criminal justice system is directing more of its attention to drug offenses and less to violent crime," warns the American Bar Association.[51] And that attention is focused much more on punishment than treatment and prevention. Murderers, child molesters and other violent offenders are actually being released early to make room for nonviolent drug offenders.[52]

"Corrections" spending, the fastest growing part of state budgets, is consuming tax dollars that once went to social services such as education, job training and drug treatment. California, for example, spent 10 percent of its state budget on higher education in fiscal 1983-84 and 4 percent on corrections. In fiscal 1994-95, higher education and corrections were each allocated 10 percent. Corrections spending is expected to rise sharply to accommodate the rise in prisons and prisoners due to "three strikes and you're out" legislation. Vincent Schiraldi, director of the Center on Juvenile and Criminal Justice, observes:

> For the cost of incarcerating one prisoner for one year, California can educate 10 community college students, five Cal State students, or two University of California students. So imposing a 40-year sentence on one Three Strikes burglar means forgoing 200 two-year community college educations. If even one of the 200 turns to crime in the absence of educational and employment opportunities, incarcerating that burglar will have failed to reduce California's crime rate. Meanwhile, it will have decreased the state's educated workforce by 200 people.[53]

Nationally, less than 15 percent of those needing publicly funded drug treatment are able to get it at any one time.[54] The 1994 budget for drug control was over $13 billion, only a third of it going to prevention and treatment. Kevin Zeese of the Drug Policy Foundation has estimated that for little over $1 billion, the nation could offer drug treatment on demand to everyone who needs it.[55]

In a 1994 study commissioned by the Clinton administration, the RAND Drug Policy Research Center concluded that to make drug policy more effective, money should be shifted from law enforcement to treatment: "Treatment is seven times more cost-effective than domestic drug enforcement in reducing cocaine use and 15 times more cost-effective in reducing the social costs of crime and lost productivity."[56] The study's government sponsors—the drug czar's office and the Army—wanted RAND to soften its recommendation to cut law enforcement funds. Failing to change the study's conclusions, the Clinton administration rejected them.

The National Center on Institutions and Alternatives observes, "[The] startling racial disparities [in arrest and imprisonment] are not due to any peculiar incorrigibility, moral deficiency, or inherent violence among African American males. Rather, they are the predictable consequence of having replaced the social safety net with a dragnet. The political rhetoric of both major political parties calling for the death penalty, removing 'weeds,' ever longer prison sentences, martial law, and even beheading [as proclaimed by former drug czar William Bennett on network television], is a poor substitute for thoughtful policy. Policymakers can no longer conceal the racial implications of demagogic stratagems which have ignored the disintegration of the inner cities while a generation of African American men is sent off to the nation's reform schools, jails, prisons, detention centers and camps."[57]

VIOLENT IMAGES

In the stereotype world, violence is largely the product of "gunsanddrugs" and gangs—namely inner city guns, drugs and gangs. That's a dangerous falsehood.[58] The United States has had the industrial world's highest homicide rates for some 150 years. The 1989-90 homicide rate for White males in the United States was at least twice as high as the overall rate for males in countries such as Canada, England and Portugal. The homicide rate for White American males, ages 15-24, was at least twice as high as the overall rate for males, ages 15-24, in 21 other countries for 1986-87, including Canada, Japan, Israel and European countries.[59] Between 1970 and 1992, the number of Whites arrested for homicide rose 67 percent, according to the FBI.[60] Most homicide victims are killed by someone of the same race. For women, the greatest threat of violent injury and death, as noted earlier, comes from so-called domestic violence by past or present boyfriends or spouses.

Black Americans have historically had higher homicide rates than Whites.[61] Research has shown that "when socioeconomic status is taken into consideration, racial differences in homicide mortality rates all but disappear."[62] A long-term study notes the linkage between violence and employment:

> According to an ongoing research project led by Delbert Elliott of the Center for the Study and Prevention of Violence at the University of Colorado, during adolescence the rates of violence for black and white young men are virtually the same. However as the study tracks the same group as they mature, the statistics show that black men between 25 and 30 years old are four times as likely to be involved in violent crimes as white men the same age. The difference is employment, Elliott says, "If you get a job, you quit your violence. If you don't get a job, you continue your violence."[63]

A series of studies for the National Commission for Employment Policy by economist Stephen Rose tracked the earnings and employment experiences of thousands of young adults over a 22-year period.

TABLE 18
Estimated Effects of Unemployment and Poverty on Social Stressors, 1975-90

Percent Rise in	Effect of a 1% Rise in Unemployment	Effect of a 0.5% Rise in Poverty
Mortality		
Heart attack	2.2	n.s.
Stroke	1.9	n.s.
Crime		
Homicide	5.6	2.8
Aggravated Assault	1.8	2.9
Forcible Rape	1.9	1.5
Larceny/Theft	2.7	1.3
Robbery	1.7	2.8
Burglary	3.7	2.0

Note: n.s. means not significant.

Source: Mishel and Bernstein, *The State of Working America 1994-95*, Table 1.37, citing report by Mary Merva and Richard Fowles (1994).

Among the findings: Nearly three-quarters of Black men were able to maintain a full-time job year-round consistently throughout the 1970s. In the 1980s, only half of Black men were able to do that.[64]

The heavily advertised legal drug alcohol is the drug most linked to violence and death (excluding deadly, addictive nicotine). Indeed, in the words of a report by Jeffrey Roth, prepared for the Justice Department's National Institute of Justice, "Of all psychoactive substances, alcohol is the only one whose consumption has been shown to commonly increase aggression." Roth notes, "For at least the last several decades, alcohol drinking—by the perpetrator of a crime, the victim, or both—has immediately preceded at least half of all violent events, including murders, in the samples studied by researchers."[65] Alcohol is associated with many more homicides nationally than illicit drugs. And almost the same number of people are killed annually by drunk drivers as are murdered; drunk drivers are overwhelmingly White males.

In contrast to drug offenders, who are disproportionately low-income Black and Latino because of the racially biased "War on Drugs," the predominantly White drunk drivers are generally charged with misdemeanors and typically receive sentences involving fines, license suspension, treatment programs and community service. In 1993, there were 1.5 million arrests for drunk driving (87 percent White) and 1.1 million arrests for drug abuse violations (60 percent White); 70 percent of all drug arrests were for possession only.[66] The racial composition of jails and prisons would look dramatically whiter if drunk driving was punished like drug possession, and if the "war on drugs" was not biased against people of color. It would be better, of course, if fair, reasonable and effective policies were applied to both.

The use of marijuana, the nation's most commonly used illegal drug, is not associated with violence or death. Indeed, "Although the misuse of over-the-counter medications such as aspirin, acetaminophen, and antihistamines each year kills hundreds of Americans, not a single death has ever been credibly attributed directly to smoking or consuming marijuana in the 5,000 years of the plant's recorded use."[67] Yet law enforcement officers and politicians indulge in modern-day "Reefer Madness." Daryl Gates, then police chief of Los Angeles, testified at a 1990 Senate hearing that those who "blast some pot on a casual basis" should be "taken out and shot."[68] We've come a long way backward since 1972 when a bipartisan commission appointed by President Nixon advocated the decriminalization of marijuana for personal use—a recommendation, not surprisingly, he rejected.[69] In 1993, about 381,000 people were arrested, by FBI count, for possession (the majority), sale or production of marijuana.[70]

In a two-part *Atlantic Monthly* series on marijuana and the law, Eric Schlosser asks, "How does a society come to punish a person more harshly for selling marijuana than for killing someone with a gun?" He notes that the average punishment for an American found guilty of murder is eight years and eight months in prison. In numerous states, possessing, selling or growing even small amounts of marijuana can land you in prison for many more years than the average murderer— and the government can seize your home, farm and other assets. Data "suggest that one of every six inmates in the federal prison system— roughly 15,000 people—has been incarcerated primarily for a marijuana offense. The number currently being held in state prisons and local jails is more difficult to estimate: a conservative guess would be an additional 20,000 to 30,000." In many states "possession of more than an ounce— roughly equal to the amount of tobacco in a pack of cigarettes" is a felony. In Oklahoma, that can get you life in prison.[71] Nonviolent drug "lifers" will become a lot more common because under federal and state "three strikes and you're out" legislation, a third drug felony can bring life in prison without parole.

Schlosser observes that in the current drug war the costs for the war on marijuana include: "$30 billion spent so far at the state, federal, and local levels to fight marijuana; two billion dollars' worth of assets seized in marijuana cases; four million Americans arrested for marijuana offenses; a quarter of a million people convicted of marijuana felonies and sent to prison for at least a year. Statistics can only suggest a portion of the truth. As I learned from the families of inmates [among them cancer and AIDS patients arrested while using marijuana to alleviate pain and nausea], the human costs are not so easily measured."[72]

Most people who "do drugs" aren't addicts, just as most people who drink aren't alcoholics. Poor addicts shouldn't go to jail while richer ones go to famous clinics. All addicts should get treatment on demand. Laws should be toughened for reckless drivers—drunk or drugged. A wide range of proposals have been developed on how to proceed with decriminalization, distinguishing between specific substances. It's time they were given a fair hearing. Marijuana is the drug most widely recommended for legalization. To those who fear a rise in drug use with decriminalization, Duke and Gross point to the experience of Holland and to the 11 U.S. states which "more or less decriminalized possession and use of marijuana" at various times. Marijuana consumption "declined at approximately the same rate in the states that decriminalized it as consumption has declined elsewhere in the United States."[73]

Most of the violence now attributed to illegal drugs is a product of their hypocritical prohibition. The so-called drug war has led to a proliferation of guns among adults and children, diverted resources better spent, endangered lives and civil liberties, and enriched organized crime. Duke and Gross contend that "possibly as much as half of our violent and property crimes—certainly a very large portion—would be eliminated by legalization."[74] As summed up by Jeffrey Roth, "Illegal drugs and violence are linked primarily through drug marketing: disputes among rival distributors, arguments and robberies involving buyers and sellers, property crimes committed to raise drug money and, more speculatively, social and economic interactions between the illegal markets and the surrounding communities."[75]

Overall homicide rates reached nearly their highest point for this century in the early 1930s, coinciding with Prohibition and the Great Depression; the peak was 1933, the year Prohibition was repealed. The highest recorded rate at this writing was in 1980.[76] Like alcohol Prohibition earlier, today's drug prohibition means profit for modern Al Capones and criminal enterprises who will use violence to control their markets. To avoid the harsh mandatory sentences of the contemporary "War on Drugs," adults have pulled younger and younger youth into drug dealing, and armed them with increasingly deadly firearms. The deepening economic depression experienced by youth of color greatly intensifies the pull of the dangerous underground economy.

Males of all races between the ages of 15 and 24 are about three times as likely as men over 25 to be arrested for violent crimes. Thus, demographics play a role in the homicide rate. The high murder rates of the 1970s partly echoed the "baby boom." Today's rates partly reflect the boomers' children.[77]

Homicide is now the second-largest killer of young people of all races, ages 15-24. Accidents, mostly motor vehicle, are first; suicide is third. For Black young people, homicide leads accidents and suicide. For Whites, accidents and suicide lead homicide. Public health specialists believe that the many fatal auto "accidents" caused by drunk and reckless driving have more in common with homicide and suicide than commonly thought. In 1990, young Black males were nearly 11 times more likely to be murdered by gunfire than their White counterparts.

The gap in their overall death rates from accidents and violence was much lower, though still terribly large at 2-to-1; that's about the same ratio as 1970.[78] After dropping in the early 1980s, the homicide rate for Black males ages 15-24 increased sharply between 1985 and 1991, especially for those 15 to 19 years old. Between 1988 and 1991, the homicide rates for young White males also rose significantly. Nearly all the increase in rates was due to firearm-related homicides.[79] Among White juveniles, the number arrested for homicide between 1970 and 1992 jumped 204 percent, the highest rate of increase among racial groups.[80]

The FBI reports an escalation of juvenile violence "evident in all races, social classes, and lifestyles." In Little Rock, Arkansas, one of many small cities where youth violence is rising, "one of the most violent gangs is composed of white middle-class children."[81] Instead of nonviolent conflict resolution, children are widely taught that violence is the way to deal with problems—through popular wars and media "entertainment," for example.

Increasingly deadly weapons designed for hunting people are produced for profit by major manufacturers and proudly defended by the National Rifle Association—which demonstrated its continued power by successfully targeting numerous politicians who had supported gun control legislation for defeat in the 1994 elections and contributing to the Republican majority. In many places, you can legally possess firearms before you can legally drink, and it's easier to buy a gun than to register to vote. Poorly regulated gun shows and dealers' licenses make a sham of the minimal restrictions on firearms that do exist.[82] Half the homes in the country contain firearms, and guns in the home greatly increase the risk of murder and suicide for family members and close acquaintances. Guns are the weapon used in more deaths by suicide than homicide. Studies have found the risk of murder to be three times higher and the risk of suicide five times higher with a gun in the home.[83] Guns also expose children to the risk of unintentional injury and death. In 1988, for example, 277 children under 15 were killed by unintentional firearm injuries such as "playing" with loaded guns in the home.[84]

As far as gun manufacturers are concerned, children are just another consumer market. The National Shooting Sports Foundation (NSSF) is the gun industry's leading trade association. As Susan Glick and Josh Sugarmann report for the Violence Policy Center, NSSF informational material asks, "How old is old enough?" to have a gun, and advises parents:

> Age is not the major yardstick. Some youngsters are ready to start at 10, others at 14. The only real measures are those of maturity and individual responsibility. Does your youngster follow directions well? Would you leave him alone in the house for two or three hours? Is he conscientious and reliable? Would you send him to the grocery store with a list and a $20 bill? If the answer to these questions or similar ones are "yes" then the answer can also be "yes" when your child asks for his first gun.

To make matters worse, NSSF activities have been subsidized by tax dollars. In 1993, the NSSF received nearly $230,000 from the U.S. Fish and Wildlife Service to revise three videos on hunting and wildlife management for school children, grades 4 through 12. As Glick and Sugarmann explain, the NSSF is using the schools to promote its pro-gun sales, anti-gun control agenda. In a 1993 issue of *S.H.O.T. Business*, the NSSF industry publication, a columnist encourages gun dealers and manufacturers: "There's a way to help ensure that new faces and pocketbooks will continue to patronize your business. Use the schools...Every decade there is a whole new crop of shining young faces taking their place in society as adults...Will [they] be for or against a local ordinance proposal to ban those bad semiautos?"[85]

Children are bombarded with pro-violence messages and desensitized to ever-more violent imagery. Between 1982 and 1988—a period when children's TV was deregulated and networks defended programs like G.I. Joe as "educational"—television time devoted to war cartoons jumped from 90 minutes to 27 hours a week. By age 18, the average American child will have seen 40,000 murders on television. Violent "superhero" shows are created expressly to sell toys to children. Virtual reality computer games are bringing even more graphic and participatory "virtual" violence. The strong consensus of private and government research is that on-screen violence contributes to off-screen violence.[86]

"In the media world, brutality is portrayed as ordinary and amusing," writes Dr. Deborah Prothrow-Stith, former Massachusetts commissioner of Public Health, in her book, *Deadly Consequences*. Violence is often merged with sex. Audiences "have learned to expect the blood to be bloodier and the gore gorier." Missing are realistic portrayals of emotion, pain, death, consequences. In the movies, "bystanders, subway riders, ordinary people get caught in shootouts, crossfires, explosions, and other violent incidents. The action moves on quickly. We're not supposed to even think about the dead and dying left behind," writes Prothrow-Stith. "In the movies, violence is limitless, and it is fun. In the same spirit as President Reagan when he urged the Libyans to 'make my day,' by attacking, the violent hero cannot wait for the opportunity to, in the words of...President Bush, 'kick ass'" in Iraq. The screen "good guys" not only use violence as a first resort, but total war is the only response to the dehumanized "bad guys" who often speak with foreign accents.[87]

"In numerous experiments based at pre-schools," Prothrow-Stith reports, "researchers have observed children at play before and after seeing violent television programs. Following the violent program the children's play is invariably more aggressive. They are much more likely to hit, punch, kick, and grab to get their way." Many parents have seen this in their own home. To take another example, "If you show a 20-year-old male a romantic movie and then ask him about a rape, he will probably empathize with the rape victim. But if you show him a violent movie—*The Texas Chainsaw Massacre*, say—and then ask him about a rape, he is likely to tell you that the rape victim deserved what she got...She was asking for it."[88]

James Alan Fox, dean of the College of Criminal Justice at Northeastern University, observes: "It is well known that positive reinforcement for pro-social behavior will always outperform negative reinforcement for anti-social behavior. And, besides, it is far cheaper to hire elementary school teachers and pay them wages commensurate with the importance of their jobs than it is to build more prisons and hire more corrections officers. Unfortunately, for some of our leaders, there remains a more immediate political payoff in advocating a return to the three R's of retribution, retaliation and revenge."[89]

Fresh from victory in the 1994 elections, Republican leaders set out to strip the Crime Bill of its minimal programs for prevention of crime and violence. Only a society heading toward chaos would continue its failed strategy of filling more prisons instead of fully implementing proven programs in preventing crime and violence.

8

GREED SURPLUS, DEMOCRACY DEFICIT

Raised in unrivaled prosperity, we inherit an economy that is still the world's strongest, but is weakened by business failures, stagnant wages, increasing inequality, and deep divisions among our people...

Communications and commerce are global; investment is mobile; technology is almost magical...

Profound and powerful forces are shaking and remaking our world, and the urgent question of our time is whether we can make change our friend and not our enemy.

This new world has already enriched the lives of millions of Americans who are able to compete and win in it. But when most people are working harder for less; when others cannot work at all; when the cost of health care devastates families and threatens to bankrupt many of our enterprises, great and small; when fear of crime robs law-abiding citizens of their freedom; and when millions of poor children cannot even imagine the lives we are calling them to lead—we have not made change our friend.

President Bill Clinton, 1992 Inaugural address.

In her reflections on the 1992 Los Angeles riots, Rep. Maxine Waters (D-CA) quoted Robert Kennedy's words from 1968: "There is another kind of violence in America, slower but just as deadly, destructive as the shot or bomb in the night...This is the violence of institutions; indifference and inaction and slow decay. This is the

violence that afflicts the poor, that poisons relations between men and
women because their skin is different colors. This is the slow destruction
of a child by hunger, and schools without books and homes without
heat in the winter." Waters added, "What a tragedy it is that America
has still...not learned such an important lesson."[1]

Indeed, lessons about "the violence of institutions, indifference
and inaction" are being unlearned. As Marian Wright Edelman of the
Children's Defense Fund observed in 1991: "One of the most corrosive
lies we face is the pervasive argument that 'nothing works,' the War on
Poverty failed, social programs don't succeed. It is as though our entire
nation has been put in one of those spirit-squelching, hope-destroying
schools in which we bury so many students...These teachings inspired
a 'can't do' spirit."[2]

Our threshold of toleration for the intolerable rises steadily as we
step around more homeless people on the streets and subways; drive
over crumbling roads and bridges; bail out S&L spendthrifts; foreclose
on family farmers; put drug addicts on long waiting lists for treatment
and casual users in overcrowded jails; and send more kids to schools
without textbooks, libraries, arts or athletics.

Every day in the United States, the Children's Defense Fund
reports, "9 children are murdered, 13 children die from guns, 27
children—a classroom—die from poverty...101 babies die before their
first birthday."[3] We can change that if we open our minds and
democratically reorder our priorities.

DISINVESTMENT AND MISINVESTMENT

The Washington-based Milton S. Eisenhower Foundation was
created, in part, by members and staff of President Johnson's National
Advisory Commission on Civil Disorders, known as the Kerner Commission. It was following the 1968 riots that the Kerner Commission
issued its famous warning that the United States was becoming "two
societies, one black, one white—separate and unequal." Twenty-five
years later, the Eisenhower Foundation issued a report concluding:
"Overall, in spite of some gains since the 1960s but especially because
of the federal disinvestments of the 1980s, the famous prophesy of the
Kerner Commission...is more relevant today than in 1968, and more
complex, with the emergence of multiracial disparities and growing
income segregation."

In the words of the Eisenhower Foundation report, "Federal tax and income policy that helped the rich was accompanied by federal disinvestment policy that hurt the poor...From 1980 to 1990, federal community development block grants to the cities were cut from over $6B[billion] to under $3B." Moreover, "from 1979 to 1990, overall federal outlays on defense skyrocketed from close to $200B per year to nearly $300B per year, while overall federal outlays for education, job training, employment and social services declined from over $50B per year to under $40B per year—an astounding drop of over twenty percent...The huge military increases were financed only in a small way by the domestic cuts. Most was paid for by running up the national debt." The Eisenhower Foundation adds:

> One exception to the federal government's domestic disinvestment was prison building...costing $37B at the federal and state levels over the decade...Because the inmates were disproportionately young, in many ways prison building became the American youth policy of choice over the mid 1980s and early 1990s...[Because they were disproportionately youth of color], in some ways prison building became part of the nation's civil rights policy. Given that the population in American prisons more than doubled over the decade, while funding for housing for the poor was cut, incredibly, by more than eighty percent from 1978 to 1991 [after accounting for inflation], and given that the cost of a new prison cell in New York State was about the average cost of a new home purchased in the U.S. nationally, in some ways prison building became the American low-income housing policy of the 1980s.[4]

The cycle of unequal opportunity has been reinforced by tax cuts rewarding the wealthy and ballooning the national debt. According to Robert Reich, "Were the tax code as progressive as it was even as late as 1977," the top 10 percent of income earners "would have paid approximately $93 billion more in taxes" than they paid in 1989.[5] How much is $93 billion? About the same amount as the combined 1989 budget for all these programs for low-income persons:

- jobs and employment training, $3.9 billion
- education aid, including Head Start, college loans, etc., $13 billion
- housing benefits, including low-rent public housing, lower-income housing assistance, etc., $15.9 billion
- food benefits, including food stamps, school lunch program, WIC (nutrition program for pregnant and nursing Women, Infants and Children), $22 billion

- AFDC, $19.7 billion
- Supplemental Security Income, SSI, $15.8 billion
- General Assistance, $2.8 billion.[6]

Corporate taxes are way down. The share that corporate income taxes contribute to federal spending dropped from an average of 23 percent during the 1960s to almost 17 percent in the 1970s to about 8 percent during much of the 1980s. "How much more would corporations have contributed each year during the 1980s had their 1970s average tax rate not been cut but merely stayed constant? $130 billion!"[7]

Lower-income Americans pay for the debt they didn't create with cutbacks and less-talked-about tax hikes. Payroll taxes, which are regressive because they tax the poor proportionally more than the rich, are up. The Social Security tax, collected on salaries up to a cap ($60,600 in 1994), increased 31 percent from 1977 to 1990, when the rate reached 7.65 percent.[8] Up also are regressive state and local sales and property taxes, in part because the federal government is shifting billions of dollars in costs to state and local government.

Clinton's tax reforms went a step in the right direction by cutting income taxes, on average, for low-income people by expanding the Earned Income Tax Credit, and raising income taxes for higher-income people. But the tax system's earlier progressivity has not been restored. The wealthiest 1 percent of families can still expect to pay about 8 percent (averaging $15,674) less in 1995 federal taxes than would have been the case under 1977 rules. The top personal income tax bracket of 39.6 percent still "remains well below the average top rate, 47%, charged by the 86 countries with an income tax." Moreover, capital gains are taxed at only 28 percent, substantial investment interest is tax-exempt and the wealthy benefit disproportionately from mortgage interest and other deductions.[9] In the *Contract With America's* absurdly titled "Job Creation and Wage Enhancement Act," Republicans promise to cut the capital gains tax in half and index it to inflation.

What about charitable giving by the wealthy? A 1987 study by Yale University's Program on Non-Profit Organizations found that "most high income Americans are modest to stingy givers and only because a tiny minority are exceptionally charitable do the wealthy have a reputation for generosity."[10] Robert Reich notes that "most voluntary contributions of wealthy Americans go to the places and institutions that entertain, inspire, cure or educate wealthy Americans—art museums, opera houses, theaters, orchestras, ballet companies, private hospitals and elite universities."[11]

While the rich were getting richer, they were also getting stingier. In the 1980s, for all wage groups who itemized deductions on their tax returns, the average charitable contributions increased by over 9 percent; average contributions by those with pretax incomes above $1 million *decreased* by nearly 39 percent, adjusting for inflation. Charitable contributions by millionaires declined from about 7 percent of income in 1979 to below 4 percent of income in 1991. Indeed, as a percent of income, Americans with the least give the most.[12] The poor are the most generous with their hard-earned money (remember that money begets money through interest, dividends and inheritance; low-income Americans are lucky to avoid paying bank fees, much less earn net interest). In 1990, households with incomes of less than $10,000 gave an average of 5.5 percent of their earnings to charity or religious organizations; those with incomes above $100,000 gave only 2.9 percent.

Robert Reich has warned of the "secession of the successful": The wealthy top fifth of Americans, who earn more than the other four-fifths put together, have withdrawn "their dollars from the support of public spaces and institutions shared by all and dedicated the savings to their own private services"—from schools to health clubs to security guards for walled-off residential communities. Reich explains:

> Of course, wealthier Americans have been withdrawing into their own neighborhoods and clubs for generations. But the new secession is more dramatic...The new elite is linked by jet, modem, fax, satellite and fiber-optic cable to the great commercial and recreational centers of the world, but it is not particularly connected to the rest of the nation...
>
> Most large cities now possess two school systems—a private one for the children of the top-earning group and a public one for the children of service workers, the remaining blue-collar workers and the unemployed...
>
> When not living in urban enclaves [subsidized by public funds supporting upscale downtown "revitalization" projects], symbolic analysts are increasingly congregating in suburbs and exurbs where corporate headquarters have been relocated, research parks have been created, and where bucolic universities have spawned entrepreneurial ventures...
>
> The secession has been encouraged by the Federal Government...At their peak, Federal grants made up 25 percent of state and local spending in the late 1970's. [As of 1991], the Federal share has dwindled to 17 percent...States have quickly transferred many of these

new expenses to fiscally strapped cities and towns, with a result that by the start of the 1990's, localities were bearing more than half the costs of water and sewage, roads, parks, welfare and public schools.[13]

Making things still worse, state and local governments are rushing to expand lotteries, video poker, casinos and other government-promoted gambling to raise revenues, again disproportionately from those with lower incomes, which they should be raising from a fair tax system. As the *Boston Globe* put it in a lengthy series, "As state after state succumbs to the perfume of gambling, the odor of desperation becomes increasingly harder to mask...An exhaustive study by two Duke University economists found that lotteries...rather than being a voluntary tax or even a nontax way to balance state budgets...prey on the poor and make gamblers of people who never before had placed a bet." [14] The growing government dependency on gambling is a sign of chaos and decline.

DEFICIT OF WILL

Just as conservatives intended, the federal budget deficit—produced by skyrocketing military spending and tax cuts favoring the wealthy—has been used as a permanent enforcer of cutbacks in social services and public works. We have a greed surplus and a justice deficit.

Clinton's campaign program to Rebuild America and "put people first" was quickly sacrificed on the altar of deficit reduction. It is as if Franklin Roosevelt talked New Deal rhetoric and continued the policies of Herbert Hoover. Behind the headlines about new commitments to Head Start, for example, overall education and training spending declined.[15] Now the Republican chainsaws are ripping away. The real misery is yet to come, as cuts cascade down in the form of spreading hunger, homelessness and pollution; unprevented death and disease; decimated youth programs, schools and communities.

The Balanced Budget Amendment, if ratified, would be used to destroy social programs built since the Great Depression of the 1930s. It would ensure that government is ever leaner and meaner toward those with the least wealth and opportunity. It would starve social spending during periods of economic growth *and* recession, and transform recessions into depressions.[16]

As economist Max Sawicky explains in a report for the Economic Policy Institute:

The ideology underlying the fiscal doctrine of unlimited, unending deficit reduction is not aimed at stable prices, full employment, and greater private investment. Rather, the motivations are to reduce the size of government, to disassemble the U.S. system of social insurance, and to maintain unyielding downward pressure on the price level. The implied economic policy is one of stagnation: a disproportionate weight is put on low inflation to the detriment of employment, investment, and general economic growth. The policy is also counter-redistributive: it favors wealth-holders at the expense of wage-earners, the elderly, and the poor. If stated outright, these goals would be manifestly unpopular, so the sales pitch for extreme deficit reduction has to focus elsewhere—on creating and perpetuating misconceptions or downright superstitions about the federal budget and the public debt.

Sawicky says that "critics of government spending have succeeded in putting across the myth that all entitlement programs are out of control," but in actuality "only the two major health programs underlie the general upward pressure on deficits." Sawicky shows why a zero-deficit approach does more harm than good and makes the case for a policy of "sustainable deficit reduction." Under this approach, "the economic burden of public debt is best reflected in the ratio of debt to gross domestic product [GDP], not by the dollar size of deficits." He points out that the United States has a lower ratio of public debt to GDP than the principal nations of the Organization for Economic Cooperation and Development (OECD). The "sustainable deficit reduction" approach entails: cost containment through structural reform of the health care system; consistent reduction of the debt/GDP ratio when unemployment is low; fiscal stimulus to relieve high unemployment; and expanded public investment in a capital budgeting framework, which spreads out the cost of a capital project over its useful life. With this approach, Sawicky argues, it is possible "to continuously 'grow our way' to lower debt-GDP ratios, as the nation did steadily for 30 years after World War II."[17]

Just as families can productively borrow money to invest in homes and education, so the government can productively run a reasonable deficit to invest in its people, the infrastructure and the environment in the long-term interest of sustainable economic growth and social well-being. Enlarging the deficit to provide tax breaks for the wealthy and unnecessary military spending was not productive. And it isn't productive to impose austerity on low-income people, or undercut the nation's health and education to balance the budget. New federal priorities are principally a matter of will, not wallet.

As *The Nation* editorialized:

> Support for the [Balanced Budget Amendment] is driven by the feeling that the federal government is growing. In fact, it's not. As a share of G.D.P., Washington's spending is lower than it was in 1983, and Clinton's own budget—which has to be seen as an upper limit—projects that by the year 2000 it will be back to 1968 levels. As a share of the population, the federal civilian work force is lower than it has been since 1941, and as a share of total employment, it's the smallest since 1934. For all levels of government combined, U.S. public spending is the lowest of any rich industrial nation, and our deficit is the smallest (tied with Japan's) of the Group of Seven [U.S., Canada, Japan, U.K., Germany, France, Italy]. Since this stinginess doesn't seem to make for a healthy economy or a happy populace, it's hard to see why even more would do the trick.
>
> Not that deficits are a good habit over the long term. Instead of taxing rich people, the government borrows from them, and pays them more than $200 billion a year in interest for the privilege. We could eliminate the deficit in all but recession years by another round of income tax increases on the richest 1 percent and by eliminating their precious tax breaks. But that's the last thing on the minds of the [Balanced Budget Amendment's] sponsors.[18]

Conservatives have managed to confuse the idea of raising taxes on the wealthy with raising taxes in general, so that any attempts to put the tax system back on more of a sliding scale, based on ability to pay, are given the politically unpopular brand tax hikes. In the guise of populist tax revolt, conservatives provide "no new taxes" insurance for those who can afford to send their kids to private day care, private school, private hospitals and private colleges. In Europe, where taxes are higher, governments invest much more in social spending and infrastructure to assure basic human needs and more widely shared economic progress. One result is less crime and violence. In Western Europe, government tax revenues as a percent of GDP in 1994 were an average 46 percent. In the United States it was 32 percent.[19]

As *The State of Working America* reports, the United States spends proportionately much less than European countries in "the provision of publicly provided job training, job creation, and subsidies. Such programs are vital in an economy experiencing a shift from manufacturing to services and a reduction in the size of the armed forces." In 1991-92, the U.S. government spent only 0.09 percent of GDP on job training and placement and direct job creation and subsidies. The percentage in other OECD countries ranged from 0.17 to 1.45 percent.[20]

There is obviously no lack of work to be done if we commit ourselves to full employment. To take one example, after the Los Angeles riots the U.S. Conference of Mayors identified in their report, *Ready to Go,* over 7,000 public works projects on hold for lack of funds. As reported by the Eisenhower Foundation, these projects would have generated over 400,000 construction jobs and, calculating the multiplier effect of such investment, over one million jobs within a year.[21]

Hillary Rodham Clinton and Secretary of Health and Human Services Donna Shalala formerly chaired the Children's Defense Fund. But because of a deficit of political will, children are still losing to "defense"—i.e. the military-industrial complex that conservative president and retired general Dwight Eisenhower warned of decades ago. President Eisenhower said in his Farewell Radio and Television Address to the American People, January 17, 1961: "This conjunction of an immense military establishment and a large arms industry is new in the American experience...In the councils of government, we must guard against the acquisition of unwarranted influence, whether sought or unsought, by the military-industrial complex. The potential for the disastrous rise of misplaced power exists and will persist."

In 1992, the United States spent four times more on the military than federal investment in education, job training, housing, economic development and environmental protection combined.[22] The 1993 military budget of $291 billion was 20 percent higher, adjusting for inflation, than the Cold War budget of 1980. In the words of the Washington-based Center for Defense Information (CDI), led by retired military officers, the Clinton administration "wants to spend an astounding $1.3 Trillion on the military over a period of just 5 years. In the final year of the plan, the downward trend will be reversed as military spending rises again." CDI warns that "Pentagon 5-year plans have long been grounded in overstated threats and understated costs." CDI urges politicians not to rationalize military spending as a jobs program, noting, "money spent on real needs will generate more jobs than are currently wasted on unneeded military programs."[23] Republicans promise to spend even more on the military.

Instead of supporting serious military-civilian conversion at home and abroad, the U.S. government is reinforcing militarism by avidly expanding weapons exports. The United States is the world's leading arms dealer and, in 1993, "about three-quarters of these sales went to governments deemed repressive or undemocratic in the State Department's own human rights reports." Behind the rhetoric about economic

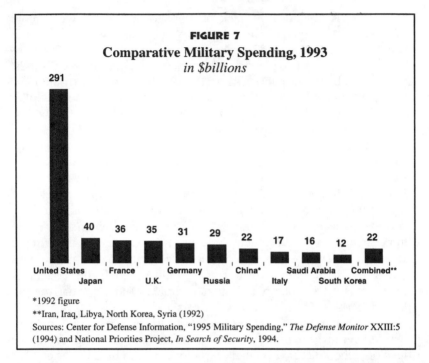

FIGURE 7

Comparative Military Spending, 1993

in $billions

291

40 36 35 31 29 22 17 16 12 22

United States   France   Germany   China*   Saudi Arabia   Combined**
        Japan   U.K.   Russia   Italy   South Korea

*1992 figure

**Iran, Iraq, Libya, North Korea, Syria (1992)

Sources: Center for Defense Information, "1995 Military Spending," *The Defense Monitor* XXIII:5 (1994) and National Priorities Project, *In Search of Security*, 1994.

benefits, "William Hartung of the World Policy Institute found that when subsidies and indirect costs are factored in, 'the net value of arms exports to the U.S. economy in a given year will range somewhere between a small net gain and a small net loss.'"[24] The real costs are even greater in terms of polluted and wasted resources, weapons proliferation and human rights. In 1992, the world spent the combined income of half the world's people—$815 billion—on the military.[25] The United States was far out front in the spending race.

Numerous military and foreign policy specialists have called for bringing the military budget down to $175 billion or less by the end of the decade. These include the Center for Defense Information, former Secretary of Defense Robert McNamara and defense analyst William Kaufman. Arms control expert Randall Forsberg, director of the Institute for Defense and Disarmament Studies, goes much further. She proposes a phased ten-year program to build a cooperative international security system with strong mechanisms for peaceful conflict resolution and a commitment to "non-offensive defense," bringing the U.S. military budget to $87 billion, for a savings of $989 billion.[26] To reduce the military budget to that level and lower, the United States has to commit itself willfully to fostering international demilitarization and nonviolent conflict resolution.

In the words of the United Nations *Human Development Report 1994,* "The world can never be at peace unless people have security in their daily lives. Future conflicts may often be within nations rather than between them—with their origins buried deep in growing socio-economic deprivation and disparities. The search for security in such a milieu lies in development, not in arms."[27]

Clinton chose the course of less security, not more, when he declared in his 1994 State of the Union address, "We must not cut defense further." As Martin Luther King warned in *Where Do We Go From Here?,* "A nation that continues year after year to spend more money on military defense than on programs of social uplift is approaching spiritual death."

DEMOCRACY OR DEMAGOGUERY

> Today's Sun Belt represents a confluence of Social Darwinism, entrepreneurialism, high technology, nationalism, nostalgia and fundamentalist religion, and any Sun Belt hegemony over our politics has a unique potential…to accommodate a drift toward apple-pie authoritarianism.
>
> Kevin Phillips, *Post-Conservative America,* 1982.[28]

The failed American Dream can give way to a new American fairness or a neofascist nightmare. It can happen in Europe. It can happen here.*

In the words of conservative Edward Luttwak of the Center for Strategic and International Studies, "Democracy, too, must become fragile when better hopes are worn away by bitter disappointment, opening the way for the strong, false remedies of demagogues. Once the politics of affluence for all—the politics of the American dream—become too blatantly unrealistic for most Americans, the politics of racist, xenophobic, or class resentment can more honestly gain votes."[29]

---

* In Sinclair Lewis's classic, *It Can't Happen Here,* the right-wing pseudo-populists devoured their more progressive populist allies and instituted a fascism which profited Big Business.

Decades ago conservative strategist Kevin Phillips helped define *The Emerging Republican Majority* which brought us Nixon, Reagan, Bush and the culmination of the Republican's Sun Belt strategy in the 1994 elections. In *The Politics of Rich and Poor*, he predicted a populist swing in the political pendulum in the face of the 1980s redistribution of wealth to the rich. And, most recently, in *Arrogant Capital*, he blasted a parasitic Washington of privileged influence-peddlers and dealmaking politicians unresponsive to the public they ostensibly serve.

In a 1992 magazine article, Phillips reflected on the contemporary "politics of frustration," antecedents such as Huey Long and Father Coughlin, and similarities and dissimilarities with Weimar Germany, a topic he had also explored years before in *Post-Conservative America*. He noted "the radicalization of the usually nonideological midsection of the population because of cultural and economic trauma," and warned: "This can lead to dangerous politics, the most terrible example being Germany in the 1920's and early 1930's, when hard times and a collapsing center produced Adolf Hitler." He continued:

> One measure of the depth of the current frustration in America is that [David] Duke could win the support of a majority of white Louisiana

---

More people are unemployed in Chemnitz, Leuna, or Frankfurt an der Oder than in 1933, when people there elected the Nazis. If we cannot overcome this [problem], we must be prepared for everything.

Former German Chancellor Helmut Schmidt.[30]

With little or no job security, we are essentially creating a new feudal system where Kafka-like authorities and a senior managerial class, with close ties to the government of the day, replace the landlord. The prospects for democracy, with advanced living conditions...grow increasingly dim...

Law and order are politicians' watchwords, deemed best to reach and appeal to a shrinking number of constituents. That is until a new deliverer appears on the scene. It need not be a Hitler...but anybody carrying the alluring promise of security and full employment will find receptive ears. All that may be asked of us in exchange is our freedom.

Thomas R. Ide and Arthur J. Cordell, "Automating Work,"
Society, September-October 1994.

voters in two straight statewide elections, notwithstanding television advertisements showing him in Ku Klux Klan robes and swastika armbands. [Presidential candidate Patrick] Buchanan took many of the same positions as Duke on immigration, race, welfare, trade and nationalism, albeit more moderately. And the charges of nativism, fascism, xenophobia and anti-Semitism inspired by his statements had little effect on his support. When a radicalizing middle class regards the establishment as bankrupt and the status quo as intolerable, normal standards fall quite easily.[31]

When not running full time for president, authoritarian demagogue Pat Buchanan enjoys a large audience as cohost of CNN's *Crossfire*, which is a microcosm of the dominant political spectrum in today's United States. "From the Right," there's Buchanan; "from the Left," there's quasi-liberal Michael Kinsley. Buchanan's heroes include Senator Joe McCarthy, Spanish dictator Francisco Franco and Chilean dictator Augusto Pinochet. He has a long track record of defending South African apartheid and Nazi war criminals, and opposing civil rights legislation.[32] In a 1991 column he made plain his support for authoritarianism—from the Third World to New York and Washington, DC.[33] Buchanan told the 1992 Republican national convention: "There is a religious war going on in this country. It is a cultural war." Delegates waved signs saying "Gay Rights Never"—the '90s version of "Segregation Forever." Referring to the then-recent rioting in Los Angeles, following the acquittal of police officers who had severely beaten a Black man, Buchanan said that as the troopers "took back the streets of Los Angeles, block by block, my friends, we must take back our cities and take back our culture and take back our country."

Clinton, a leader of the "moderate" and conservative "New Democrats," whose policies often make Nixon look liberal, catapulted into office with populist rhetoric and imagery—capped off by the inaugural poetry of Maya Angelou. Many mistaken pundits are blaming the Democratic Party's rout in the 1994 mid-term elections as evidence that Clinton's first two years were too liberal and have urged him on in shifting right. Wrong.

As Kevin Phillips pointed out in *Arrogant Capital*, Clinton did not "represent that famous old cement of New Deal coalition-building known as 'interest-group liberalism.'" Phillips writes, "If it had weakened under Democrat Jimmy Carter in 1977-81, it expired under Bill Clinton...What Clinton has done is to shift his party from so-called interest group liberalism to 'interest-group centrism'—away from the pro-spending liberal-type lobbies that represented *people* (labor, sen-

> Previously passive or unorganized groups in the population,
> blacks, Indians, Chicanos, white ethnic groups, students, and women
> now embarked on concerted efforts to establish their claims to oppor-
> tunities, positions, rewards, and privileges, which they had not consid-
> ered themselves entitled [sic] before.
>
> ...
>
> The effective operation of a democratic political system usually
> requires some measure of apathy and noninvolvement on the part of
> some individuals and groups.
>
> Samuel Huntington, The Crisis of Democracy,
Trilateral Commission, 1975.[34]

iors, minorities, and urban) to a more upscale centrist (or center-right) group that represents *money* (multinational business, banks, investment firms, trial lawyers, trade interests, superlobbyists, investors, the bond market, and so on)."[35]

Voters often face a choice between timid Democratic tinkerers and hot-button pushing Republicans who thrive on divide-and-rule politics. Many Democratic politicians behave like defense lawyers who plea bargain every case, no matter the particulars of guilt or innocence. Who wants a lawyer with a track record of pleading their clients "part guilty"?

Phillips quotes the late Lee Atwater, the Bush Campaign manager who remarked after the 1988 election, "The way to win a presidential race against the Republicans is to develop the class warfare issue, as Dukakis did at the end. To divide up the haves and have-nots and to try to reinvigorate the New Deal coalition and to attack."[36]

Instead, Democrats keep dividing the have-nots. Modern Demo-crats know how to defeat themselves better than anyone. Their favorite strategy is a well-tested failure: the best defense is a good sellout. Sell out labor and environmentalists on NAFTA and GATT; dump Lani Guinier, Joycelyn Elders and numerous others deemed politically incorrect by right-wingers; scapegoat single mothers; make court appointments courting conservatives; and so on. The Clinton admini-stration even managed to give health care reform a bad name—leaving the current system free to insure profits by cutting health care.

Imagine Franklin Roosevelt winning reelection as Hoover Lite, offering unpaid family leave and an earned income tax credit, say, instead of Social Security and the WPA (Works Progress Administration). Clinton could see the 1994 electoral rebuke coming, as seen in this exchange from April 1993 recounted in Bob Woodward's *The Agenda*. But he badly underestimated the ramifications and led his party into defeat instead of away:

> "Congress thinks it can run in '94 on this budget, plus GATT and NAFTA," he added, referring to the two pending trade agreements. "*They're crazy...*"
>
> "Where are all the Democrats?" Clinton bellowed. "I hope you're all aware we're all Eisenhower Republicans," he said, his voice dripping with sarcasm. "We're Eisenhower Republicans here, and we are fighting the Reagan Republicans. We stand for lower deficits and free trade and the bond market. Isn't that great."...
>
> The room was silent once more.
>
> He erupted again, his voice severe and loud. "I don't have a goddamn Democratic budget until 1996. None of the investments, none of the things I campaigned on...We must have something for the common man. It won't hurt me in '94, and I can put enough into '95 and '96 to crawl through to reelection.
>
> "At least we'll have health care to give them, if we can't give them anything else," he added.[37]

The Democrats have reaped the scapegoating divisions they have sown with their moves to the right on "welfare reform," immigration and so on. They divide their electoral base of workers, Blacks and women, and wonder why Republicans conquer. As if to show he learned nothing from the 1994 election, when Clinton met the press the next day, the first initiative he asked Republicans to join him in passing was GATT. He opened the door wide to the welfare wrecking crew, allowing right-wingers to achieve what they had only been able to dream under Nixon, Ford, Bush and Reagan. The impossible process of multiplication by division is now being repeated with the sellout of affirmative action.

The Democrats deserved to lose in 1994, but the Republicans did not deserve to win. Their *Contract With America* is part II of their murder contract on the American Dream begun under Reagan and Bush. Right-wing politicians won in 1994 because their base (mostly religious conservative Republicans, but also like-minded Independents and Democrats) was mobilized to turn out in force—and there was no Perot to divert them—while the more liberal and moderate Democratic base was demoralized and turned off.

Look at differences in the electorate for the 1992 presidential election and the 1994 mid-term election, where conservative candidates made strong gains at the national, state and local levels. According to a report by the Roper Center for Public Opinion Research, the proportion of the *electorate* (not a representative sample of the larger population) calling themselves conservative increased 7 points nationally. In New York, 33 percent of the electorate identified as conservative in 1994, compared to 25 percent in 1992; the liberal share remained at 23 percent, but the moderate portion fell from 52 percent in 1992 to 43 percent in 1994. In California, 36 percent of the electorate identified as conservative, up sharply from 26 percent in 1992; the liberal portion changed from 23 percent in 1992 to 20 percent in 1994, while the moderate share fell from 50 percent in 1992 to 44 percent in 1994. In Florida, the conservative portion was 39 percent in 1994, up from 33 percent in 1992, while in New Jersey it was 38 percent in 1994 compared to 26 percent in 1992. In Illinois, the portion of the electorate identified as conservative was 40 percent, up from 26 percent in 1992. Independent voters, according to national exit poll data, backed Republican candidates by a 58 percent to 42 percent margin.[38]

Right-wing candidates were effectively groomed and promoted by forces such as the Christian Coalition, Newt Gingrich's GOPAC and the National Rifle Association. They were aided by a growing number of rabid right-wing radio and television talk show hosts, among whom Rush Limbaugh was the most famous nationally. Before the 1994 election, House Speaker-to-be-Newt Gingrich called Clinton Democrats "the enemy of normal Americans." Ronald Reagan had a similarly successful strategy. As a June 1984 Reagan Campaign strategy memo advised: "*Paint RR as the personification of all that is right with, or heroized by, America…*where an attack on Reagan is tantamount to an attack on America's idealized image of itself—*where a vote against Reagan is, in some subliminal sense, a vote against a mythic 'America.'*" (Italics in original.)

Gingrich trained many of the new Republican House members to describe Democrats with words such as "traitors," "sick," "antifamily," "greed" and "lie." Of the 75 Republicans elected to the House in 1994, "GOPAC officials said that at least 33 were educated by Gingrich's training method, including many who were recruited by him to be candidates several years ago."[39]

The Christian Coalition is led by Pat Robertson. Chip Berlet, an analyst at Political Research Associates, which studies right-wing movements, explains that the Free Congress Foundation—led by theocrat Paul Weyrich and founded with money from the Coors Beer family fortune—"is the key strategic think tank backing Robertson's Christian Coalition, which is building a grass-roots movement to wage the Culture War." Berlet warns that "the Christian Coalition could conceivably evolve into a more mainstream conservative political movement or— especially if the economy deteriorates—it could build a mass base for fascism similar to the clerical fascist movements of mid-century Europe."

Looking more broadly at the growing Right, Berlet explains: "Since the 1960s, the secular, corporate, and religious branches of the Right have spent hundreds of millions of dollars to build a solid national right-wing infrastructure that provides training, conducts research, publishes studies, produces educational resources, engages in network- ing and coalition building, promotes a sense of solidarity and possible victory, shapes issues, provides legal advice, suggests tactics, and tests and defines specific rhetoric and slogans. Today, the vast majority of 'experts' featured on television and radio talk shows, and many syndicated print columnists, have been groomed by the right-wing infrastructure [they downplay their influence by promoting the myth of leftist domination of the mass media]."[40]

As journalist Marc Cooper summed it up, "at least 60 percent of the 600 conservative Christian candidates running from coast to coast [in 1994] had been elected, up from 40 percent just two years ago." Colorado Springs Christian Coalition activist Chuck Gosnell boasted to Cooper, "One-third of the votes cast nationally were from Christian conservatives. We helped elect the candidates God wants in office."[41]

Looking back on the origins of the modern Religious Right, Kevin Phillips recalls how "in 1978 and 1979, the three key national New Right strategists, Richard Viguerie [who handled George Wallace's direct-mail operations in 1972], Paul Weyrich and Howard Phillips" had, in the words of *Conservative Digest*, "decided that the millions of fundamen- talists in America were a political army waiting to be mobilized." The Moral Majority and the Religious Roundtable were early outcomes. Kevin Phillips writes of his amazement at how few have appreciated their historic achievement of building a right-leaning coalition of Christians of Protestant, Catholic, Baptist and other denominations.[42]

According to the Roper Center report, 19 percent of the 1994 electorate—one out of five voters—identified themselves as part of "the *religious right political movement.*"[43] (Italics added.) Berlet explains that "the Religious Right's ideal is a theocracy in which Christian men interpret God's will as law in a hierarchy where women are helpmates, children are property of their parents, and the Earth must submit to the dominion of those to whom God has granted power. People are basically sinful, and must be restrained by harsh punitive laws. Social problems are caused by Satanic conspiracies aided and abetted by liberals, homosexuals, feminists, and secular humanists. These forces must be exposed and neutralized."[44]

Crime is one of the demagogues' main issues. "Just two years ago, only 3 percent of Americans listed crime as the nation's top problem, according to the Times Mirror Center for the People and the Press. By July [1994], the number of people listing crime as the top problem had soared to 26 percent. This jump in fear came as the rate of most crimes actually decreased."[45]

Using the "War on Drugs" as justification, legal protections such as those against unwarranted search and seizure have been greatly eroded, especially among people of color. The *Contract With America's* "Taking Back Our Streets Act" goes further down the slippery slope. As part of the headlong rush to implement the *Contract,* the House passed a bill that would allow incriminating evidence seized illegally, without a search warrant, to be used in Federal Court if the police acted in "good faith." Fundamental constitutional protections are portrayed as minor technicalities to be undone for the sake of justice. *New York Times* columnist Anthony Lewis observes:

> In 1914 the Supreme Court held unanimously that Federal prosecutors could not use evidence seized in violation of the Fourth Amendment's rule against unreasonable searches and seizures. Justice William R. Day wrote:
> "If letters and private documents can thus be seized and held and used in evidence against a citizen accused of an offense, the protection of the Fourth Amendment declaring his right to be secure against such searches and seizures is of no value and, so far as those thus placed are concerned, might as well be stricken from the Constitution."
> This week the House of Representatives...voted to do what the conservative Supreme Court of 1914 evidently thought unimaginable. It passed a bill that would effectively strike the search-and-seizure protections of the Fourth Amendment from the Constitution.[46]

Scapegoating fuels fear and fear fuels scapegoating. It is not far-fetched to see the seeds of "ethnic cleansing"—the awful euphemism for genocide in the former Yugoslavia—in the widespread support given California's Proposition 187. Think about how successful the Big Lie technique has been when it comes to women on welfare.

How easy it has been to roll back civil liberties with the excuse of fighting a "War on Drugs." How accustomed the United States has grown to being a leader among the world's jailers. How easy it's become to spend more money on prisons and less on education.

Think about how far to the right the political "center" has shifted. Views once considered extremist Far Right are now considered ordinary, views once considered centrist are now considered ultraliberal and views genuinely to the left are largely ignored in the mass media. A nation that committed genocide against Native Americans, enslaved Blacks and imprisoned Japanese Americans should never doubt that authoritarianism can happen here. Today, with little opposition, a right-wing majority in Congress is voting away pieces of the Bill of Rights and cornerstones of 20th century progress. How would the nation enter the 21st century with a right-wing president, a right-wing Congress and a conservative Supreme Court?

The tyranny of this dictatorship isn't primarily the fault of Big Business, nor of the demagogues who do their dirty work. It's the fault of Doremus Jessup! Of all the conscientious, respectable, lazy-minded Doremus Jessups who have let the demagogues wriggle in, without fierce enough protest.

Sinclair Lewis, *It Can't Happen Here* (1935).

In Germany, the Nazis came for the Communists, and I didn't speak up because I wasn't a Communist. Then they came for the Jews, and I didn't speak up because I wasn't a Jew. Then they came for the trade unionists, and I didn't speak up because I wasn't a trade unionist. Then they came for the Catholics, and I didn't speak up because I was a Protestant. Then they came for me, and by that time there was no one left to speak for me.

Attributed to Protestant pastor Martin Niemoeller, who voted for the Nazi party in 1933 and was imprisoned in a concentration camp from 1938 to 1945.

As Martin Luther King warned in *Where Do We Go From Here?*, "History is cluttered with the wreckage of nations and individuals who pursued [the] self-defeating path of hate." King was assassinated while organizing the Poor People's Campaign, which was intended as a building block for an ongoing alliance of people of all races around economic justice.

It is time to strip away the camouflage of scapegoating from the upward redistribution of wealth. It is time to stop shredding social safety nets and demanding that people do paid work for their living without assuring full employment or living wages. If we revert increasingly to separate and unequal, we will surely self-destruct. It is time to stop pretending that the problem is people with cultures of poverty and not the prevailing economy of impoverishment. It is time to pose a true alternative to the dangerous false populism of the Right.

9

ECONOMICS FOR EVERYONE

WE THE PEOPLE of the United States, in Order to form a more perfect Union, establish Justice, insure domestic Tranquillity, provide for the common defense, promote the general Welfare, and secure the Blessings of Liberty to ourselves and our Posterity, do ordain and establish this Constitution for the United States of America.

Constitution of the United States, 1787.

Economic rights are fundamental to the establishment of Justice, Tranquillity, the promotion of the general Welfare and securing the Blessings of Liberty to ourselves and our posterity. Economic rights are fundamental human rights. Yet half a century after President Roosevelt proposed an Economic Bill of Rights for the United States and the United Nations adopted the Declaration of Human Rights, including economic rights, the welfare and justice of people are being sacrificed for the liberty of global corporations. Two decades after the United Nations adopted a Declaration and Program of Action on the Establishment of a New International Economic Order respecting national sovereignty and dedicated to the redress of inequalities and injustices, most of the world has come under the domain of the Global Corporate Order in which people and nations are merely means to further elite profit.

"Free trade" agreements such as NAFTA and GATT can be understood as economic bills of rights for corporations. So can the

Republican *Contract With America*. We must come together nationally and internationally to promote an economic bill of rights for people. Democracy cannot survive, much less thrive, in a world where people are secondary to corporate power.

CORPORATE BILLS OF RIGHTS

The public and leaders of most countries continue to live in a mental universe which no longer exists—a world of separate nations—and have great difficulties thinking in terms of global perspectives and interdependence.

The liberal premise of a separation between the political and economic realm is obsolete: issues related to economics are at the heart of modern politics.

Richard N. Cooper, Karl Kaiser, Masataka Kosaka, *Towards a Renovated International System*, Trilateral Commission, 1977.

As others have noted, unrestrained growth is the ideology of the cancer cell.

Muhammad Yunus, "Redefining Development."[1]

The rapacious global corporate model of development exploits and endangers both people and the environment. "The North, with 20% of world population, uses up 80% of world resources and has a per capita income on average 15 times higher than that of the South," writes economist Martin Khor Kok Peng, editor of *Third World Resurgence* and director of the Malaysia-based Third World Network. There is a "socio-ecological crisis." As Earth's resources are exhausted and contaminated, "much of the world's output and income are channeled to a small elite (mostly in the North but also in the South), while a large part of humanity (mostly in the South, but also a growing minority in the North) has insufficient means to satisfy its needs."[2]

"During the past five decades, world income increased sevenfold (in real GDP) and income per person more than tripled (in per capita GDP)," reports the United Nations Development Program. "But this gain has been spread very unequally—nationally and internationally—and the inequality is increasing. Between 1960 and 1991, the share of world income for the richest 20% of the global population rose from 70% to 85%. Over the same period, all but the richest quintile saw their share of world income fall—and the meager share for the poorest 20% declined from 2.3% to 1.4%." In 1960, the richest 20 percent of the

world's population had 30 times as much income as the poorest 20
percent. By 1991, the richest 20 percent had 61 times as much income
as the poorest 20 percent. "More than one billion people survive on a
daily income of less than $1." Some 800 million people go hungry,
although there is food enough to provide everyone with more than the
basic minimum.[3]

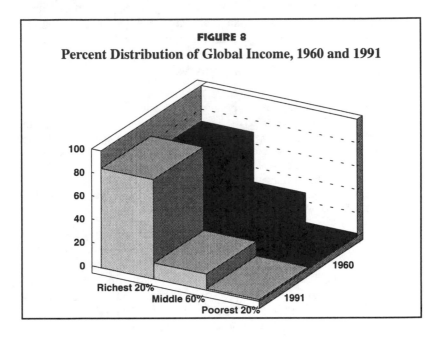

FIGURE 8
Percent Distribution of Global Income, 1960 and 1991

    The Republican *Contract With America* is, in part, a national
corporate bill of rights. It contains many provisions—now steamrolling
through Congress—to roll back environmental, health and safety, and
civil rights protections without telling people that's their intent. For
example, under the Orwellian "Job Creation and Wage Enhancement
Act," the *Contract* seeks to require all "federal agencies to issue an
annual report projecting the cost to the private sector of compliance
with all federal regulations. The cost of the regulations will then be
capped below its current level forcing agencies to (1) find more
cost-effective ways to reach goals and (2) identify regulatory policies
whose benefits exceed their costs to the private sector." Private
economic interests, not public health and safety, will rule the regula-

tions. The underfunded, understaffed regulators would be swamped in red tape, while the polluters would be given all benefit of doubt.

Similarly, under the rubric of "unfunded mandate reform," the *Contract With America* calls for capping the cost of federal mandates for state and local governments at below their levels for the preceding year. Through these caps and other provisions, contract proponents want to ensure cutbacks and block new regulations in crucial areas ranging from the cleanup of toxic waste and enforcement of clean air and water standards, to implementing gun control regulations and antidiscrimination mandates such as the Americans with Disabilities Act. One reporter highlighted the issue this way:

> Go back now to June 22, 1969, when the Cuyahoga River in Cleveland finally became so polluted it actually caught fire.
> Local and state officials simply had not been able to "buck the political pressure of the steel mills and chemical companies," opposed to cleanup measures because they would cut into profits, Rep. George Miller, D-Calif., told the House...
> "I think you have to ask yourself if that is what we want to go back to," Miller said, recalling it required passage of the federal Clean Water Act to finally clean up the Cuyahoga.[4]

Another *Contract* provision demands that the government compensate property owners financially for federal regulations that reduce the value of their business or property by even a small percentage. It seeks to drastically expand the sweep of the Fifth Amendment clause which states that private property shall not "be taken for public use without just compensation." This has traditionally been used to ensure that owners are paid market value when the government takes private land to build a highway or subway, for example. As author David Helvarg explains, the *Contract With America* "compensation plan is one of several attempts by the 'property rights' wing of the anti-environmental backlash to use a radical reinterpretation of the Fifth Amendment to gut a generation of environmental laws and land-use reforms...Developers and property owners are arguing that any protection of nature that affects the dollar value of real estate is a 'taking' that must be financially compensated for by the government. The instigators of these efforts figure that such treasury-busting compensation would quickly lead to the dismantling of broadly popular environmental laws like the Clean Air, Clean Water and Endangered Species acts." Helvarg observes:

The first suit against a "regulatory taking" was brought in 1887 by a Kansas beer brewer named Peter Mugler, who argued that a prohibition law passed in his state was a taking under the Fifth Amendment because it put him out of business. The Supreme Court ruled that "a government can prevent a property owner from using his property to injure others without having to compensate the owner for the value of the forbidden use."

This "nuisance clause" is the basis on which the government has been able to establish health and safety regulations, labor codes and consumer and environmental protections without having to pay out vast sums of money for individual compensation.

What more than a century of this precedent has tended to show is that for every form of regulatory "taking" there are far more "givings." The land-use plan or "taking" that prevents a property owner from dumping garbage, manure or chemicals into a river may be seen as a "giving" by property owners downstream whose land values increase with improved water quality.[5]

If the deregulators have their way, we will have to pay people to *stop* polluting and destroying the environment. "If environmentalists are panicked now, though, conservative activists say, they haven't seen anything yet," the *Boston Globe* reports. For example, Jerry Taylor of the increasingly influential Cato Institute recommends selling off all the national forests and opening up public land, such as the Arctic National Wildlife Refuge, to oil and gas developers.[6] The anti-environment backlash begun under Reagan has returned with a vengeance.

The GATT is a global corporate bill of rights, and under the World Trade Organization (WTO)—the GATT's successor—enforcement will be even stronger. Corporations are freer to exploit workers, consumers and the environment throughout the world. For the Third World it is a form of recolonization.[7] For the major industrial nations, it means further repolarization into haves and have-nots.

Around the world, the corporatist WTO will undermine small farmers, speed up ecological crisis and threaten the health and safety of workers and consumers. It will undermine Third World sovereignty, reward the production of cash crops for export over food needed for local consumption and tighten corporate control over culture, technology and resources, including seeds and medicinal plants. It will endanger livelihoods and undercut democratic government.

One need not be wary of global corporations to see the GATT/WTO potential for disaster. Peter Kassler is head of planning for Shell International Petroleum Co. in London. As *Business Week* reports, he can see a very positive post-GATT trade liberalization scenario bringing rising global living standards and strong growth. "However, Kassler and other Shell executives also can sketch a far more ominous— and equally plausible—outcome. Under a Shell scenario labeled 'Barricades,' the [GATT] produces social and economic chaos. Global trade liberalization triggers unrelenting job cuts and downward pressure on wages in industrialized nations. From Kansas to Kuala Lumpur, entrenched interests team up with religious, nationalist, and other blocs to close borders. 'Globalization,' says Kassler, 'may lead to strife among people who don't get the rewards they think they deserve.'"[8]

Instead of holding new technology to high social, health and environmental standards and sharing the profits of rising productivity, corporations are using technology, much of it harmful, to dispose of more workers and intensify the work of those remaining. Meanwhile, an international elite of financial investors and speculators—generally known in the United States as the Bond Market—is using the latest computer capabilities to electronically sweep the world for ready profit, often at the expense of long-run investment, not to mention workers' livelihoods. In *Business Week's* words:

> As traders pump up their supercomputers and merge physics, math, and money to create ever-more-complex instruments and techniques, capital markets will turn more cruelly efficient and risky than ever. Financial volatility will become "a fact of life," says World Bank Managing Director Ernest Stern, who believes that the once-staid global market for government debt has already turned into a $16 trillion casino that behaves more and more like the rough-and-tumble market for stocks.
>
> In this new battleground for savings, market players will become a new class of stateless legislators. With the power of the purse, they will check governments' ability to tax, spend, borrow, or depreciate their debts through inflation. To be sure, money mavens sitting at computer screens already vote their portfolios on issues as diverse as the value of the Mexican peso, U.S. trade imbalances with Japan, and Sweden's struggle to maintain the archetype of the European welfare state. But that's only the starting point.
>
> As more countries and companies hook themselves up to the global financial network, this shifting and stateless corps of fund managers and traders will not only be passing judgment. To preserve the value of their investments, they will become more and more directly involved in day-to-day affairs of state, meting out guidance, encouragement, and discipline on a daily basis. "The very sovereignty of nation-

states," says London-based economist David C. Roche, "is being defeated."[9]

Former Citicorp Chair Walter Wriston has boasted of how "200,000 monitors in trading rooms all over the world" now conduct "a kind of global plebiscite on the monetary and fiscal policies of the governments issuing currency...There is no way for a nation to opt out."[10] No way, that is, under the rigged rules of corporate domination.

PUTTING ECONOMICS IN HUMAN RIGHTS

Labor is prior to, and independent of, capital. Capital is only the fruit of labor, and could never have existed if labor had not first existed. Labor is the superior of capital, and deserves much the higher consideration.

President Abraham Lincoln, Message to Congress, December 3, 1861.

The time has come for us to civilize ourselves by the total, direct and immediate abolition of poverty...
A true revolution of values will soon cause us to question the fairness and justice of many of our past and present policies. We are called to play the good samaritan on life's roadside; but...one day the whole Jericho road must be transformed so that men and women will not be beaten and robbed as they make their journey through life. True compassion is more than flinging a coin to a beggar; it understands that an edifice which produces beggars needs restructuring.

Martin Luther King Jr., *Where Do We Go From Here: Chaos or Community?*

In the United States and around the world, people are working together—acting locally, nationally and internationally—to oppose the trends discussed here and promote just alternatives: from human rights organizations to international trade unions; from women's economic literacy and economic development projects to credit unions and environmental organizations; from urban community land trusts to agricultural cooperatives; from fair trade campaigns and consumer boycotts to alternative technology and people-to-people trading; from local campaigns to stop toxic dumping to the growing movement against environmental racism; from community-based organizations to cross-border coalitions and international Non-Governmental Organiza-

THE VIEW FROM THE JANITORS AT THE WORLD BANK

Working as a janitor in downtown Washington, D.C., [Maria Elena Flores, an immigrant from El Salvador] earns the D.C. minimum wage ($4.75 an hour) and has no health insurance. To make ends meet, she shares a small apartment with three other adults.

"The pay is not much," she said..."and if you are one minute late, they take away money."

The building Flores works to clean five nights a week is one of several housing the Washington headquarters of...the World Bank...

The people whose offices Flores cleans have good jobs. They are engineers, economists and technical experts...They come from all over the world. Their pay is generous, and so are their benefits and health coverage...

There are about 250 janitors who clean the Bank's office buildings. They, too, come from all over the world—from Ghana, Egypt, Brazil, Jamaica, Sierra Leone, Nigeria, as well as from El Salvador and the United States. Most are women. And, like Flores, many are from countries to which the Bank has made development loans.

Employed by a private cleaning contractor, these janitors are offered only part-time work. Their pay averages about $115 a week, or less than $6,000 a year. This forces some of them to rely on public assistance. An example is Denise Speed, 24. While working as a janitor at the World Bank, Speed had to live in a homeless shelter for several months. Now she lives in an apartment subsidized by the D.C. government and qualifies for food stamps.

The World Bank janitors are overwhelmingly in favor of a campaign for union representation begun in 1988 by SEIU (Service Employees International Union) Local 525 in Washington. (The Bank used to have a unionized cleaning contractor, but changed to a nonunion contractor several years ago.)...[World Bank officials] indicated that, should the cleaning firm sign a union contract with the janitors, the Bank might switch to another cleaning company. In addition to union recognition, the janitors have sought a pay increase to $6.50 an hour, health insurance, paid sick days and holidays...

At one point, eight [prounion] protestors were arrested in a peaceful sit-in demonstration at the Bank building's main entrance. But the janitors and their union haven't given up.

Margie Snider, "Fighting Poverty at the World Bank," in Kevin Danaher, ed., *50 Years is Enough: The Case Against the World Bank and the International Monetary Fund* (1994).

tion (NGO) forums. In their diverse ways, these groups and movements practice solidarity and demonstrate the everyday viability of alternative economic policies and practices. In the United States, there are growing efforts to organize state and national electoral alternatives to the corporatist politics of Republicans and Democrats, and to right-wing pseudo-populism outside and inside the Republican Party.

We have to understand the growing linkage between working conditions and wages in the United States and those abroad. Wages and costs in many Third World countries are kept low by denying workers the right to organize unions, or recognizing only subservient unions. Health and safety regulations are minimal or nonexistent. Repression is widespread. But there is also widespread activism. American workers have a direct stake in supporting better wages and working conditions for Third World workers; otherwise corporations will continue freely trading on cheap labor to transfer jobs and diminish wages and working conditions in the United States.

Calling for a "global new deal," Richard Barnet and John Cavanagh explain: "In the 1930s, as the United States was building a national market that integrated prospering and less developed regions of the United States, the Roosevelt administration established a new set of social standards to soften the destructive side effects of becoming a more integrated nation. For the first time the federal government, prodded by a powerful labor movement, prescribed a minimum wage, maximum hours of work and later a comprehensive set of health, safety and environmental regulations...One purpose in establishing uniform labor standards was to prevent the likely alternative, a spiraling down of wages and working conditions across the nation."[11]

Bills of economic rights have been spelled out before, as in the Roosevelt proposal (1944), the United Nations Declaration of Human Rights (1948) and the International Covenant on Economic, Social and Cultural Rights (1976). They are being elaborated and expanded in many forums today, enriched by antiracist, feminist, indigenous and ecological perspectives, such as Agenda 21, adopted at the 1992 Earth Summit. These alternatives take a variety of shapes, from social and environmental charters to detailed democratic and sustainable development strategies.[12]

What is sustainable development? The United Nations Development Program provides a useful explanation:

> To address the growing challenge of human security, a new development paradigm is needed that puts people at the center of

We have come to a clear realization of the fact that true individual freedom cannot exist without economic security and independence...We have accepted...a second Bill of Rights under which a new basis of security and prosperity can be established for all—regardless of station, race, or creed.

Among these are:

The right to a useful and remunerative job...

The right to earn enough to provide adequate food and clothing and recreation...

The right of every family to a decent home;

The right to adequate medical care and the opportunity to achieve and enjoy good health;

The right to adequate protection from the economic fears of old age, sickness, accident, and unemployment;

The right to a good education.

President Franklin Roosevelt introducing an Economic Bill of Rights, annual message to Congress, 1944.

All human beings are born free and equal in dignity and rights...

Everyone has the right to work...and to protection against unemployment.

Everyone, without any discrimination, has the right to equal pay for equal work.

Everyone who works has the right to just and favorable remuneration ensuring for himself [sic] and his family an existence worthy of human dignity, and supplemented, if necessary, by other means of social protection.

Everyone has the right to form and to join trade unions...

Everyone has the right to rest and leisure, including reasonable limitation of working hours and periodic holidays with pay.

Everyone has the right to a standard of living adequate for the health and well-being of himself and of his family, including food, clothing, housing, and medical care and necessary social services, and the right to security in the event of unemployment, sickness, disability, widowhood, old age, or other lack of livelihood in circumstances beyond his control...

All children, whether born in or out of wedlock, shall enjoy the same social protection...

Everyone is entitled to a social and international order in which the rights and freedoms set forth in this Declaration can be fully realized...

Universal Declaration of Human Rights, adopted by the United Nations General Assembly, 1948.

development, regards economic growth as a means and not an end, protects the life opportunities of future generations as well as the present generations and respects the natural systems on which all life depends...

A major restructuring of the world's income distribution, production and consumption patterns may therefore be a necessary precondition for any viable strategy for sustainable human development.

In the final analysis, sustainable human development is pro-people, pro-jobs and pro-nature. It gives the highest priority to poverty reduction, productive employment, social integration and environmental regeneration...And sustainable human development empowers people—enabling them to design and participate in the processes and events that shape their lives.[13]

KEYS FOR THE FUTURE

We can and must invest in people, the environment and the future. It's time to break the cycle of unequal opportunity. Here are key elements of national and international policies fostering fair and sustainable development.

• *All-Age Social Security.* Societies with no ceiling on the private accumulation of wealth have a special obligation to provide a solid foundation upon which all people may build. Without that foundation, there is nothing remotely approaching "equal opportunity." As Martin Luther King urged, "The time has come for us to civilize ourselves by the total, direct and immediate abolition of poverty." We should set a realistic basic human needs level and assure adequate income to meet it through the tax system and government programs such as universal health care. All-Age Social Security would succeed piecemeal and inadequate income support programs such as AFDC.

• *Fair Taxation and Income Support.* Bring everyone's income up to the basic human needs level with a refundable tax credit (adjusted for number of dependents). Those with incomes below the basic human needs line would get a cash grant to make up the difference, payable in regular installments, whether they are in the paid workforce or not (unlike the Earned Income Tax Credit). For people with incomes above the line, the tax credit would ensure they do not fall below it after taxes; it would serve as a greatly enhanced version of the personal and dependent deductions now in existence. Restore real progressivity to the tax system by increasing the range and number of personal income tax rates, with lower bottom rates and higher top rates, indexed for inflation. The rates would reflect wide-ranging differences in income and wealth. Lower the Social Security tax rate and remove the cap on taxable income. Raise corporate taxes. It's time to stop the pretense that the rich—who hold an oligarchic share of the nation's wealth—are being drained by high taxes.

• *Work Fair and Full Employment.* A decent job at fair pay should be a right, not a privilege. Society can't demand that people work for a living, but deny many a living wage. Today we have the absurd situation of high unemployment at a time when millions of people need work and urgent work needs people—from repairing bridges and building mass transit, to cleaning up pollution and converting to renewable energy, to teaching and staffing after-school programs and community centers, to building and renovating affordable housing and so on. In the words of New Initiatives for Full Employment, "a nation that intones the work ethic has the ethical obligation to provide an opportunity for gainful and productive employment to all."[14] The minimum wage must be raised and must keep pace with the basic human needs level. A global minimum wage must be established to protect livelihoods in a global economy.

• *Shorter Work Hours, Share the Work.* Mandatory overtime should be prohibited and a shorter standard work week of 30 hours should be implemented. In the 1930s, American labor called on the nation to "share the work." The idea of a shorter work week is one whose time has come again. Representative John Conyers of Michigan introduced legislation supporting a 30-hour week in 1979. The 1993 AFL-CIO convention turned renewed attention to the issue of reduced hours. Former Rep. Lucien Blackwell's bill, "The Full Employment Act of 1994," called for a 30-hour week and a large rise in the minimum wage. Numerous companies in the United States and Europe are operating successfully with reduced hours today—sometimes with full pay, sometimes with reduced pay.15 In contrast to European countries, which mandate four to five weeks of vacation each year, the United States mandates no paid vacation and averages a measly nine days. Instead of encouraging the Europeans to follow the U.S. lead and give up their social welfare advances, the United States should learn from them.

• *Workers' Rights* including the right to a livable wage, organize and bargain collectively, strike without fear of permanent replacement workers, occupational health and safety, and the right to participate in workplace decisions. All workers should have the same rights and benefits be they full-time or contingent workers, domestic workers, farm workers or others.

• *Environmentally Sustainable Development.* Instead of "harmonizing" standards to low common denominators in the name of "free trade," high standards would be promoted in the name of health and safety. Localities, states and nations, including indigenous nations, must have the right to establish and enforce tougher regulations on pesticides, toxic waste disposal, etc., than those set internationally. Prohibit the export of toxic and hazardous substances that are banned in the country of origin. "The right of Nations to establish national food and agriculture policies in order to eradicate hunger and ensure food security should be explicitly recognized. There should be no patenting of life forms."[16] National and international aid and financing should encourage, rather than undermine, renewable energy, appropriate technology and organic farming. Democratize or abolish such national and international institutions as the antiworker U.S. Federal Reserve Board, the International Monetary Fund, World Bank, World Trade Organization, etc. End the imposition of "structural adjustment" programs. Write off or reduce Third World debt. It is time to recognize that the "debt" has been more than repaid through colonialism, neocolonialism and usurious interest; funds stolen by dictators should be tracked and recovered. Respect indigenous land, water and other resource rights.

• *Conversion of the Military-Industrial Economy.* Give sustained support for comprehensive conversion of military and environmentally hazardous production to socially responsible uses. Sharply reduce the military budget, aiming at a true bottom-up restructuring such as the "nonoffensive defense" and cooperative security model mentioned earlier. Immediately stop the sale of military and military-related equipment to repressive regimes. Instead of maintaining interventionist militarism with the popular post-Cold War rationale of protecting jobs for American defense workers, everyone should be able to count on an effective system of income support, education and training—be they defense workers, soldiers or teachers, loggers or construction workers, computer assemblers or farm workers.

Robert Pollin explains: "In *Making Peace With the Planet*, Barry Commoner estimated that it would cost $1 trillion—a little more than what the Pentagon spends in three years—to transform the existing production system in the United States. This would entail an epoch-defining reconstruction of our mode of production—the substitution of solar for fossil fuel energy; high performance organic farming for pesticides; and a range of alternatives for most petrochemical products...It says don't lower environmental standards to save jobs; rather, create jobs by investing in the technological transformations that will raise environmental standards."[17]

• *Nonviolent Conflict Resolution.* Make nonviolent conflict resolution part of the core school curriculum at every grade. Support community programs dedicated to peaceful conflict resolution. Strengthen international bodies such as the International Court of Justice (World Court). End the double standard for big powers now undermining international law.

• *Codes of Conduct* mandating social and ecological responsibility. To stop the "downward spiral" of city versus city, state versus state and nation versus nation bidding wars for business, national and global standards should be set and enforced for minimum wages, labor practices, consumer safety, environmental regulation and so on. No corporation should receive tax breaks or other public subsidies without adhering to these standards, such as those already set by the International Labor Organization and the Generalized System of Preferences. Violations should be enforced through civil and criminal penalties. As President Roosevelt declared in a message to Congress on the 1937 Fair Labor Standards Act, the first nationally applicable law setting minimum labor standards and outlawing child labor: "Goods produced under conditions which do not meet a rudimentary standard of decency should be regarded as contraband and ought not to be able to pollute the channels of interstate commerce."[18]

• *Corporate Accountability.* As the Los Angeles-based Labor/Community Strategy Center puts it, "government funds are a public trust, and business cannot receive funds and then operate contrary to broader public interests." In exchange for public subsidies business should accept contractual prohibitions against capital flight. If they violate these agreements, they should repay government funds.[19]

• *Community Investment and Redevelopment.* End all redlining and other discrimination by banks and insurance companies. Strengthen the Community Reinvestment Act and pass counterpart legislation for insurance companies. Support community development banks, credit unions and loan funds. The successful Grameen Bank of Bangladesh, for example, which lends mostly to rural women, rejected the traditional banking approach of "the more you have, the more you can borrow" and affirms instead, "the less you have, the higher your priority."[20] Rechannel pension funds into investments that enhance workers' interests rather than undermine them. Provide incentives for nonprofit and democratically-controlled enterprises such as cooperatives, employee-owned firms, community land trusts, credit unions, etc., including incentives for the international trade of goods and services provided by such enterprises. The focal point of the kind of financial and other assistance typically provided corporations through "free trade zones" or domestic enterprise or "empowerment" zones—in the name of benefiting the community—should be representative community organizations, not corporations and government planners. As innovative and successful organizations like the Dudley Street Neighborhood Initiative of Boston show, there can be no community "empowerment" without organizing and community power. And without community organizing, planning and long-term control, there will be no sustainable, comprehensive community development. [21]

• *Nondiscrimination* on the basis of race, gender, national origin, ethnicity, religion, age, disability, marital status, sexual orientation, immigration status or political beliefs. Strong enforcement of current laws and passage of new ones.

• *Child Caring.* Most parents work outside the home as well as inside it. Government must provide the support necessary to assure affordable, quality child care with decent wages for home- and center-based providers. End the pretense that most mothers are home in the afternoon and make after-school programs a part of every school. The United States is the only industrialized nation except Australia that doesn't provide paid and job-protected maternity leave (varying between 50 and 100 percent of salary and from 6 to 65 weeks), with most countries providing at least 4 months. Some countries provide paternity leave. All should.

• *Universal Health Care.* The rationing of health care by income is obscene. To make matters worse, private insurance companies may deny coverage to those who most need protection because of pre-existing conditions—from cancer to having been battered by a spouse. Many nations have managed to show they care for their people with a single-payer system of universal coverage. The United States should join them.

- *Equal Educational Opportunity* from preschool to college to adult education. End the discriminatory financing of public schools through private property taxes. Schools should be better utilized as community centers for lifelong learning, culture and recreation. Public financing should assure that no one forgoes college for economic reasons. Sabbaticals should be a right of all workers, not just those in academia.

- *Participatory Democracy.* Make the principle of one-person, one-vote meaningful by taking the power of money out of politics. Public financing of local, state and federal campaigns is essential. So are universal voter registration and free media for in-depth debate among candidates and voters. Establish a federal Voting Day holiday to encourage maximum voting turnout and participation. Eliminate the structural biases against independents and third parties.

CHAOS OR COMMUNITY?

It is time to stop scapegoating and start solving our shared problems. Successful communities and nations are greater than the sum of their parts—and not torn apart.

It is a sure sign of impending chaos when children are increasingly seen as the Other, as the Enemy—and not our hope for the future. Our national destiny will reflect our children's destinies. It will reflect their opportunities—and disadvantages. Their successes—and failures. Their dreams—and nightmares. All kids must have fair opportunities to succeed. Second chances can't just be a privilege of the more affluent. It is time to stop building more prison cells and instead build the preventative foundation of income security, child care and education.

It is time to stop building walls between us and start building bridges. It is time to envision our nation as a mutually-beneficial community, not a zero-sum game of winners and losers. Let's take the path of cooperation for mutual progress. Let's take the path of community.

We cannot build communities in economic quicksand. It is time to start using technological advances to free human labor for leisure, family, community and more socially productive work, culture, learning and so on. Technology can help us build real and "virtual communities" within neighborhoods and across local and national boundaries. Or it can destroy real communities while promoting cyberspace communities of people increasingly afraid to leave their homes or gated enclaves.

Without a change in course, the high-tech world will be a high-oppression world. The kind of world envisioned in stories like *1984, Virtual Light* and *Blade Runner.* A world in which some people live in futuristic splendor, and millions live in medieval squalor. A violent world of crumbling cities sprinkled with high-tech gadgets. A world of voice-mail mazes and fewer interactions with real people. A world where children are free to explore their computers, if they have one, but not their neighborhoods. A world where bosses are organized and workers are not. Where corporate executives earn millions and workers struggle to find jobs paying living wages. A world of virtual reality travel and plundered natural wonders. A world in which prisons are the fastest-growing government service. A world of virtual democracy, at best, without real choice, much less accountability. Or an overtly authoritarian world of virulent demagoguery.

Together, we can choose democracy over demagoguery. We can choose community over chaos. The time is now.

NOTES

INTRODUCTION

1. Martin Luther King Jr., *Where Do We Go From Here: Chaos or Community?*, 1967, in James Melvin Washington, ed., *A Testament of Hope: The Essential Writings of Martin Luther King, Jr.* (New York: Harper & Row, 1986), pp. 630-33.

CHAPTER ONE: WEALTH AND POVERTY

1. Kevin Phillips, *The Politics of Rich and Poor: Wealth and the American Electorate in the Reagan Aftermath* (New York: Random House, 1990), p. 10.
2. Sam Roberts, "Gap Between Rich and Poor Widens in New York," *New York Times*, December 24, 1994.
3. Lawrence Mishel and Jared Bernstein, *The State of Working America 1994-95* (Washington, DC: Economic Policy Institute, 1994, press edition), pp. 238-40, 244, 248-49, citing reports by Edward Wolff.
4. *The Forbes Four Hundred Richest People in America,* October 17, 1994.
5. Donald L. Barlett and James B. Steele, America: What Went Wrong (Kansas City: Andrews and McMeel, 1992), p. ix.
6. Editorial, "Executive Pay: It Doesn't Add Up" and "Executive Pay: The Party Ain't Over Yet," *Business Week*, April 26, 1993; "What, Me Overpaid? CEOs Fight Back," *Business Week*, May 4, 1992; Labor Research Association, *The American Labor Yearbook 1993* (New York: Labor Research Association, 1993), p. 35. 1980-93 pay, price and profit comparisons from "CEO Pay Soars," *Solidarity* (UAW), September 1994.
7. "Executive Pay: It Doesn't Add Up," *Business Week.*
8. "That Eye-Popping Executive Pay: Is Anybody Worth This Much?" and editorial, "CEO Pay: A Skyrocket That Could Backfire," *Business Week*, April 25, 1994.
9. "That Eye-Popping Executive Pay," *Business Week.*
10. Graef S. Crystal, *In Search of Excess: The Overcompensation of American Executives* (New York: W.W. Norton, 1992), pp. 23, 213.
11. Arloc Sherman, *Wasting America's Future: The Children's Defense Fund Report on the Costs of Child Poverty* (Boston: Beacon Press, 1994), pp. 6, 8.
12. Children's Defense Fund and Northeastern University's Center for Labor Market Studies, *Vanishing Dreams: The Economic Plight of America's Young Families* (Washington, DC: Children's Defense Fund, 1992), p. 22; Clifford M. Johnson, et al., *Child Poverty in America* (Children's Defense Fund, 1991), pp. 13-15, 25.
13. U.S. Bureau of the Census (hereafter Census Bureau), *Studies in Household and Family Formation: When Households Continue, Discontinue, and Form* (1992), pp. 29-30.

14. John E. Schwarz and Thomas J. Volgy, *The Forgotten Americans: Thirty Million Working Poor in the Land of Opportunity* (New York: W.W. Norton, 1992), pp. 38-46, 61-62 and "Above the Line—But Poor," *The Nation*, February 15, 1993. Also see, Census Bureau, *Money Income of Households, Families, and Persons in the United States: 1991.* Patricia Ruggles likewise concluded that the 1990 poverty line would have had to rise by over $6,000 to a level of $16,685 for a family of three just to match the original poverty formula. Patricia Ruggles, *Drawing the Line: Alternative Poverty Measures and their Implications for Public Policy* (Washington, DC: Urban Institute Press, 1990), presented in Tim Wise, "Being Poor Isn't Enough," *Dollars & Sense*, September 1990. Child care figure from Children's Defense Fund, *The State of America's Children 1992*, p. 19 and other sources. Low-rent units/low-income renters figures from Center on Budget and Policy Priorities, *Funding for Low-Income Programs in FY 1994*, p. 6. HUD considers housing affordable if it costs no more than 30 percent of household income, but it is often not available. In a study of 44 major metropolitan areas for 1989, affordable housing was so scarce that four out of five poor renters spent more than 30 percent of their income on housing costs (rent and utilities) and more than one out of two spent at least half their income on housing. More than two out of three poor homeowners spent more than 30 percent and 43 percent spent more than half their incomes on housing. Two-thirds of poor people are renters, one-third are homeowners, many of them elderly. Paul A. Leonard and Edward B. Lazere, *A Place To Call Home: The Low Income Housing Crisis In 44 Major Metropolitan Areas* (Washington, DC: Center on Budget and Policy Priorities, November 1992), pp. 1, 5-8.

15. Sherman, *Wasting America's Future*, p. 5.

16. Household assistance figures from Census Bureau, *Poverty in the United States: 1992* (1993), pp. xvii-xviii, Tables F and G, and "Health Insurance Coverage—1993," *Statistical Brief*, October 1994.

17. For female-headed families with children living at 125 to 150 percent of the official poverty line, the average 1989 amount of in-kind income received in food stamps and housing assistance was $312. For male-present families with children, the average amount was $170. Schwarz and Volgy, *The Forgotten Americans*, fn. 14, pp. 178-79.

18. Campaign For An Effective Crime Policy, *Evaluating Mandatory Minimum Sentences* (Washington, DC: October 1993), p. 5, citing National Conference of State Legislatures, "State Budget and Tax Actions 1993," *City & State*, August 16, 1993.

19. Isaac Shapiro and Robert Greenstein, *Selective Prosperity: Increasing Income Dispari-ties Since 1977* (Center on Budget and Policy Priorities, July 1991), pp. 22-23, citing the Luxembourg Income Study of the U.S., Australia, Britain, Canada, Germany, Israel, the Netherlands, Norway, Sweden and Switzerland. Also see Mishel and Bernstein, *The State of Working America 1994-95*, pp. 308-19.

20. Latino infant mortality rates are higher than for non-Latino Whites and lower than for Blacks. The Black-White infant mortality gap is growing. Reuters, "Baby deaths for blacks 2.5 times white rate," *Boston Globe*, December 10, 1993; Children's Defense Fund, *Decade of Indifference: Maternal and Child Health Trends* (March 1993 press edition), pp. 7-8, Tables B and C, Table 22 and Joseph Tiang-Yau Liu, et al., *The Health of America's Children 1992* (Children's Defense Fund, 1992), pp. 12-13.

CHAPTER TWO: BREAKDOWN OF THE PAYCHECK

1. Steven Rattner, "Volcker Asserts U.S. Must Trim Living Standards," *New York Times*, October 18, 1979.

2. Mishel and Bernstein, *The State of Working America 1994-95,* pp. 71-74, 188-91. Also see "Spiraling down: The fall of real wages," *Dollars & Sense*, April 1992.

3. Children's Defense Fund, *Vanishing Dreams*, pp. 2-3, 10-17, 23, Tables in Appendix.

4. Mishel and Bernstein, *The State of Working America 1994-95*, pp. 108-13, 137.

5. Jeremy Rifkin, *The End of Work* (New York: Jeremy P. Tarcher/Putnam, 1995), p. 91.

6. "The Real Truth About the Economy," *Business Week*, November 7, 1994, pp. 113, 116.

7. Myron Magnet, "The Productivity Payoff Arrives," *Fortune*, June 27, 1994.

8. Jaclyn Fierman, "When Will You Get a Raise?" *Fortune*, July 12, 1993.

9. Ibid.

10. "That Eye-Popping Executive Pay," *Business Week*, April 25, 1994, p. 53.

11. Fierman, "When Will You Get a Raise?"

12. Census Bureau, "The Earnings Ladder: Who's at the Bottom? Who's at the Top?" *Statistical Brief*, March 1994. Also see Census Bureau, *Workers With Low Earnings: 1964 to 1990* (1992) and *Trends in Relative Income: 1964 to 1989* (1991).

13. Richard B. Freeman and Lawrence F. Katz, "Rising Wage Inequality: The United States VS. Other Advanced Countries," in Richard Freeman, ed., *Working Under Different Rules* (New York: Russell Sage Foundation, 1994), p. 30.

14. William E. Spriggs and Bruce W. Klein, *Raising the Floor: The Effects of the Minimum Wage on Low-Wage Workers* (Economic Policy Institute, 1994), pp. 1-4. Data also from Mishel and Bernstein, *The State of Working America 1994-95*, pp. 169-71 and Robert A. Rankin, Knight-Ridder Service, *Boston Globe*, "Clinton calls for minimum wage boost," February 4, 1995.

15. Mishel and Bernstein, *The State of Working America 1994-95*, pp. 14-16, 141, 191-95. Also see Lawrence Mishel and Jared Bernstein, "Declining Wages For High School AND College Graduates: Pay and Benefits Trends by Education, Gender, Occupation, and State, 1979-1991," Economic Policy Institute, *Briefing Paper*, May 1992 and Lawrence Mishel and Ruy A. Teixeira, *The Myth of the Coming Labor Shortage: Jobs, Skills, and Incomes of America's Workforce 2000* (Economic Policy Institute, 1991).

16. Mishel and Bernstein, *The State of Working America 1994-95*, p. 198.

17. John Greenwald, "Bellboys with B.A.s," *Time*, November 22, 1993, p. 36, sidebar to George Church, "Jobs in an Age of Insecurity."

18. John B. Judis, "Why Your Wages Keep Falling," *The New Republic*, February 14, 1994.

19. Ibid.

20. "The New World of Work," *Business Week*, October 17, 1994, p. 87.

21. U.S. Department of Labor, Bureau of Labor Statistics, *Employment and Earnings*, January 1995, Table 41, p. 215.

22. Quote from Labor Research Association, *American Labor Yearbook 1993*, p. 4; Mishel and Bernstein, *The State of Working America 1994-95,* p. 168.

23. Labor Research Association, *American Labor Yearbook 1993*, p. 6.

24. "Why America Needs Unions But Not The Kind It Has Now," *Business Week,* May 23, 1994, p. 78.

25. Labor Research Association, *American Labor Yearbook 1993,* p. 12.

26. George Will, "The Porcelain Presidency," *Newsweek,* July 25, 1994.

27. Bureau of Labor Statistics, *Employment and Earnings,* January 1995, Table 40, p. 214; *The World Almanac and Book of Facts 1993,* "U.S. Union Membership, 1930-1991," p. 160.

28. Labor Research Association, *American Labor Yearbook 1993,* p. 16.

29. "Why America Needs Unions But Not The Kind It Has Now," *Business Week,* pp. 70-71.

30. Commission on the Future of Worker-Management Relations, *Fact Finding Report* (U.S. Department of Labor/U.S. Department of Commerce: May 1994), p. 19. Also see *The OECD Jobs Study: Facts, Analysis, Strategies* (Paris/Washington, DC: Organization for Economic Cooperation and Development, 1994), pp. 22-23.

31. Labor Research Association, *American Labor Yearbook 1993,* p. 44.

32. "The New World of Work," *Business Week,* pp. 76-77.

33. Lance Morrow, "The Temping of America," *Time,* March 29, 1993, pp. 40-41.

34. Labor Research Association, *American Labor Yearbook 1993,* p. 35.

35. See, for example, U.S. General Accounting Office (GAO), *Workers At Risk: Increased Numbers in Contingent Employment Lack Insurance, Other Benefits* (March 1991); Janice Castro, "Disposable Workers," *Time,* March 29, 1993; S. C. Gwynne, "The Long Haul," *Time,* September 28, 1992; Bruce D. Butterfield, "'Leasing' employees: a growing discount service," *Boston Globe,* March 21, 1993; Camille Colatosi, "A Job without a Future," *Dollars & Sense,* May 1992; Peter T. Kilborn, "A Disrupting Change Hits Workers After Recession," *New York Times,* December 26, 1992.

    The definition of "contingent work" has varied and so has the counting. See, for example, Anne E. Polivka and Thomas Nardone, "On the Definition of 'Contingent Work,'" *Monthly Labor Review,* December 1989 and Ann Crittenden, "Temporary Solutions," *Working Woman,* February 1994. Polivka and Nardone, economists with the Bureau of Labor Statistics, proposed this definition of contingent work: "Any job in which an individual does not have an explicit or implicit contract for long-term employment or one in which the minimum hours worked can vary in a nonsystematic manner."

36. "Business gives in to temptation," *U.S. News & World Report,* July 4, 1994. Also see "The new migrant workers," in the same issue.

37. Lawrence Mishel and Jared Bernstein, "The Joyless Recovery: Deteriorating Wages and Job Quality in the 1990s," Economic Policy Institute, *Briefing Paper,* September 1993, pp. 2, 15-16, 20. Figures for 1979-89 from Mishel and Bernstein, *The State of Working America 1994-95,* pp. 151-55, 220-21.

38. Gary Blonston, "Workers' Role in '90s Efficiency," *Philadelphia Inquirer,* August 8, 1993.

39. Kenneth C. Crowe, *Newsday,* "Full-Time Workers Vs. the Part-Timers: A New Battleground," *Philadelphia Inquirer,* June 1, 1994. Also see U.S. Department of Labor, *Issues in Labor Statistics,* "Part-time Work: A Choice or A Response," October 1994.

40. United Nations Development Program (UNDP), *Human Development Report 1994* (New York: Oxford University Press, 1994), p. 25. Some data from United Nations

Department of Economic and Social Information and Policy Analysis, *World Economic and Social Survey 1994* (New York: United Nations, 1994), Table VI.6, p. 170.

41. Reuters, "China Set to Be World's Top Investment Destination," October 26, 1994.

42. Mishel and Bernstein, *The State of Working America 1994-95*, pp. 221-23; Bruce D. Butterfield, "Diminished jobs, added worry," *Boston Globe*, March 21, 1993 and "When work is stripped to the bone," January 17, 1993.

43. Janet Novack, "Is lean, mean?" *Forbes*, August 15, 1994.

44. Castro, "Disposable Workers," pp. 43-47.

45. Jaclyn Fierman, "The Contingency Work Force," *Fortune*, January 24, 1994.

46. Tannette Johnson-Elie, "Workers of Future Must Be Flexible, Temp Agency Executive Says," *The Milwaukee Sentinel*, November 3, 1994.

47. Interview by Sherri Eng, "How Changing Landscape Affects Today's Worker," *San Jose Mercury News*, October 31, 1994.

48. Guy Gugliotta, "The Minimum Wage Culture," *Washington Post Weekly*, October 3-9, 1994.

CHAPTER THREE: COMPETING FOR GLOBAL CORPORATIONS

1. *Left Business Observer*, No. 61, December 13, 1993.

2. On global corporate strategies and long-term planning, see Holly Sklar, ed., *Trilateralism: The Trilateral Commission and Elite Planning for World Management* (Boston: South End Press, 1980).

3. John A. Garraty and Peter Gay, eds., *The Columbia History of the World* (New York: Harper & Row, 1972/Dorset Press edition, 1983), p. 624.

4. George Ball, "Cosmocorp: The Importance of Being Stateless," *Columbia Journal of World Business* 2:6 (November-December 1967), pp. 26, 28.

5. Major General Smedley D. Butler, "America's Armed Forces," Part 1, "Military Boondoggling," *Common Sense*, October 1935, pp. 6, 7, 10. Butler, Part 2, "'In Time of Peace': The Army," p. 8.

6. Quote from Richard J. Barnet and John Cavanagh, *Global Dreams: Imperial Corporations and the New World Order* (New York: Simon & Schuster, 1994), p. 275. Also see *Left Business Observer*, No. 61, December 13, 1993. Figure on 70 percent of world trade from UNDP, *Human Development Report 1994*, p. 87.

7. United Nations Conference on Trade and Development (UNCTAD), Division on Transnational Corporations and Investment, *World Investment Report 1994: Transnational Corporations, Employment and the Workplace* (New York: United Nations, 1994), p. xxi.

8. Ibid., Tables I.1 and I.2, Box I.1.

9. "Business Rolls the Dice," *Business Week*, October 17, 1994, p. 90.

10. Reuters, "China Set to Be World's Top Investment Destination."

11. UNCTAD, *World Investment Report 1994*, pp. 26, 68.

12. Bennett Harrison, *Lean and Mean: The Changing Landscape of Corporate Power in the Age of Flexibility* (New York: Basic Books, 1994), pp. 8-12, 20, 47; chapter 6.

13. Ibid., pp. 206-07.

14. Quotes from Frederic M. Biddle and Josh Hyatt, "City, state at odds on Stride Rite plan," *Boston Globe*, December 19, 1992. Roxbury figure from Diane E. Lewis, "Rebuild Roxbury," *Boston Globe*, March 30, 1993, citing Boston Redevelopment Authority.

15. Lois Marie Gibbs and Pamela K. Stone, "Corporate Tax Breaks: The Real Welfare Scam," in *Everyone's Backyard* (Center for Environmental Justice, Citizens Clearinghouse for Hazardous Waste: 1992), p. 3. Cited in Eva Gladstein, "Livelihoods in Jeopardy," American Friends Service Committee working paper, Philadelphia, 1994.

16. Robert Goodman, *The Last Entrepreneurs: America's Regional Wars for Jobs and Dollars* (Boston: South End Press, 1982), p. 4.

17. Rebecca Smith and Thomas Farragher, "Why California Lost in Bid for Intel Plant," *San Jose Mercury News*, April 4, 1993.

18. Joseph Pereira, "Split Personality: Social Responsibility and Need for Low Cost Clash at Stride Rite," *Wall Street Journal*, May 28, 1993; Tolle Graham, "Plant Closings in Boston," *The Labor Page* (City Life, Boston), March-April 1993.

19. Steve Bailey, "Kentucky Blues," *Boston Globe*, September 27, 1994 and editorial, "Stride Rite's footprints," *Boston Globe*, September 29, 1994.

20. Laurie Udesky, "The 'Social Responsibility' Gap: Sweatshops Behind the Labels," *The Nation*, May 16, 1994. Also see letters exchange, August 8/15, 1994.

21. "Europe: The Push East," *Business Week*, November 7, 1994, p. 48.

22. Charles T. Jones, "Temp Worker Agencies See Need for Better-Prepared U.S. Workforce," *The Daily Oklahoman*, October 31, 1994.

23. "High-Tech Jobs All Over the Map," *Business Week/21st Century Capitalism*, Special 1994 Bonus Issue, p. 113.

24. Paul Lima, *Computer Dealer News* (Canada), June 1, 1994.

25. Edward A. Gargan, "India Among the Leaders In Software for Computers," *New York Times*, December 29, 1993.

26. "The Mexican Worker: Smart, Motivated, Cheap," *Business Week*, April 19, 1993. Also see Harley Shaiken, "Advanced Manufacturing and Mexico: A New International Division of Labor?" *Latin American Research Review* 29:2, 1994.

27. Richard J. Barnet and John Cavanagh, "A Global New Deal," in John Cavanagh, Daphne Wysham and Marcos Arruda, eds., *Beyond Bretton Woods: Alternatives to the Global Economic Order* (Boulder, CO: Pluto Press/Institute for Policy Studies and Transnational Institute, 1994), p. 179.

28. Richard Rothstein, "Who Will Buy?" *CEO/International Strategies*, December 1993/January 1994, p. 24.

29. See Annette Fuentes and Barbara Ehrenreich, *Women in the Global Factory* (Boston: South End Press, 1983) and Rachel Kamel, *The Global Factory* (Philadelphia: American Friends Service Committee, 1990).

30. UNCTAD, *World Investment Report 1994*, p. 191.

31. Charles Kernaghan, The National Labor Committee in Support of Worker and Human Rights in Central America, *Paying to Lose Our Jobs* (New York: September 1992), pp. 54-55.

32. Charles Kernaghan, The National Labor Committee in Support of Worker and Human Rights in Central America, *Free Trade's Hidden Secrets: Why We Are Losing Our Shirts* (New York: November 1993), pp. 1-2, Appendix 1.

33. Ted Plafker, "Brown, in China, stresses trade over rights," *Boston Globe*, August 30, 1994.

34. See, for example, Steve Askin and Carole Collins, "Kick-backs and kleptocracy" and Steve Askin, "Odious debts," *The New Internationalist*, September 1994, an issue devoted to global robber barons.

35. GAO, *U.S. Has Made Slow Progress in Involving Women in Development*, December 1993, pp. 61-62, citing, for example, Ron Hood, et al., *Gender and Adjustment*, the Mayatech Corporation, prepared for the Bureau of Research and Development, Agency for International Development, October 1992.

36. United Nations Children's Fund (UNICEF), *The State of the World's Children 1989*, p. 15. Also see UNICEF, *The State of the World's Children 1994*, pp. 50-51.

37. Linda Gray MacKay, "World Bank and IMF have failed, and the poor pay the price," *Boston Globe*, July 14, 1994.

38. ILO estimate in Anna Quindlen, "Out of the Hands of Babes," *New York Times*, November 23, 1994.

39. See, for example, "A Child's Crusade Against Sweater Sweatshops," *Solidarity* (UAW), November 1994 and "Lesly Goes Back to School; Honduran Workers Win a Union," *Solidarity*, January-February 1995. These articles tell the story of Honduran teenager Lesly Rodriguez, who is organizing against the exploitation of child labor with the support of the UAW and the National Labor Committee in Support of Worker and Human Rights in Central America.

40. Rothstein, "Who Will Buy?" p. 25.

41. Harrison, *Lean and Mean*, p. 205.

CHAPTER FOUR: FULL OF UNEMPLOYMENT

1. Quoted in Jacqueline Jones, *The Dispossessed: America's Underclasses from the Civil War to the Present* (New York: Basic Books, 1992), p. 289.

2. Census Bureau, *Statistical Abstract of the United States 1993* (hereafter *Statistical Abstract* with year), Tables 625, 629, 635; Bureau of Labor Statistics, *Employment and Earnings*, January 1995, Table 1, p. 162.

3. Edward S. Herman, "The Natural Rate of Unemployment," *Z Magazine*, November 1994, p. 64.

4. Hobart Rowen, "Alan Blinder as Inflation Hawk," *Washington Post*, December 1, 1994.

5. Max B. Sawicky, *Up From Deficit Reduction* (Economic Policy Institute, 1994), p. 56.

6. Labor Research Association, *American Labor Yearbook 1993*, p. 35.

7. "Hats Off! It was a Heck of a Year," *Fortune*, April 18, 1994, pp. 210-13. Part of the annual special issue on the *Fortune* 500 largest U.S. industrial corporations.

8. "Hot Damn! They Did It Again" and "What's Making Those Margins So Fat?" *Business Week*, November 14, 1994.

9. American Management Association, *1994 AMA Survey on Downsizing and Assistance to Displaced Workers* (New York: 1994), p. 7 and "Summary of Key Findings," p. 4. Also see B. J. Phillips, "The addiction of the layoff," *Philadelphia Inquirer*, January 7, 1994.

10. "The New World of Work," *Business Week*, p. 85.

11. Ibid.

12. David Bacon, "Another Sellout of the Workers? Labor Law 'Reform,'" *The Nation*, May 30, 1994.

13. Judis, "Why Your Wages Keep Falling."

14. Blonston, "Workers' Role in '90s Efficiency."

15. American Management Association, *1994 AMA Survey on Downsizing and Assistance to Displaced Workers*, p. 5.

16. Juliet Schor, "A Sustainable Economy for the Twenty-First Century," paper prepared for the New Party, July 1994. Also see Schor, *The Overworked American: The Unexpected Decline of Leisure* (New York: Basic Books, 1991).

17. Adam Levy, "Overtime Wearing Thin Across the U.S. Production is Up, Employment Isn't," *Philadelphia Inquirer*, October 4, 1994.

18. Andy Neather and Dave Elsila, "The LONGEST Day: Excessive Overtime is Taking Its Toll," *Solidarity* (UAW), November 1994, p. 10

19. Press Briefing by Secretary of Labor Robert Reich and Assistant to the President for Economic Policy Bob Rubin, November 4, 1994; address by President Clinton to the National Association of Realtors convention, Anaheim, California, November 5, 1994.

20. Levy, "Overtime Wearing Thin Across the U.S." Also see George J. Church, "We're #1 And It Hurts," *Time*, October 24, 1994.

21. Andy Neather, "UAW Wins: New Hires at GM," *Solidarity* (UAW), November 1994.

22. "The New World of Work," *Business Week*, p. 84.

23. "The Real Truth About the Economy," *Business Week*, November 7, 1994, pp. 110-11.

24. David Dembo and Ward Morehouse, *The Underbelly of the U.S. Economy: Joblessness and the Pauperization of Work in America* (New York: Council on International and Public Affairs, 1994), pp. 7-17, 41-46. Also see *Statistical Abstract 1993*, Table 657.

25. Jane Sasseen et al., "Europe's Job Crunch," *International Management*, December 1993.

26. Robert D. Hershey Jr., "Jobless Rate Underestimated, U.S. Says, Citing Survey Bias," *New York Times*, November 17, 1993. While useful for reporting the gender bias, this article misrepresents the impact of redefining the discouraged worker category.

27. Data from U.S. House of Representatives, Committee on Ways and Means, *1994 Green Book: Overview of Entitlement Programs*, July 1994, p. 1096. Hereafter *Green Book* with year. Quote from Mishel and Bernstein, *The State of Working America 1994-95*, p. 202.

28. Patricia Kirkpatrick, "Triple Jeopardy: Disability, Race and Poverty in America," *Poverty & Race*, Poverty & Race Research Action Council, Washington, DC, May/June 1994. Also see Chicago Tribune, "Joblessness is on the Rise among Disabled," *San Jose Mercury News*, January 29, 1995.

29. John M. McNeil, *Americans With Disabilities: 1991-92* (Census Bureau, December 1993), p. 12 and Table 24.

30. *1994 Green Book*, p. 1102. GAO, *Unemployment Insurance: Program's Ability to Meet Objectives Jeopardized*, September 1993. Only one out of three of the official unemployed received benefits on average from 1984 to 1989; the figure rose to 42 percent in 1991 and 52 percent in 1992, still much less than the 76 percent who received benefits during the 1975 recession. The figure dropped to 48 percent in 1993. Isaac Shapiro and Marion Nichols, *Far From Fixed: An Analysis of the Unemployment Insurance System* (Center on Budget and Policy Priorities, March 1992), pp. 1-7, 16; *1994 Green Book*, pp. 266-67, 1102; *1993 Green Book*, pp. 490-523.

31. Shapiro and Nichols, *Far From Fixed*, p. 25. Also see Iris J. Lav, et al., *The States and the Poor: How Budget Decisions Affected Low Income People in 1992* (Washington, DC: Center on Budget and Policy Priorities and Albany, NY: Center for the Study of the States, 1993).

32. "The New World of Work," *Business Week*, p. 80.

33. Martin Khor, "Worldwide unemployment will reach crisis proportions, says social expert," Third World Network, *Briefings for the Social Summit*, No. 9, August 1994.

34. Rifkin, *The End of Work*, p. 109.

35. Jeremy Rifkin, "Dangers in Pinning Our Hopes on Trickle Down Technology," *USA Today Magazine*, May 1994.

36. Rifkin, *The End of Work*, p. 84.

37. Ibid., pp. 25-29.

38. Schor, *The Overworked American*, pp. 154-55.

39. Rifkin, *The End of Work*, pp. 85-86. Rifkin cites, for example, David Noble, *Forces of Production: A Social History of Industrial Automation* (New York: Alfred A. Knopf, 1984).

40. Rifkin, *The End of Work*, pp. 81-82.

41. Ibid., p. 261.

42. Gretchen Morgenson, "The Fall of the Mall," *Forbes*, May 24, 1993.

43. Kristin Downey Grimsley, "Where Have All the Salespeople Gone? Survey Shows Number of Retail Stores Growing in Area, but Employees Declining," *Washington Post*, November 26, 1994.

44. Sara Silver, Associated Press, "A Year After Free Trade Treaty, No Job Boom for Mexicans," December 17, 1994.

45. Paul Lima, *Computer Dealer News* (Canada), June 1, 1994.

46. Rifkin, *The End of Work*, p. 78.

CHAPTER FIVE: THE SNAKE OIL OF SCAPEGOATING

1. Children's Defense Fund, *Vanishing Dreams*, p. 10.

2. Schwarz and Volgy, *The Forgotten Americans*, p. 11.

3. "Compassion's Short Supply," *Boston Globe* editorial, September 21, 1990 and "Birth in the 'Death Zones,'" September 10, 1990.

4. Jon Meacham, "Down and Out," *The Washington Monthly*, November 1993, p. 26.

5. Mead quoted in Richard A. Cloward and Frances Fox Piven, "The Fraud of Workfare," *The Nation*, May 24, 1993. Mishel and Bernstein, *The State of Working America 1994-95*, pp. 272, 277-93.

6. Mike Davis, "Who Killed L.A.?: The War Against the Cities," *Crossroads*, June 1993, p. 8.

7. Herbert Gans, "Deconstructing the Underclass," in Paula S. Rothenberg, ed., *Race, Class, and Gender in the United States: An Integrated Study*, 3rd edition (New York: St. Martin's Press, 1995), pp. 51-52.

8. Lynne Duke, "But Some of My Best Friends Are...," *Washington Post Weekly*, January 14-20, 1991.

9. Ruth Hubbard and Elijah Wald, *Exploding the Gene Myth* (Boston: Beacon Press, 1993), p. 14.

10. Ibid., p. 16.

11. Ibid., p. 21.

12. Ibid., pp. 21, 25, also citing Helen Rodriguez-Trias, "Sterilization Abuse," in Ruth Hubbard, Mary Sue Henifin and Barbara Fried, eds., *Biological Woman—The Convenient Myth* (Cambridge, MA: Schenkman Publishing Co., 1982), p. 149.

13. Hubbard and Wald, *Exploding the Gene Myth,* pp. 17-18.

14. Michael Lind, "Brave New Right," The New Republic, October 31, 1994, p. 24. Also see *Business Week*, "Behind *The Bell Curve*: The Pioneer Fund backs even more racist-rousing research," November 7, 1994, p. 36.

15. Quote from Scott Anderson and Jon Lee Anderson, *Inside the League* (New York: Dodd, Meade & Co., 1986), pp. 92-103. Also see Holly Sklar, *Washington's War on Nicaragua* (Boston: South End Press, 1988), pp. 78-79.

16. Adam Miller, "Professors of Hate," *Rolling Stone,* October 20, 1994.

17. FAIR (Fairness & Accuracy in Reporting), "Questions About Source in Immigration Debate: Group Has Links to Racist Fund," press advisory, September 8, 1994; Lind, "Brave New Right," p. 24.

18. Lisa Duran, Bill Gallegos, Eric Mann and Glenn Omastu, *Immigrant Rights and Wrongs* (Los Angeles: The Labor/Community Strategy Center, 1994).

19. David Cole, "The New Know-Nothingism: Five Myths About Immigration," *The Nation*, October 17, 1994, citing a 1994 report by the Urban Institute and studies cited by the 1994 ACLU Immigrants' Rights Project report. See Elizabeth Kadetsky, "'Save Our State' Initiative: Bashing Illegals in California"; Leslie Marmon Silko, "America's Iron Curtain: The Border Patrol State"; and Peter Kwong, "Wake of the Golden Venture: China's Human Traffickers," in the same issue of *The Nation*. Also see Ashley Dunn, "Greeted at Nation's Front Door, Many Visitors Stay on Illegally," *New York Times*, January 3, 1995.

20. Margot Hornblower, "Hot Lines and Hot Tempers," *Time*, November 28, 1994, p. 36.

21. Stephen Jay Gould, "Curveball," *The New Yorker*, November 28, 1994, p. 139.

22. Paul Hoffman, "The Science of Race," *Discover*, November 1994. Also see, for example, articles by Stephen Jay Gould, Jared Diamond and James Shreeve in the same issue.

23. Lawrence Wright, "One Drop of Blood," *The New Yorker*, July 25, 1994, p. 53.

24. Charles Murray and Richard J. Herrnstein, "Race, Genes and I.Q.—An Apologia," *The New Republic*, October 31, 1994, p. 37. On the "Wise Use" movement, see, for example, David Helvarg, "The War on Greens: Anti-Enviros Are Getting Uglier," *The Nation*, November 28, 1994; William Kevin Burke, "The Wise Use Movement: Right-Wing Anti-Environmentalism," *The Public Eye* (Political Research Associates), June 1993 and Political Research Associates, "Corporate Roots of Attacks on the Environmental Movement," resource packet, Cambridge, MA.

25. John Carey, "Clever Arguments, Atrocious Science," *Business Week*, November 7, 1994, pp. 16, 18.

26. Hubbard and Wald, *Exploding the Gene Myth*, p. 129.

27. Richard Lacayo, "For Whom the Bell Curves," *Time*, October 24, 1994, p. 67.

28. Book jacket for Richard J. Herrnstein and Charles Murray, *The Bell Curve: Intelligence and Class Structure in American Life* (New York: The Free Press, 1994).

29. "The White Underclass: Does the rise in out-of-wedlock babies and white slums foretell a social catastrophe?" *U.S. News & World Report*, October 17, 1994; Brian McGrory, "Sharp rise in births to unmarried whites stirs welfare worries," *Boston Globe*, January 3, 1994.

30. Jason DeParle, "Daring Research or 'Social Science Pornography?'" *New York Times Magazine*, October 9, 1994.

31. Quoted by Henry Louis Gates Jr., "Why Now?" *The New Republic*, October 31, 1994, p. 10.

32. Thomas H. O'Connor, "A city of 'foreigners': then and now," *Boston Globe*, January 24, 1993; Oscar Handlin, *Boston's Immigrants: 1790-1880* (Belknap/Harvard University Press, 1991 revised ed.), pp. 43-48, 52, 117-23, 261, 332, fn. 87. On the Massachusetts registry, see Dolores Kong, "Vital records speak volumes on tougher times," *Boston Globe*, December 27, 1992.

33. Carey, "Clever Arguments, Atrocious Science," p. 16.

34. Black per capita income was 59 percent of White income in 1993; Latino income was 53 percent of White income. Census Bureau, *Income, Poverty, and Valuation of Noncash Benefits: 1993*, prepublication press excerpts (October 1994).

35. Coramae Richey Mann, *Unequal Justice: A Question of Color* (Bloomington, IN: Indiana University Press, 1993), pp. 222, 251-54; Manning Marable, *How Capitalism Underdeveloped Black America* (Boston: South End Press, 1983), pp. 109-123; W. E. B. Du Bois, "The Black Codes," in Rothenberg, ed., *Race, Class, and Gender in the United States*.

36. Robert C. Hayden, "An Historical Overview of Poverty Among Blacks in Boston: 1850-1990," in James Jennings, ed., *Perspectives on Poverty in Boston's Black Community* (The Boston Persistent Poverty Project, The Boston Foundation, February 1992), pp. 5, 7-11.

37. Mimi Abramovitz, *Regulating the Lives of Women: Social Welfare Policy From Colonial Times to the Present* (Boston: South End Press, 1988), pp. 233-35, 249-60, 292-304, 368-76.

38. Jill Quadagno, *The Color of Welfare: How Racism Undermined the War on Poverty* (New York: Oxford University Press, 1994), pp. 20-22, 24.

39. See Peter Medoff and Holly Sklar, *Streets of Hope: The Fall and Rise of an Urban Neighborhood* (Boston: South End Press, 1994).

40. Gregory D. Squires, "Community Reinvestment: An Emerging Social Movement," in Squires, ed., *From Redlining to Reinvestment: Community Responses to Urban Disinvestment* (Philadelphia: Temple University Press, 1992), p. 5.

41. Dennis R. Judd, "Segregation Forever?" *The Nation*, December 9, 1991.

42. Ibid.

43. Hillel Levine and Lawrence Harmon, *The Death of An American Jewish Community: A Tragedy of Good Intentions* (New York: Free Press, 1992), p. 167, citing "Building the American City," report of the National Commission on Urban Problems, December 1968, pp. 100-102.

44. Charles Finn, *Mortgage Lending in Boston's Neighborhoods 1981-1987*, study commissioned by the Boston Redevelopment Authority (University of Minnesota: Hubert H. Humphrey Institute of Public Affairs, December 1989), p. 1.

45. Ibid., pp. 9-10.

46. Alicia H. Munnell, et al., *Mortgage Lending in Boston: Interpreting HMDA Data*, Working Paper No. 92-7, Federal Reserve Bank of Boston, October 1992, pp. 1, 3. A subsequent report by other investigators not only confirmed the Federal Reserve report findings, it found that the data supported an even stronger case of discrimination. James H. Carr and Isaac F. Megbolugbe, "The Federal Reserve Bank of Boston Study on Mortgage Lending Revisited," *Fannie Mae Working Paper*, Fannie Mae Office of Housing Research, Washington, DC, 1993. Also see "Your Loan is Denied," *Frontline*, WGBH-TV, Boston, June 23, 1992.

47. Rep. Joseph P. Kennedy II, chairman, House Banking Subcommittee on Consumer Credit and Insurance, Statement at Hearing on Insurance Redlining, February 24, 1993; also see testimony by Rev. Charles Cummings Jr., treasurer, Washington, DC chapter of ACORN and by Professor Gregory D. Squires. Also see Kimberly Blanton, "Nice home, WRONG BLOCK," *Boston Globe*, March 23, 1993, which looked at insurance redlining of the Roxbury, Dorchester and Mattapan neighborhoods of Boston.

48. William W. Goldsmith and Edward J. Blakely, *Separate Societies: Poverty and Inequality in U.S. Cities* (Philadelphia: Temple University Press, 1992), pp. 119-22; Census Bureau, *The Black Population in the United States: March 1991*, Table 3.

49. Richard Lacayo, "This Land is Your Land," *Time*, May 18, 1992, p. 3.

50. The HUD statistic is 59 percent. Penda D. Hair, "Civil Rights," in Citizens Transition Project, Mark Green, ed., *Changing America: Blueprints for the New Administration* (New York: Newmarket Press, 1992), pp. 341-42.

51. Author's conversation with Mimi Abramovitz, December 23, 1992.

52. Patricia Hill Collins, *Black Feminist Thought* (New York: Routledge, 1991), pp. 70-75. Also see Jewell Handy Gresham and Margaret B. Wilkerson, eds., *The Nation* special issue, "Scapegoating the Black Family: Black Women Speak," July 24/31, 1989.

53. Susan Faludi, *Backlash: The Undeclared War Against American Women* (New York: Crown, 1991), pp. 51-52.

54. Stephanie Coontz, *The Way We Never Were: American Families and the Nostalgia Trap* (New York: Basic, 1993), pp. 32, 35.

55. Faludi, *Backlash*, pp. 53-54.

56. Abramovitz, *Regulating the Lives of Women*, p. 335.

57. Collins, *Black Feminist Thought*, pp. 76-77.

58. Cited by A. Leon Higginbotham Jr., "Race and the American Legal Process," in Rothenberg, ed., *Race, Class, and Gender in the United States*, p. 301.

59. Ricki Solinger, *Wake Up Little Susie: Single Pregnancy and Race Before Roe V. Wade* (New York: Routledge, 1992), pp. 17, 24-28.

60. Ibid., pp. 41-57, 148, 193-94.

61. See, for example, "Saying No to Norplant," *People*, November 7, 1994 and Barbara Kantrowitz and Pat Wingert, "The Norplant Debate," *Newsweek*, February 15, 1993. A long campaign to stop sterilization abuse—which heavily targeted Black, Puerto Rican, Chicana and Native American women—led, for example, to federal regulations regarding sterilization in 1979. Regulations are poorly enforced, and work to end sterilization abuse continues.

62. See Holly Sklar, "The Upperclass and Mothers N the Hood," *Z Magazine*, March 1993. Also see, for example, Nancy Gibbs, "The War on Welfare Mothers: Reform may put them to work, but will it discourage illegitimacy?" *Time*, June 20, 1994; "Endangered Family," *Newsweek*, August 30, 1993.

63. Senator John Kerry, "Race, Politics and the Urban Agenda," Yale University, March 30, 1992, transcript excerpted in Holly Sklar, "Reaffirmative Action," *Z Magazine*, May 1992.

64. Arthur L. Kellermann and James A. Mercy, "Men, Women, and Murder: Gender-Specific Differences in Rates of Fatal Violence and Victimization," *The Journal of Trauma* 33:1, July 1992. Also see Bureau of Justice Statistics, *Violence Between Intimates*, November 1994 and Lynda Gorov and John Ellement, "Most women's deaths laid to intimates," *Boston Globe*, January 3, 1993.

65. Ronet Bachman, Bureau of Justice Statistics, *Violence Against Women: A National Crime Victimization Survey Report*, January 1994, p. 8.

66. U.S. Senate Judiciary Committee, *Violence Against Women: A Week in the Life of America*, report prepared by the Majority Staff, October 1992, pp. ix, 1-3.

67. Coontz, *The Way We Never Were*, p. 247. Also see Adolph Reed Jr., "The Underclass as Myth and Symbol: The Poverty of Discourse About Poverty," *Radical America* 24:1, January 1992 and Adolph Reed Jr. and Julian Bond, "Equality: Why We Can't Wait" and other articles in *The Nation* special issue, "The Assault on Equality: Race, Rights and the New Orthodoxy," December 9, 1991.

68. "Shalala speaks on teen mothers," *Boston Globe*, July 15, 1994; Judith Stacey, "Dan Quayle's Revenge: The New Family Values Crusaders," *The Nation*, July 25/August 1, 1994.

69. Solinger, *Wake Up Little Susie*, pp. 41, 148.

70. Coontz, *The Way We Never Were*, p. 223; also see pp. 221-28. Coontz critiques Judith Wallerstein's famous study of children of divorced parents.

71. During the 1970s and 1980s, the birth rates of unmarried (never-married, divorced, widowed) Black women fell while the rates for unmarried White women rose. The 1990 birth rate of unmarried Black women was higher than it was in 1980, but lower than it was in 1970. GAO, *Poverty Trends, 1980-88: Changes in Family Composition and Income Sources Among the Poor* (September 1992), pp. 4, 35-38, 40-43, 53; *Statistical Abstract 1993*, Tables 101 102; *1993 Green Book*, pp. 1138-1146. Also see Mishel and Bernstein, *The State of Working America 1994-95*, pp. 272-76.

The teenage birth rate (ages 15-19) was 90.3 per 1,000 females in 1955. It reached an all-time low of 50.2 in 1986 and has risen since to 62.1 in 1991. Center for Law and Social Policy (Washington, DC), *Adolescent Mothers, AFDC and Jobs: facts,* March 1994, p. 1. Also see Statistical Abstract 1994, Table 92.

72. At least 80 percent "of the increase in single parents between 1981 and 1983 is attributable to technical refinements in survey procedures that were introduced early in the 1980's. This represents 10 to 15 percent of the total increase between 1970 and 1993 (or 20 to 25 percent of the increase since 1980)." Steve W. Rawlings, Census Bureau, *Household and Family Characteristics: March 1993* (June 1994), pp. VI-VII, XIV-XVIII.

73. *1992 Green Book,* pp. 1086-87; Arlene F. Saluter, Census Bureau, *Marital Status and Living Arrangements: March 1993* (May 1994), pp. VII-IX, Table 8. The Census Bureau count of same-sex partners with and without children is considered to be very low.

74. GAO, *U.S. Has Made Slow Progress in Involving Women in Development,* pp. 53, 56, citing, for example, Rae Lesser Blumberg, *Making the Case by the Gender Variables: Women and the Wealth and Well-Being of Nations* (Washington, DC: 1989). UNICEF, *The Progress of Nations* (New York: 1993), pp. 41, 43.

75. Quote from *1993 Green Book,* p. 1116; data from *Statistical Abstract 1994,* Table 1358. Also see *1992 Green Book,* pp. 1077, 1288-1300.

76. Census Bureau, Table L, "Poverty Status of Families, by Type of Family, Presence of Related Children, Race, and Hispanic Origin: 1959 to 1993."

77. Karin Stallard, Barbara Ehrenreich and Holly Sklar, *Poverty in the American Dream: Women and Children First* (Boston: South End Press, 1983), p. 9, citing Patricia C. Sexton, *Women and Work,* R. and D. Monograph No. 46, U.S. Department of Labor, Employment and Training Administration (1977).

78. GAO, *Mother-Only Families: Low Earnings Will Keep Many Children in Poverty* (April 1991), pp. 3, 6. Also see Heidi Hartmann, et al., "Raising Wages: The Family Issue of the 90's," *Equal Means,* Winter 1991.

79. Carrie Teegardin, "Recession Took Bite out of Workers' Pay," *The Atlanta Journal and Constitution,* Knight-Ridder/Tribune Business News, January 13, 1995.

80. Labor Research Association, *American Labor Yearbook 1993,* p. 38.

81. Census Bureau, *Household and Family Characteristics: March 1993,* Tables B and 15. Women now make up 46 percent of all multiple-wage earners, up from 15 percent in 1970. Many multiple-wage earners work a full-time job and at least one part-time job. S. A. Reid, "Number of Women Moonlighting on the Rise," *The Atlanta Journal and Constitution,* October 28, 1994.

82. Editorial, "An investment in child care," *Boston Globe,* November 22, 1994.

83. *1994 Green Book,* pp. 706-7; GAO, *Tax Expenditures Deserve More Scrutiny* (June 1994), p. 50. In 1991, about 81 percent of the $37 billion in tax benefits from deductible mortgage interest went to the top 20 percent of households with incomes above $50,000. See Edward B. Lazere, Paul A. Leonard, Cushing N. Dolbeare and Barry Zigas, *A Place to Call Home: The Low Income Housing Crisis Continues* (Center on Budget and Policy Priorities/Low Income Housing Information Service, December 1991), pp. 27, 30-31, 34-35.

84. The Boston Foundation Carol R. Goldberg Seminar on Child Care, *Embracing Our Future: A Child Care Action Agenda* (Boston: Boston Foundation, 1992), pp. 39, 54-5;

Children's Defense Fund, *State of America's Children 1992*, pp. 18-22; Barbara Presley Noble, "Worthy Child-Care Pay Scales," *New York Times*, April 18, 1993; Child Care Employee Project, *The National Child Care Staffing Study Revisited: Four Years in the Life of Center-Based Child Care* (Oakland, CA: 1993).

85. Boston Foundation, *Embracing Our Future*, p. 31. Also see Carol Stevenson and Marcy Whitebook, "Child Care in America: Is Nap Time Over?" *Equal Means*, Fall 1993.

86. GAO, *Child Care Subsidies Increase Likelihood That Low-Income Mothers Will Work* (December 1994), p. 2.

87. Rosemary L. Bray, "So How Did I Get Here?" New York Times Magazine, November 8, 1992.

88. Frances Fox Piven and Richard A. Cloward, *Regulating the Poor: The Functions of Public Welfare* (New York: Vintage, 1971), pp. 192-95.

89. Unemployment rate from *Statistical Abstract 1994*, Table 646. Other data from *1994 Green Book*, pp. 390, 399-403.

90. Barbara Presley Noble, "An Increase in Bias is Seen Against Pregnant Workers," *New York Times*, January 2, 1993; Editorial, "Women, Children and Work," *New York Times*, January 12, 1993. Health insurance study in Robert Moffitt and Barbara Wolfe, "The Effect of the Medicaid Program on Welfare Participation and Labor Supply," National Bureau of Economic Research, Working Paper N. 3286 (Cambridge, MA: 1990), cited in GAO, *Mother-Only Families*, p. 6, fn. 7.

91. Jordana Hart, "Few in Area Use Leave Law, Parents Can't Afford Time Off," *Boston Globe*, July 22, 1994.

92. There is no federally prescribed minimum for the AFDC benefit which is set by states. The median monthly benefit for a family of three in 1994 was $366 which, at $4,392 a year, is much less than that year's official poverty threshold for a single individual. *1994 Green Book*, pp. 231, 374-77; Lav, et al., *The States and the Poor*, pp. 11-14; also see House Ways and Means Committee, *Background Material on Family Income and Benefit Changes*, pp. 7-8.

93. Leonard and Lazere, *A Place To Call Home*, pp. 1, 5-8, 36-41; *1993 Green Book*, p. 712; U.S. Department of Health and Human Services (HHS), Office of Family Assistance, *Characteristics and Financial Circumstances of AFDC Recipients: FY 1990*, p. 8 and *FY 1992*, p. 1.

94. GAO, *Poverty Trends, 1980-88*, p. 52. "In 1972, all States paid AFDC benefits to a family with wages equal to 75 percent of the poverty threshold; by 1991, only 5 States paid AFDC to such a family. Average tax rates on such earnings increased from 52 to 69 percent from 1972 to 1984, and then fell to 56 percent in 1991." House Ways and Means Committee, *Background Material on Family Income and Benefit Changes*, pp. 7-8, 36.

95. Harvard School of Public Health, Henry J. Kaiser Family Foundation and KRC, "National Election Night Survey," November 1994. Also see Robin Toner, "Pollsters See a Silent Storm That Swept Away Democrats," *New York Times*, November 16, 1994. Actual FY 1995 budget figures from *1994 Green Book*, Table J-6, p. 1255.

96. Catherine Lerza, "Sex, Lies & Welfare Reform," *Equal Means*, Spring 1992; Robin Toner, "Politics of Welfare: Focusing on the Problems," *New York Times*, July 5, 1992.

97. The *1993 Green Book* explains variations among different measures of length of time on welfare and why, though over time most recipients are short-term recipients, at any

one point in time there will be a large proportion of long-term recipients on the rolls. See pp. 685-97, 699, 705, 708, 714-18. Also see HHS, *Characteristics and Financial Circumstances of AFDC Recipients: FY 1991* and *FY 1992*, pp. 1-4. Most families on AFDC have one child (43 percent) or two children (30 percent); only 10 percent have more than three children.

98. *1993 Green Book*, pp. 721-23. Not surprisingly, though, given impoverished schools and other impediments, a higher percentage of daughters who were on welfare receive it as young adults than those who weren't.

99. In 1900, Black women's labor force participation rate was 40.7 percent, White women's 16 percent. The 1960 rates were 42.2 percent for Black women and 33.6 percent for Whites; in 1970, 49.5 percent for Blacks and 42.6 percent for Whites; in 1980, 53.2 percent and 51.2 percent respectively; and in 1991 they converged at nearly 58 percent. Teresa L. Amott and Julie A. Matthaei, *Race, Gender & Work* (Boston: South End Press, 1991), Appendix C, Table C-1; *Statistical Abstract 1992*, Table 609.

100. HHS, *Characteristics and Financial Circumstances of AFDC Recipients FY 1992*, pp. 42-43; *1993 Green Book*, pp. 696-98, 706, 727-28; Will Marshall and Elaine Ciulla Kamarck, "Replacing Welfare with Work," in Will Marshall and Martin Schram, eds., *Mandate for Change* (New York: Berkeley Books/for The Progressive Policy Institute of the Democratic Leadership Council, 1993), p. 224.

101. GAO, *Families on Welfare: Sharp Rise in Never-Married Women Reflects Societal Trend*, May 1994, p. 3.

102. Jodie Levin-Epstein, *Understanding the Clinton Welfare Bill: Teen Pregnancy Prevention and Teen Parents* (Washington, DC: Center for Law and Social Policy, July 27, 1994) p. 7.

103. Census Bureau, *Income, Poverty, and Valuation of Noncash Benefits: 1993*, Table 4. Also see Coontz, *The Way We Never Were*, pp. 262 and 367-68, fn. 17, on the biased reporting of women as "marrying out" of welfare, even if they left because of a job and only later married.

104. For children under 14, the 1989 female-male ratio is 100 to 105 for Whites, 103 for Blacks and 104 for Latinos. For 14 to 24 year olds, the female-male ratio is 100 to 103 for Whites, 98 for Blacks and 104 for Latinos. For 25 to 44 year olds, the female-male ratio is 100 to 101 for Whites, 87 for Blacks and 107 for Latinos. For 45 to 64 year olds, the female-male ratio is 100 to 94 for Whites, 82 for Blacks and 90 for Latinos. For those 65 and over, the female-male ratio is 100 to 69 for Whites, 67 for Blacks and 71 for Latinos. *Statistical Abstract 1991*, Table 20; the 1992-1994 editions do not differentiate by race.

105. Theresa Funiciello, *Tyranny of Kindness: Dismantling the Welfare System to End Poverty in America* (New York: Atlantic Monthly Press, 1993), pp. 56-57; also see Stallard, Ehrenreich and Sklar, *Poverty in the American Dream*.

106. Alison Mitchell, "Posing as Welfare Recipient, Agency Head Finds Indignity," *New York Times*, February 5, 1993.

107. Mark Greenberg, *Beyond Stereotypes: What State AFDC Studies on Length of Stay Tell Us About Welfare as a "Way of Life,"* Center for Law and Social Policy, July 1993, p. 23.

108. Roberta M. Spalter-Roth, Heidi Hartmann and Linda Andrews, *Combining Work and Welfare: An Alternative Anti-Poverty Strategy*, A Report to the Ford Foundation (Washington, DC: Institute for Women's Policy Research, 1992). Also see the Institute for Women's Policy Research reports, *The Real Employment Opportunities of Women*

Participating in AFDC: What the Market Can Provide (October 1993) and *Dependence on Men, the Market, or the State: The Rhetoric and Reality of Welfare Reform* (November 1993).

109. 1988 federal study cited in Children's Defense Fund, "Myths About AFDC," in *The State of America's Children 1992*, p. 31; child care exemptions, p. 20. Work exemption figures and children's ages from HHS, *Characteristics and Financial Circumstances of AFDC Recipients: FY 1990*, pp. 2, 5.

110. Census Bureau, "Ratio of Income to Poverty Level Distribution, by Selected Characteristics: 1993," unpublished Table 17.

111. House Republican Conference, *Contract With America*, Legislative Digest, September 27, 1994.

112. Quoted in "The Myths of Charity," *U.S. News & World Report*, January 16, 1995, p. 39.

113. Dale Russakoff and Dan Balz, "Play Rough and Never Say Die," *Washington Post Weekly*, January 2-8, 1995, p. 11.

CHAPTER SIX: CYCLE OF UNEQUAL OPPORTUNITY

1. See Ellen Teninty, "Corporate Taxes: The Return for Our Public Investment," *Equal Means*, Fall 1993.

2. Dan Goodgame, "Welfare for the Well-Off," *Time*, February 22, 1993.

3. Mark Muro, "Class Privilege," *Boston Globe*, September 18, 1991.

4. Ellis Cose, *The Rage of a Privileged Class* (New York: HarperCollins, 1993), pp. 111-12.

5. Coontz, *The Way We Never Were*, p. 69.

6. Editorial, "In Congress, Give Peace a Chance," *Business Week*, November 21, 1994, p. 138.

7. Evan Thomas, "Goodbye Welfare State," *Newsweek*, November 21, 1994, p. 44.

8. Michael Wines, "Taxpayers Are Angry: They're Expensive, Too," *New York Times*, November 20, 1994.

9. Thomas F. Jackson, "The State, the Movement, and the Urban Poor: The War on Poverty and Political Mobilization in the 1960s," in Michael B. Katz, ed., *The 'Underclass' Debate: Views from History* (Princeton, NJ: Princeton University Press, 1993), p. 411.

10. See, for example, Abramovitz, *Regulating the Lives of Women*, pp. 368-73.

11. Dean Baker, "Generations at War: The real problems with Social Security," *Dollars & Sense*, November 1990, p. 16. The gap in White and Black life expectancies widened to seven years as Black life expectancy actually dropped in the 1980s. The life expectancy for Black men in 1991 was 64.6 years while it was 72.9 for White men. The life expectancy for Black women was 73.8 years compared with 79.6 years for White women. *Statistical Abstract 1994*, Tables 114-115.

12. Jonathan Kozol, *Savage Inequalities: Children in America's Schools* (New York: Crown Publishers, 1991), pp. 54-55.

13. William Celis 3d, *New York Times*, November 18 and December 4, 1992.

14. Kozol, *Savage Inequalities*, pp. 193-94.

15. Ibid., p.76.

16. Robert B. Reich, "Secession of the Successful," *New York Times Magazine*, January 20, 1991.

17. Jeff P. Howard, "The Third Movement: Developing Black Children for the 21st Century," in National Urban League, *The State of Black America 1993* (New York: 1993), pp. 20-21.

18. Jean Caldwell, "Ending Tracking: Difficult and Controversial," *Boston Globe*, November 14, 1993.

19. Deborah Prothrow-Stith, *Deadly Consequences: How Violence is Destroying Our Teenage Population and a Plan to Begin Solving the Problem* (New York: Harper Perennial, 1991/1993), pp. 164-66, 169-71.

20. Kozol, *Savage Inequalities* and *Death At An Early Age: The Destruction of the Hearts and Minds of Negro Children in the Boston Public Schools* (New York: Plume/Penguin, 1967). Also see, for example, Alexis Jetter, "Mississippi Learning," *Boston Globe Magazine*, February 21, 1993, on the Algebra Project led by Bob Moses.

21. Robert Kominski and Andrea Adams, Census Bureau, *Educational Attainment in the United States: March 1993 and 1992* (May 1994), Table 2. The percentage of Blacks (ages 25 to 29), who are high school graduates or more has steadily climbed from 22.3 percent in 1947 (before the Supreme Court outlawed school segregation) to 76.6 percent in 1980 to 81.7 percent in 1991, while Whites went from 54.9 percent in 1947 to 86.9 percent in 1980 to 85.8 percent in 1991. The percentage of Blacks (ages 25 to 29) with four or more years of college has risen from 2.8 percent in 1947 to 11.6 percent in 1980 to 13.4 percent in 1990, while Whites rose from 5.9 percent in 1947 to 23.7 percent in 1980 and 24.2 percent in 1990. Census Bureau statistician, February 17, 1993, citing *Current Population Reports*.

22. "Inequality: How the Gap Between Rich and Poor Hurts the Economy," *Business Week*, August 15, 1994, p. 79. Congressional commission cited in Mary Jordan, *Washington Post*, "Panel to call for new student-aid system," *Boston Globe*, February 3, 1993. Associated Press, "US college costs still rising faster than income," *Boston Globe*, September 22, 1993.

23. Judith Gaines, "Work, study: High costs shift college priorities," *Boston Globe*, September 16, 1994.

24. People for the American Way, *Democracy's Next Generation II: A Study of American Youth on Race* (Washington, DC: 1992), pp. 41, 161. Also see Lynne Duke, "Just When You Thought It Was the 20th Century...," *Washington Post Weekly*, January 6-12, 1992; Tom W. Smith, "Ethnic Images in the United States," *The Polling Report* 7:11, May 27, 1991.

25. Duke, "Just When You Thought It Was the 20th Century..."

26. ABC News, *PrimeTime Live*, "True Colors," September 26, 1991, Journal Graphics transcript.

27. Diane E. Lewis, "Employment testing: Useful tool, or entrapment?" *Boston Globe*, April 11, 1993.

28. Mishel and Bernstein, *The State of Working America 1994-95*, pp. 185-86).

29. Margery Austin Turner, et al., *Opportunities Denied, Opportunities Diminished: Racial Discrimination in Hiring* (Washington, DC: Urban Institute Press, 1991), pp. 2, 56-57.

30. Between July 1990 and March 1991, Blacks were the only racial group to suffer a net loss in jobs at companies that provide employment statistics to the Equal Employment Opportunity Commission. Elaine Ray, "Another depression," *Boston Globe*, September 24, 1993 and Meg Vaillancourt, "Figures show large job loss among blacks," *Boston Globe*, September 15, 1993, citing *Wall Street Journal* study. *Wall Street Journal* quote from Acel Moore, "Recession Hit Blacks the Hardest—Why is that Not Surprising?" *Philadelphia Inquirer*, September 28, 1993.

31. GAO, *Displacement Rates, Unemployment Spells, and Reemployment Wages by Race*, September 1994.

32. Editorial, "Federal Racism: Blacks are Fired from Jobs at a Higher Rate than Whites," *San Jose Mercury News*, October 26, 1994.

33. Editorial, "Race and the Workplace: A Study of Firings Raises Old Questions Anew," *Philadelphia Inquirer*, December 18, 1993. Also see Stephen Barr, "The Shrinking Federal Work Force," *Washington Post Weekly*, September 19-25, 1994.

34. Steven A. Holmes, "Programs Based on Sex and Race are Under Attack" and Peter T. Kilborn, "Women and Minorities Still Face 'Glass Ceiling,'" *New York Times*, March 16, 1995, citing Federal Glass Ceiling Commission, *Good For Business: Making Full Use of the Nation's Human Capital* (1995). Also see Diane E. Lewis, "No Break in Glass Ceiling Found," *Boston Globe*, March 16, 1995.

35. Ellis Cose, "To the Victors, Few Spoils," *Newsweek*, March 29, 1993, p. 54; also see David Gates, "White Male Paranoia," in the same issue.

36. Diana Bilimoria and Sandy Kristin Piderit, "Sexism on High: Corporate Boards," *New York Times*, February 5, 1995.

37. Anne B. Fisher, "When Will Women Get To The Top?" *Fortune*, September 21, 1992, p. 45; also see "Corporate Women: Progress?," *Business Week*, June 8, 1992; Judith H. Dobrzynski, "The 'Glass Ceiling': A Barrier to the Boardroom, Too," *Business Week*, November 22, 1993; U.S. Labor Department, *Report on the Glass Ceiling Initiative*, 1991.

38. Faludi, *Backlash*, pp. xiii-xiv.

39. Alicia C. Shepard, "High Anxiety," *American Journalism Review*, November 1993, pp. 20, 24.

40. Gates, "White Male Paranoia," p. 49 and Cose, "To the Victors, Few Spoils," p. 54.

41. Faludi, *Backlash*, p. 375.

42. Times Mirror Center for The People & The Press, "The People, the Press & Politics: The New Political Landscape," News Release, September 21, 1994; Richard L. Berke, "U.S. Voters Focus on Selves, Poll Says," *New York Times*, September 21, 1994.

CHAPTER SEVEN: LOCKING UP "SURPLUS" LABOR

1. Marc Mauer, *Americans Behind Bars: The International Use of Incarceration, 1992-1993* (Washington, DC: The Sentencing Project, September 1994).

2. U.S. Department of Justice, Bureau of Justice Statistics, *Criminal Victimization in the United States: 1973-92 Trends, A National Crime Victimization Survey Report* (July 1994); *Criminal Victimization in the United States, 1992*, (March 1994); *Highlights from*

20 Years of Surveying Crime Victims: The National Crime Victimization Survey, *1973-92* (October 1993).

3. Racial composition figures from Bureau of Justice Statistics, *Prisoners in 1993* (June 1994); Caroline Wolf Harlow, Bureau of Justice Statistics, *Comparing Federal and State Prison Inmates* (September 1994); Craig Perkins, Bureau of Justice Statistics, *National Corrections Reporting Program, 1992* (October 1994), p. 83; *Survey of State Prison Inmates, 1991* (March 1993). Also see Patrick A. Langan, Bureau of Justice Statistics, *Race of Prisoners Admitted to State and Federal Institutions, 1926-86* (May 1991).

4. Editorial, "Young Black Men," *New York Times*, May 7, 1992.

5. Hubert Williams and Patrick V. Murphy, "The Evolving Strategy of Police: A Minority View," *Perspectives on Policing*, U.S. Department of Justice (January 1990), p. 2. Also see National Minority Advisory Council on Criminal Justice, *The Inequality of Justice: A Report on Crime and the Administration of Justice in the Minority Community* (U.S. Department of Justice, January 1982).

6. The 1989 figures for women were 1 in 37 Blacks, 1 in 56 Latinas and 1 in 100 Whites. Mark Mauer, *Young Black Men and the Criminal Justice System* (The Sentencing Project, 1990); Mauer, *Americans Behind Bars: The International Use of Incarceration.*

7. Jerome C. Miller, *Hobbling A Generation: Young African American Males In Washington, DC's Criminal Justice System* (Alexandria, VA: National Center on Institutions and Alternatives, April 17, 1992), pp. 1, 5; National Center on Institutions and Alternatives, *Hobbling a Generation: Baltimore, Maryland* (September 1992), pp. 1-4.

8. Carol Stocker and Barbara Carton, "GUILTY...of being black," *Boston Globe*, May 7, 1992.

9. James M. Shannon, Stephen A. Jonas and Marjorie Heins, *Report of the Attorney General's Civil Rights Division on Boston Police Department Practices*, December 18, 1990, pp. 14-15, citing Judge Mather in *Commonwealth v. Phillips & Woody*. Also see *Commonwealth v. Carr et al.*

10. John Demeter and Holly Sklar, "'Dark' and White," *Z Magazine*, May 1990.

11. Prothrow-Stith, *Deadly Consequences*, pp. 33-34.

12. Jesse J. Holland, "False Image of Abductor Strained Race Relations," Associated Press, November 5, 1994.

13. Mann, *Unequal Justice*, p. 33, citing R. L. McNeely and Carl E. Pope, *Race, Crime and Criminal Justice* (Beverly Hills, CA: Sage Publications, 1981).

14. Mike Davis, *City of Quartz: Excavating the Future in Los Angeles* (New York: Vintage Books edition, 1992), p. 284, citing *Los Angeles Times*, May 8, 1988. Gates has also said that a disproportionate number of Blacks died as a result of police chokeholds because they didn't have veins in their necks "like normal people." See Mann, *Unequal Justice*, p. 152.

15. ABC News, *20/20*, "Presumed Guilty." November 6, 1992, Journal Graphics transcript.

16. Mann, *Unequal Justice*, pp. 167-71, 181-84, 213-14.

17. Ibid., p. 188, citing Joan Petersilia, "Racial Disparities in the Criminal Justice System: A Summary," *Crime and Delinquency* 31:1, 1985.

18. Douglas C. McDonald and Kenneth E. Carlson, *Sentencing in the Federal Courts: Does Race Matter? The Transition to Sentencing Guidelines, 1986-90*, A Discussion Paper from the Bureau of Justice Statistics Federal Justice Statistics Program, December 1993, pp. 8-10, 13-14, passim.

19. Staff Report by the Subcommittee on Civil and Constitutional Rights, Committee on the Judiciary, U.S. House of Representatives, *Racial Disparities in Federal Death Penalty Prosecutions 1988-1994* (March 1994), p. 1, citing Blackmun's dissent in *Callins v. Collins*, No. 93-7054, February 22, 1994.

20. Ibid., pp. 1, 5.

21. Ron Harris, "Blacks Feel Brunt of Drug War," *Los Angeles Times*, April 22, 1990.

22. Ibid.

23. Neil Steinberg, "The Law of Unintended Consequences," *Rolling Stone*, May 5, 1994, p. 33.

24. The U.S. Department of Health and Human Services, National Institute on Drug Abuse (NIDA) produces regular detailed surveys on drug use. See, for example, *Preliminary Estimates from the 1993 National Household Survey on Drug Abuse* (July 1994) and *National Household Survey on Drug Abuse: Population Estimates 1992* (October 1993). For prison data in text see, Drugs and Crime Data Center, Bureau of Justice Statistics, *Drugs and Crime Facts, 1993* (August 1994); *Statistical Abstract 1993*, Table 316; FBI, *Crime in the United States 1992* (October 1993), p. 235; FBI, *Crime in the United States 1993* (December 1994), pp. 216, 235-37; Bureau of Justice Statistics, *Survey of State Prison Inmates, 1991* and *Correctional Populations in the United States, 1992* (January 1995); U.S. Department of Justice statisticians, citing 1993 federal statistics.

25. Diana R. Gordon, *The Return of the Dangerous Classes: Drug Prohibition and Policy Politics* (New York: W.W. Norton, 1994), p. 143.

26. Harris, "Blacks Feel Brunt of Drug War."

27. Gordon, *The Return of the Dangerous Classes*, pp. 24-26. Also see Mann, *Unequal Justice*, pp. 58-62.

28. Gordon, *The Return of the Dangerous Classes*, p. 126.

29. Special Series, "Is the Drug War Racist?" Sam Vincent Meddis, "Disparities suggest the answer is yes," *USA Today*, July 23-25, 1993; also see other articles in series.

30. Ira J. Chasnoff, et al., "The Prevalence of Illicit-Drug or Alcohol Use During Pregnancy and Discrepancies in Mandatory Reporting in Pinellas County, Florida," *New England Journal of Medicine*, April 26, 1990, pp. 1202-06.

31. On drug treatment, see GAO, *ADMS Block Grant: Women's Set-Aside Does Not Assure Drug Treatment for Pregnant Women* (May 1991), p. 1. Also see *1992 Green Book*, p. 1120; Katha Pollitt, "Fetal Rights: A New Assault on Feminism," *The Nation*, March 26, 1990; Joseph B. Treaster, "For Children of Cocaine, Fresh Reasons for Hope," *New York Times*, February 16, 1993.

32. U.S. Department of Health and Human Services, *HHS News Release*, May 13, 1992. Also see GAO, *Teenage Drug Use: Uncertain Linkages with Either Pregnancy or School Dropout* (January 1991); Michael Isikoff, "Contrary to Popular Belief: Study finds white students are most likely to use drugs," *Washington Post Weekly*, March 4-10, 1991; and National Institute on Drug Abuse, *National Household Survey on Drug Abuse: Main Findings 1990; Population Estimates 1990; Highlights 1990; NIDA Capsules: Summary of Findings from the 1991 National Household Survey on Drug Abuse.*

33. America's Black Forum, "America's War on Drugs," August 1, 1992, Journal Graphics transcript.

34. Harris, "Blacks Feel Brunt of Drug War."

35. American Bar Association (ABA), Section of Criminal Justice, *The State of Criminal Justice: An Annual Report* (Chicago: ABA, February 1993).

36. National Center on Institutions and Alternatives, *Hobbling a Generation: Baltimore*, pp. 5-6.

37. FBI, *Crime in the United States 1991* (August 1992), p. 286.

38. Lois G. Forer, *A Rage to Punish: The Unintended Consequences of Mandatory Sentencing* (New York: W.W. Norton, 1994), p. 85.

39. Harris, "Blacks Feel Brunt of Drug War."

40. Steven B. Duke and Albert C. Gross, *America's Longest War: Rethinking Our Tragic Crusade Against Drugs* (New York: Jeremy P. Tarcher/Putnam, 1993), p. 125.

41. United States Sentencing Commission, Special Report to the Congress, *Mandatory Minimum Penalties in the Federal Criminal Justice System*, Washington, DC, August 1991, pp. 9, 31, Appendix A; Campaign For An Effective Crime Policy, "Evaluating Mandatory Minimum Sentences," October 1993, p. 4, citing Dennis Cauchon, "Sentences for Crack Called Racist," *USA Today*, May 26, 1993; Clarence Lusane, *Pipe Dream Blues: Racism and the War on Drugs* (Boston: South End Press, 1991), pp. 44-46; *Los Angeles Times*, April 22, 1990, cited in Davis, *City of Quartz*, p. 288; United States Code, Title 21, Sections 841 and 844 (drug offenses and penalties). On the Minnesota case see Mark Mauer, *Americans Behind Bars: One Year Later* (The Sentencing Project, February 1992), p. 12, citing *State v. Russell*, decided December 13, 1991; U.S. Sentencing Commission, *Mandatory Minimum Penalties*, Appendix H-17-19. When crack was introduced it was purposefully marketed to poor inner city neighborhoods, before the suburbs, and one study found that earlier differences in use between Whites and Blacks were related to availability. The rates of current crack use among Blacks, Whites and Latinos in 1991 were less than 1 percent and past-year use was 1.5 percent or less. Marsha Lillie-Blanton, et al., "Probing the Meaning of Racial/Ethnic Group Comparisons in Crack Cocaine Smoking," *Journal of the American Medical Association* 269:8, February 24, 1993; U.S. Department of Health and Human Services, *HHS News*, December 19, 1991, p. 3 and *NIDA Capsules: Summary of Findings from the 1991 National Household Survey on Drug Abuse*, p. 3.

42. U.S. Sentencing Commission, *Mandatory Minimum Penalties*, pp. ii, 10, 50-54, 76, 82, 91.

43. Barbara S. Vincent and Paul J. Hofer, *The Consequences of Mandatory Minimum Prison Terms: A Summary of Recent Findings* (Washington, DC: Federal Judicial Center, 1994), p. 13.

44. Barbara S. Meierhoefer, *The General Effect of Mandatory Minimum Prison Terms: A Longitudinal Study of Federal Sentences Imposed* (Washington, DC: Federal Judicial Center, 1992), p. 20.

45. U.S. Sentencing Commission, *Mandatory Minimum Penalties*, p. 107.

46. Forer, *A Rage to Punish*, p. 3.

47. Eric Schlosser, "Marijuana and the Law," *The Atlantic Monthly*, September 1994, p. 94.

48. March 23, 1993 remarks cited in Vincent and Hofer, *The Consequences of Mandatory Minimum Prison Terms*, p. 11.

49. Forer, *A Rage to Punish*, p. 64.

50. See, for example, Vincent and Hofer, *The Consequences of Mandatory Minimum Prison Terms*, p. 21.

51. Between 1986 and 1991, the average length of federal prison sentences for drug offenses increased 22 percent to 85 months (over seven years) while sentences for violent offenses decreased 30 percent to 91 months (seven and a half years). ABA, *The State of Criminal Justice*, p. 5.

52. See, for example, the report by Leslie Stahl on CBS, *60 Minutes*, April 11, 1993, which highlighted the overcrowding, early release problem while obscuring the cause and pointing only to solutions such as more prisons and more overcrowding.

53. Vincent Schiraldi, "Trading Books for Bars," *Dollars & Sense*, January-February 1995, p. 43.

54. Mathea Falco, "Toward A New National Drug Strategy," in Citizens Transition Project, *Changing America*, pp. 366-68. Also see U.S. Senate Committee on the Judiciary, Majority Staff Report, *Fighting Crime in America: An Agenda for the 1990s* (March 12, 1991), p. 22; Sean P. Murphy, "Few inmates get drug rehab," *Boston Globe*, January 8, 1993; Drugs and Crime Data Center & Clearinghouse, U.S. Department of Justice, *Fact Sheet: Drug Data Summary*, November 1992.

55. Francis Wilkinson, "A Separate Peace," *Rolling Stone*, May 5, 1994, p. 29.

56. Dennis Cauchon, "White House Balks at Study Urging More Drug Treatment," *USA Today*, June 14, 1994; Clarence Lusane, "Congratulations, It's A Crime, Bill," *CovertAction Quarterly*, November 1994, p. 22, citing "Treatment Far More Cost-Effective Than Control in Cutting Cocaine Use, Social Costs, RAND Says," *The National Report on Substance Abuse*, No. 15, July 1, 1994.

57. National Center on Institutions and Alternatives, *Hobbling a Generation: Baltimore*, p. 7.

58. See, for example, Albert J. Reiss Jr. and Jeffrey A. Roth, eds., National Research Council, *Understanding and Preventing Violence* (Washington, DC: National Academy Press, 1993), pp. 139-45; Prothrow-Stith, *Deadly Consequences*, pp. 103-106; Jeffrey A. Roth, "Understanding and Preventing Violence," National Institute of Justice, *Research in Brief*, February 1994; FBI, *Crime in the United States 1992*, pp. 17-21; FBI, *Crime in the United States 1993*, p. 285. According to the FBI, although juvenile gang-related homicides have been rising, less than 4 percent of the 1992 nationwide homicides were known to be juvenile gang-related, and the perpetrator may have been an adult gang leader rather than a juvenile. Also see Carolyn Rebecca Block and Richard Block, "Street Gang Crime in Chicago," National Institute of Justice, *Research in Brief*, December 1993, pp. 4-7.

59. Lois A. Fingerhut, "The Impact of Homicide on Life Changes: International, Intranational and Demographic Comparisons," in Carolyn Rebecca Block and Richard L. Block, eds., *Questions and Answers in Lethal and Non-Lethal Violence: Proceedings of the Second Annual Workshop of the Homicide Research Working Group*, FBI Academy, Quantico, VA, June 13-17, 1993 (National Institute of Justice Research Report); Lois A. Fingerhut and Joel C. Kleinman, "International and Interstate Comparisons of Homicide Among Young Males," *Journal of the American Medical Association* 263:24, June 27, 1990. Also see Prothrow-Stith, *Deadly Consequences*, p. 14; Senate Judiciary Committee, *Fighting Crime in America*; Coontz, *The Way We Never Were*, p. 5.

60. FBI, *Crime in the United States 1993*, p. 286.

61. *Statistical Abstract 1993*, Tables 134, 138. The age-adjusted Black male homicide rate was 82.1 per 100,000 in 1970, 71.9 in 1980, 50.2 in 1985, 68.7 in 1990 and 72.5 in 1991. The age-adjusted White male rates in 1970 and 1991 were 7.8 and 9.4 respectively. The

age-adjusted Black female homicide rate was 15 per 100,000 in 1970, 13.7 in 1980, 10.9 in 1985, 13 in 1990 and 13.9 in 1991. The age-adjusted White female rates in 1970 and 1991 were 2.2 and 3. "Homicide Deaths and Rates Per 100,000, for Years 1985-1991," Table provided by Centers for Disease Control, citing National Center for Health Statistics Mortality Data Tapes and Census Bureau population data; *Statistical Abstract 1993*, Tables 129, 134, 138.

62. Centers for Disease Control, *Homicide Surveillance: High Risk Racial and Ethnic Groups—Blacks and Hispanics, 1970-1983*, Atlanta, November 1986, p. 7. Also see Reiss and Roth, eds., *Understanding and Preventing Violence*, pp. 14-15, 129-33. On overall mortality disparities, see Gregory Pappas, et al., "The Increasing Disparity in Mortality Between Socioeconomic Groups in the United States, 1960 and 1986," *New England Journal of Medicine* 329:2, July 8, 1993.

A report by the Massachusetts Department of Public Health analyzing the period 1977-83 found: "When poor white urban neighborhoods were compared with middle income neighborhoods, the gaps between murder rates were as dramatic as those between races. For instance, Charlestown, a low-income Boston neighborhood, has a homicide rate 10 times higher than that of nearby Malden, a moderate-income suburban area. Both communities are over 97% white...In fact, South Boston, the most exclusively white neighborhood in Boston, has a homicide rate equal to that of South Dorchester/Mattapan, a poor community that is nearly 50% black." The highest murder rates in that period were in Roxbury and North Dorchester, areas of "staggering poverty and a large youth population." Massachusetts Department of Public Health, *Violence in Massachusetts: The Epidemiology of Homicide in Massachusetts, 1977-1983* (Boston, September 1987), pp. 24-25, 27, 29. This report was being updated at the time of this writing.

63. Symposium moderated by Bob Herbert, "Who Will Help the Black Man?" *New York Times Magazine*, December 4, 1994, p. 74.

64. Anthony Carnevale, "Trickle Down and Out; Low-Tech Reality: How Workers Get Hurt in Our Flexible Economy," *Washington Post*, November 27, 1994.

65. Jeffrey A. Roth, "Psychoactive Substances and Violence," U.S. Department of Justice, National Institute of Justice, *Research in Brief*, February 1994. Over 400,000 people a year die from smoking cigarettes in the United States. Hal Kane, "Overall Cigarette Production Rises," in Lester R. Brown, et al., *Vital Signs 1994* (World Watch Institute/New York: W.W. Norton, 1994), pp. 100-01.

66. Motor vehicle fatalities are the leading cause of death for people between the ages of 5 and 34—including 40 percent of all teenage deaths—and half of all road deaths are due to drunk drivers. Of the approximately 70,000 deaths due to alcohol and other drug-related overdoses, disease and injury other than drunk driving road crashes, 64,000 are attributed to alcohol. Cathy Shine and Marc Mauer, *Does the Punishment Fit the Crime? Drug Users and Drunk Drivers: Questions of Race and Class* (Washington, DC: The Sentencing Project, March 1993), pp. 4, 6, 11, 17, passim. Also see Duke and Gross, *America's Longest War*, pp. 32-42; Reiss and Roth, eds., *Understanding and Preventing Violence*, pp. 13-14, 182-203; FBI, *Crime in the United States 1993*, pp. 216-17, 235; Prothrow-Stith, *Deadly Consequences*, p. 9; Robert L. Flewelling, "Assessing the Relationship Between Drugs and Violence: An Aggregate-Level Analysis," in Block and Block, eds., *Questions and Answers in Lethal and Non-Lethal Violence: Proceedings of the Second Annual Workshop of the Homicide Research Working Group*; Paul J. Goldstein, "Drugs and Violence," in Block and Block, eds., *Questions and Answers in*

Lethal and Non-Lethal Violence: Proceedings of the First Annual Workshop of the Homicide Research Working Group, Ann Arbor, MI, June 14-16, 1992 (National Institute of Justice Research Report); Paul J. Goldstein, et al., "Drug-Related Homicide in New York: 1984 and 1988, *Crime and Delinquency* 38:4, October 1992, pp. 467-68, 473; Drugs and Crime Data Center, *Fact Sheet: Drug Data Summary*, July 1994; Drugs and Crime Data Center, *Drugs and Crime Facts, 1993*, pp. 8-9.

Studies have found rates of drug-related homicides—variously excluding or including alcohol—ranging from 10 percent nationally to one-fourth to over one-half in particular cities at particular times, such as one-third in Boston in 1988. GAO, *The War on Drugs: Arrests Burdening Local Criminal Justice Systems* (April 1991), pp. 2-3, 47; Reiss and Roth, eds., *Understanding and Preventing Violence*, pp. 187-88; Bureau of Justice Statistics, *Drugs, Crime, and the Justice System* (December 1992), pp. 5-6, 59. In a narrower category, the FBI lists 6 percent of homicides as known to be involving narcotics felonies. Public Health Professor Paul Goldstein links peaks in the homicide rates during 1979-1981 and the mid-to-late 1980s to Cocaine Wars I (powder) and II (crack), when "New York City and Washington, DC replaced Miami as the nation's murder capitals." Paul J. Goldstein, "Drugs and Homicide: Questions For The Future," *CESAR Reports* (Center for Substance Abuse Research), Winter 1992, p. 3 and conversation with author, March 4, 1993. Also see Goldstein et al., "Drug-Related Homicide in New York"; Goldstein, "Drugs and Violent Crime" in N.A. Weiner and M.E. Wolfgang, eds., *Pathways to Criminal Violence* (Beverly Hills: Sage Publications, 1989). By contrast, Detroit and Los Angeles experienced decreases in their murder rates during their "crack epidemics" in the 1980s. Roth, "Psychoactive Substances and Violence," p. 6.

67. Schlosser, "Reefer Madness," p. 48. Also see Duke and Gross, *America's Longest War*, pp. 43-54.

68. Gordon, *The Return of the Dangerous Classes*.

69. Schlosser, "Reefer Madness," p. 49.

70. FBI, *Crime in the United States 1993*, pp. 216-17.

71. Schlosser, "Reefer Madness," pp. 45-46, 55.

72. Eric Schlosser, "Marijuana and the Law," *The Atlantic Monthly*, September 1994, p. 94.

73. Duke and Gross, *America's Longest War*, p. 242. Also see Gordon, *The Return of the Dangerous Classes*, pp. 213-17 and Ethan Nadelmann and Jann S. Wenner, "Toward a Sane National Drug Policy," *Rolling Stone*, May 5, 1994.

74. Duke and Gross, *America's Longest War*, p. 234. Also see Gordon, *The Return of the Dangerous Classes*, p. 6.

75. Roth, "Psychoactive Substances and Violence," p. 1.

76. Bureau of Justice Statistics, "Violent Crime," *Selected Findings*, April 1994.

77. James Alan Fox, "Murder most common," *Boston Globe*, January 31, 1993.

78. See Prothrow-Stith, *Deadly Consequences*, p. 136, citing J. T. Gibbs, "The New Morbidity: Homicide, Suicide, Accidents and Life-Threatening Behavior," in Gibbs, ed., *Young, Black Male in America* (Dover, MA: Auburn House, 1988). Also see Carol W. Runyan and Elizabeth A. Gerken, "Epidemiology and Prevention of Adolescent Injury: A Review and Research Agenda," *Journal of the American Medical Association* 262:16, October 27, 1989. Rates from *Statistical Abstract 1993*, Tables 127-29, 134 and *Statistical Abstract 1994*, Table 126; Children's Safety Network, *A Data Book of Child and*

Adolescent Injury (Washington, DC: National Center for Education in Maternal and Child Health, 1991).

79. The homicide rate for Black males, ages 15-19, went from 46.6 per 100,000 in 1985 to 51.8 in 1986, 60.5 in 1987, 78.1 in 1988, 93.7 in 1989, 115.7 in 1990 and 135.3 in 1991. The rate for Black males, ages 20-24, went from 85 in 1985 to 105.9 in 1986, 110.4 in 1987, 125.4 in 1988, 135.4 in 1989, 162.2 in 1990 and 184.4 in 1991. The homicide rate for White males, ages 15-19 went from 7.2 in 1985 to 8.5 in 1986, 7.2 in 1987, 7.9 in 1988, 9.4 in 1989, 12.5 in 1990 and 14.5 in 1991. The rate for White males, ages 20-24 went from 14.2 in 1985 to 15.5 in 1986, 14.4 in 1987, 14.3 in 1988, 15.1 in 1989, 18.1 in 1990 and 19 in 1991. "Homicide Deaths and Rates Per 100,000, for Years 1985-1991," Table provided by Centers for Disease Control. Also see Centers for Disease Control, "Homicides Among 15-19-Year-Old Males—United States, 1963-1991, *Morbidity and Mortality Weekly Report* 43:40, October 14, 1994; Fox Butterfield, "Teen-Age Homicide Rate Has Soared," *New York Times*, October 14, 1994; Lois A. Fingerhut, "Firearm Mortality Among Children, Youth, and Young Adults 1-34 Years of Age, Trends and Current Status: United States, 1985-90," National Center for Health Statistics, *Advance Data* 231, March 23, 1993 and Lois A. Fingerhut and Joel C. Kleinman, "Firearm Mortality Among Children and Youth," *Advance Data* 178, November 3, 1989.

    For historical perspective, among Black males ages 15-24, homicide rates went from 46.4 per 100,000 in 1960 to 102.5 in 1970 to 84.3 in 1980 and 66.1 in 1985 and 101.8 in 1988. Among Black males ages 25-34 rates went from 92 in 1960 to 158.5 in 1970 to 145.1 in 1980 to 94.3 in 1985 and 108.8 in 1988. Christopher Jencks, *Rethinking Social Policy: Race, Poverty, and the Underclass* (Cambridge, MA: Harvard University Press, 1992), pp. 181-83.

80. FBI, *Crime in the United States 1993*, p. 286.

81. FBI, *Crime in the United States 1991*, p. 279. Erik Eckholm, "Teen-Age Gangs Are Inflicting Lethal Violence on Small Cities," *New York Times*, January 31, 1993. Also see "Why Johnny Gets a Gun," *Time*, August 2, 1993.

82. On the profitable, poorly regulated civilian weapons trade, see, for example, the *Boston Globe's* three-part series, "Guns: aiming for profits," beginning with Gregg Krupa, "Gun firms spur market," December 19, 1993 and ending with Krupa, "Spotty oversight, potential for abuse mark weapons sales," December 21, 1993. Also see Violence Policy Center, *Female Persuasion: A Study of How the Firearms Industry Markets to Women and the Reality of Women and Guns* (Washington, DC: 1994).

83. Arthur L. Kellermann, et al., "Gun Ownership as a Risk Factor For Homicide in the Home" and Jerome P. Kassirer, "Guns in the Household," editorial, *New England Journal of Medicine*, October 7, 1993; Nancy Gibbs, "Up In Arms," *Time*, December 20, 1993, p. 24, citing remarks by Secretary of Health and Human Services Donna Shalala.

84. GAO, *Accidental Shootings: Many Deaths and Injuries Caused by Firearms Could be Prevented* (March 1991), pp. 2-3; Children's Safety Network, *A Data Book of Child and Adolescent Injury*, p. 30.

85. Susan Glick and Josh Sugarmann, "Why Johnny can shoot," *Mother Jones*, January/February 1995, p. 15, excerpted from Violence Policy Center, *Use the Schools: How Federal Tax Dollars Are Spent to Market Guns to Kids*.

86. David Barry, "Screen Violence: It's Killing Us," *Harvard Magazine*," November-December 1993. Also see Prothrow-Stith, *Deadly Consequences*; U.S. House of Repre-

sentatives, Committee on the Judiciary, *Hearings on the issue of violence on television*, witness statements, December 15, 1992; "Violence on TV, special report, *TV Guide*, August 22, 1992; "Violence in Our Culture," *Newsweek*, April 1, 1991; Christina Robb, "Are we hooked on media violence? Scientists say yes," *Boston Globe*, July 8, 1991; Reiss and Roth, eds., *Understanding and Preventing Violence*, p. 371.

87. Prothrow-Stith, *Deadly Consequences*, pp. 30-31, 34-36.

88. Ibid., pp. 44-45.

89. Fox, "Murder most common."

CHAPTER EIGHT: GREED SURPLUS, DEMOCRACY DEFICIT

1. Rep. Maxine Waters, Testimony before the Senate Banking Committee, May 14, 1992.

2. Quoted in *Mother Jones*, May/June 1991.

3. Fact sheet with Children's Defense Fund, *The State of America's Children: Yearbook 1994* (Washington, DC: prepublication press edition, 1994).

4. Lynn A. Curtis and Vesta Kimble, *Investing in Children and Youth, Reconstructing Our Cities: Doing What Works to Reverse the Betrayal of American Democracy* (Washington, DC: The Milton S. Eisenhower Foundation, 1993), pp. 12-14, 157-58.

5. Robert B. Reich, *The Work of Nations* (New York: Alfred A. Knopf, 1991), pp. 199, 260.

6. Refers to federal, state, local expenditures. *Statistical Abstract 1992*, Table 565.

7. The Labor/Community Strategy Center, *Reconstructing Los Angeles From the Bottom Up* (Los Angeles, 1993), p. 41, citing Citizens for Tax Justice.

8. Donald L. Barlett and James B. Steele, *America: Who Really Pays the Taxes?* (New York: Touchstone, 1994), pp. 95-109.

9. Quote from John Miller, "The Clinton Budget: New Voodoo and Old Snake Oil," *Dollars & Sense*, November/December 1993, p. 32; 1995 figure from Mishel and Bernstein, *The State of Working America 1994-95*, pp. 93-94. See Barlett and Steele, *America: Who Really Pays the Taxes?* on tax-exempt investment, etc..

10. *The Non-Profit Times*, November 1987.

11. Reich, "Secession of the Successful."

12. Felicity Barringer, "Giving by the Rich Declines, on Average," *New York Times*, May 24, 1992; *Statistical Abstract 1993*, Table 615.

13. Reich, "Secession of the Successful."

14. Mitchell Zuckoff and Doug Bailey, "US turns to betting as budget fix," *Boston Globe*, September 26, 1993, first of five-part series, "Easy Money: America's Big Gamble."

15. Todd Schafer, "Still Neglecting Public Investment: The FY94 Budget Outlook," Economic Policy Institute, *Briefing Paper*, September 1993. Also see Miller, "The Clinton Budget" and Robert Greenstein and Paul Leonard, *A New Direction: The Clinton Budget and Economic Plan* (Center on Budget and Policy Priorities, March 1993).

16. See, for example, Louis Uchitelle, "The Pitfalls of a Balanced Budget: Dismantling a Decades-Old System for Softening Recessions," *New York Times*, February 21, 1995.

17. Sawicky, *Up From Deficit Reduction*, pp. 3-4, 7, 20, 35, 37, 42-43, 50-52, 56.

18. Editorial, "Unbalancing," *The Nation*, March 13, 1995.

19. Nathaniel C. Nash, "Europeans Shrug as Taxes Go Up," *New York Times*, February 16, 1995.

20. Mishel and Bernstein, *The State of Working America 1994-95*, pp. 325-28.

21. Curtis and Kimble, *Investing in Children and Youth, Reconstructing Our Cities*, p. 199.

22. National Priorities Project and Peace Action, *In Search of Security: Reducing America's Military: Rebuilding America's Communities* (Northampton, MA: 1994), p. 2.

23. Center for Defense Information, "Cutting Unnecessary Military Spending: Going Further and Faster," *The Defense Monitor* XXI: 3 (1993) and "Reduce Military Spending: Create More Jobs," *The Defense Monitor* XXIII:6 (1994).

24. Eyal Press, "Arms Sales and False Economics: Prez Pampers Peddlers of Pain," *The Nation*, October 3, 1994.

25. UNDP, *Human Development Report 1994*, p. 48.

26. See, for example, National Priorities Project and Peace Action, *In Search of Security* and Randall Forsberg's articles in the *Boston Review*: "Wasting Billions," April/May 1994; "Creating a Cooperative Security System," November/December 1992; "Defense Cuts and Cooperative Security in the Post-Cold War World," May-July 1992.

27. UNDP, *Human Development Report 1994*, p. 1.

28. Kevin Phillips, *Post-Conservative America: People, Politics, and Ideology in a Time of Crisis* (New York: Vintage Books edition, 1983), p. 239.

29. Edward N. Lutttwak, *The Endangered American Dream* (New York: Touchstone, 1993), p. 127.

30. Quoted in Paul Hofheinz, "How Germany is Attacking Recession," *Fortune*, June 14, 1993.

31. Kevin Phillips, "The Politics of Frustration," *New York Times Magazine*, April 12, 1992, p. 41. Also see Phillips, *Post-Conservative America*, Part Three.

32. For various articles by and about Buchanan, see "Patrick J. Buchanan," a collection of source materials compiled by Political Research Associates, Cambridge, MA.

33. Patrick Buchanan, "Disillusionment with Democracy," *Washington Inquirer*, January 18, 1991 and "Worship Democracy? A Dissent," *From the Right* (Buchanan's newsletter), January 25, 1991.

34. Michael J. Crozier, Samuel P. Huntington and Joji Watanuki, *The Crisis of Democracy: Report on the Governability of Democracies to the Trilateral Commission* (New York: New York University Press, 1975), pp. 61-62, 114.

35. Keven Phillips, *Arrogant Capital*, p. 44.

36. Phillips, *The Politics of Rich and Poor*, p. 30.

37. Bob Woodward, *The Agenda: Inside the Clinton White House* (New York: Simon & Schuster, 1994), p. 165.

38. Everett Carll Ladd, ed., *America at the Polls: 1994*, a Roper Center Databook (Roper Center for Public Opinion Research/University of Connecticut, Storrs, 1995), pp. 16-17.

39. Michael Kranish, "Gingrich rise to power fueled by PAC money, master plan," *Boston Globe*, November 20, 1994; Howard Fineman, "Revenge of the Right," *Newsweek*, November 21, 1994, p. 40.

40. Chip Berlet, "The Right Rides High, *The Progressive*, October 1994. Political Research Associates is based in Cambridge, Massachusetts.

41. Marc Cooper, "God and Man in Colorado Springs," *The Nation*, January 2, 1995. Also see Sara Diamond, *Spiritual Warfare: The Politics of the Christian Right* (Boston: South End Press, 1989) and "It's Political Power, Stupid?" *Z Magazine*, January 1995.

42. Phillips, *Post-Conservative America*, pp. 190-91.

43. Ladd, ed., *America at the Polls: 1994*, pp. 72-73.

44. Berlet, "The Right Rides High," p. 22.

45. Steven Thomma and Angie Cannon, "Angst Casts a Vote," *San Jose Mercury News*, October 30, 1994.

46. Anthony Lewis, "Out With The Bath Water," *New York Times*, February 10, 1995.

CHAPTER NINE: ECONOMICS FOR EVERYONE

1. Muhammad Yunus, "Redefining Development," in Kevin Danaher, ed., *50 Years is Enough: The Case Against the World Bank and the International Monetary Fund* (Boston: South End Press/Global Exchange, 1994).

2. Martin Khor Kok Peng, "Reforming North Economy, South Development, and World Economic Order," in Jeremy Brecher, John Brown Childs and Jill Cutler, eds., *Global Visions: Beyond the New World Order* (Boston: South End Press, 1993) pp. 164-65.

3. UNDP, *Human Development Report 1994*, pp. 18, 26-27, 35.

4. Norm Brewer, "Newest Washington Jargon: Unfunded Mandates, " Gannett News Service, January 21, 1995.

5. David Helvarg, "Legal Assault on The Environment," *The Nation*, January 30, 1995.

6. Also see Scott Allen, "Contract reframes issue of environment's worth," *Boston Globe*, February 6, 1995.

7. See Chakravarthi Raghavan, *Recolonization: GATT, the Uruguay Round & the Third World* (Penang, Malaysia: Third World Network, 1990) and Third World Network's monthly magazine, *Third World Resurgence*.

8. Douglas Harbrecht, "GATT: Tales from the Dark Side," *Business Week*, December 19, 1994, p. 52.

9. "Borderless Finance: Fuel for Growth," *Business Week/21st Century Capitalism*, Special 1994 Bonus Issue, p. 41.

10. Quoted in Jeremy Brecher, "Global Village or Global Pillage?," *The Nation*, December 6, 1993.

11. Barnet and Cavanagh, "A Global New Deal," p. 176.

12. See, for example, Schor, "A Sustainable Economy for the Twenty-First Century"; Sheila D. Collins, Helen Ginsburg and Gertrude Schaffner Goldberg, *Jobs for All in a Nation That Works: A Plan for the Economic and Social Revitalization of America* (New York: New Initiatives for Full Employment, 1993); Jeremy Brecher and Tim Costello, *Global Village or Global Pillage: Economic Reconstruction from the Bottom Up* (Boston: South End Press, 1994); Brecher, Childs and Cutler, eds., *Global Visions*; Cavanagh, Wysham and Arruda, eds., *Beyond Bretton Woods*; Dan Luria and Joel Rogers, *Metro Futures: A High Wage, Democratic Development Strategy for America's Cities and Inner Suburbs* (Chicago: Midwest Consortium for Economic Development Alternatives, 1994); Harry Browne and Beth Sims, *Runaway America: U.S. Jobs and Factories on the Move*

(Albuquerque: Resource Center Press, 1993), chapter 4; Gilda Haas, *Plant Closures: Myths, Realities and Responses* (Boston: South End Press, 1985); The Labor/Community Strategy Center, *Reconstructing Los Angeles From the Bottom Up*, official draft and final declarations and NGO proposals for the March 1995 World Summit for Social Development.

13. UNDP, *Human Development Report 1994*, p. 4.

14. Collins, et al., *Jobs for All in a Nation That Works*, p. 62.

15. Juliet Schor points to the Medtronic Corporation in Minneapolis, which found output increased after providing its workers 40 hours' pay for 36 hours of work. "On balance, the company saved money." Other firms have showed rising productivity. "A British study of a variety of companies reached similar conclusions. Far from being costly, nearly all these workweek reductions paid for themselves, even when workers' incomes were held steady." Schor, *The Overworked American*, p. 155.

   When Germany's BMW introduced a four-day, 36-hour week at one of its plants in 1990, "the productivity gains more than offset the cost of taking on more workers, so there was no need for a wage cut." In France "it has been estimated that the universal adoption of a four-day, 33-hour work week with an average 5% reduction in salary would create around two million new jobs—and save $28 billion in unemployment insurance." UNDP, *Human Development Report 1994*, p. 39.

16. "Twelve points to Save the Social Summit," An NGO statement for the second session of the preparatory Committee of the Social Summit, August 25, 1994.

17. Robert Pollin, "Use Conversion to Create Jobs," *The Nation*, July 12, 1993.

18. Terry Collingsworth, J. William Goold and Pharis J. Harvey, "Time for a Global New Deal," *Foreign Affairs*, January/February 1994, p. 10.

19. The Labor/Community Strategy Center, *Reconstructing Los Angeles From the Bottom Up*, p. 17.

20. Yunus, "Redefining Development," and Jessica Matthews, "Little World Banks," in Danaher, ed., *50 Years is Enough*.

21. See Medoff and Sklar, *Streets of Hope*.

INDEX

ABOUT THE AUTHOR

Holly Sklar's previous books include the highly acclaimed *Streets of Hope: The Fall and Rise of an Urban Neighborhood* (co-authored with Peter Medoff); *Trilateralism: The Trilateral Commission and Elite Planning for World Management*, the best-selling book that foretold the global corporate economy; and *Washington's War on Nicaragua*, winner of an Outstanding Book Award from the Gustavus Myers Center for the Study of Human Rights in the United States. Sklar is a columnist for *Z Magazine* and has contributed to numerous anthologies, newspapers and magazines such as *The Nation*, the *Philadelphia Inquirer* and *USA Today*.

OTHER TITLES OF INTEREST FROM SOUTH END PRESS

Streets of Hope: The Fall and Rise of an Urban Neighborhood
Peter Medoff and Holly Sklar

*Trilateralism: The Trilateral Commission
and Elite Planning for World Management*
edited by Holly Sklar

Washington's War on Nicaragua
Holly Sklar

*Reagan, Trilateralism, and the Neoliberals:
Containment and Intervention in the 1980s*
Holly Sklar

Poverty in the American Dream: Women and Children First
Karin Stallard, Barbara Ehrenreich, and Holly Sklar

Collateral Damage: The "New World Order" at Home and Abroad
edited by Cynthia Peters
(with an overview by Holly Sklar)

*Global Village or Global Pillage:
Economic Reconstruction from the Ground Up*
Jeremy Brecher and Tim Costello

South End Press is a nonprofit, collectively run book publisher with over 150 titles in print. For a free book catalog or information about our membership program—which offers two free books and a 40% discount on all titles—please write to South End Press, 116 Saint Botolph Street, Boston, MA 02115, or call 1-800-533-8478.